# DYNAMIC GROUP-PIANO TEACHING

*Dynamic Group-Piano Teaching* provides future teachers of group piano with an extensive framework of concepts upon which effective and dynamic teaching strategies can be explored and developed. Within fifteen chapters, it encompasses learning theory, group process, and group dynamics within the context of group-piano instruction. This book encourages teachers to transfer learning and group dynamics theory into classroom practice. As a piano pedagogy textbook, supplement for pedagogy classes, or resource for graduate teaching assistants and professional piano teachers, the book examines learning theory, student needs, assessment, and specific issues for the group-piano instructor.

**Pamela D. Pike** is Aloysia L. Barineau Associate Professor of Piano Pedagogy at Louisiana State University.

# DYNAMIC GROUP-PIANO TEACHING

## Transforming Group Theory into Teaching Practice

*Pamela D. Pike*

Routledge
Taylor & Francis Group

NEW YORK AND LONDON

First published 2017
by Routledge
711 Third Avenue, New York, NY 10017

and by Routledge
2 Park Square, Milton Park, Abingdon, Oxon OX14 4RN

*Routledge is an imprint of the Taylor & Francis Group, an informa business*

© 2017 Taylor & Francis

The right of Pamela D. Pike to be identified as the author of this work
has been asserted by her in accordance with sections 77 and 78 of the
Copyright, Designs and Patents Act 1988.

*Library of Congress Cataloging-in-Publication Data*
Names: Pike, Pamela D., author.
Title: Dynamic group piano teaching : transforming group theory into
    practice / Pamela D. Pike.
Description: New York ; London : Routledge, 2017.
Identifiers: LCCN 2016053787 | ISBN 9781138241428 (hardback) |
    ISBN 9781138241435 (pbk.)
Subjects: LCSH: Piano—Instruction and study.
Classification: LCC MT220 .P636 2017 | DDC 786.2071—dc23
LC record available at https://lccn.loc.gov/2016053787

ISBN: 978-1-138-24142-8 (hbk)
ISBN: 978-1-138-24143-5 (pbk)
ISBN: 978-1-315-28037-0 (ebk)


Typeset in Baskerville
by Apex CoVantage, LLC

To past, present, and future leaders of the group-piano teaching community.

# CONTENTS

CONTENTS

CONTENTS

CONTENTS

# FIGURES

# PREFACE

Early in my master's program, the music education professor asked me to teach his "piano for music education" class while he was at a conference. I prepared thoroughly and excitedly walked into the piano lab. I had no idea how that teaching experience would change my life. As I taught in the vintage Wurlitzer piano lab, with a Visualizer that took up an entire wall of the classroom, I saw how students were engaging with one another and using musical knowledge, theory concepts, and keyboard skills in a way that was not possible in their other music courses. I enjoyed the technology (even though it was dated) and realized that it could add a new dimension to the educational experience. Although I had previously led performance classes and had endured uninspiring keyboard-skills classes as an undergraduate, those first group-teaching experiences in the piano lab offered me a glimpse into the potential of group-piano for engaging students in meaningful educational experiences. By the end of that week, I knew that teaching group piano would be an important part of my professional life.

I have now spent half of my life teaching group piano. Still, as I walk into the piano lab, I experience the twinge of anticipation. I love the challenge of engaging students, of helping them collaborate, and the joy that I feel when I see them construct knowledge and make music together at the keyboard is indescribable. Like most group-piano professionals, I devote myself to improving my teaching techniques, to using technology in meaningful ways, and to learning how to empower my students to achieve success at the piano; it will be a lifelong pursuit. Many teachers come to group piano in the way that I did: during graduate school when teaching group piano is a typical assistantship assignment. Other teachers recognize that they would like to work with children or adults in a group setting after they complete their formal music training. Not all novice group-piano teachers have mentors to guide their early experiences, and most of us did not participate in group piano as students, so we have little precedent to draw upon. While the topic is addressed in most piano pedagogy courses, as a teaching community, we need more resources to help us as we develop the craft and skills associated with teaching group piano.

*Dynamic Group-Piano Teaching: Transforming Group Theory into Teaching Practice* is meant to be a resource for students learning how to teach group piano, as well as for preservice interns, and novice studio teachers. While one book cannot contain all of the answers, I hope that the scope is comprehensive enough and the issues raised are thought-provoking enough to encourage effective and reflective teaching of piano in groups. This is meant to be a handbook or starting point for further research, exploration, and development of group-teaching technique. The topics explored are ones that I have pondered and sought out more information about time and again as I've worked with various groups of students in the piano class.

## Organization

The book is divided into four sections:

- The first deals with the background of group piano and working with piano groups in general. Topics include learning theory, addressing individual learning styles within the group, harnessing the power of group dynamics, and creating groups that work well together. While this pithy review is not intended to be a complete source of information on the topic, it should provide a broad overview that will enable future and current group-piano teachers to recognize the stages of learning and the types of individual learners that they encounter in group-piano classes. This section lays the groundwork for how instructors can begin to address the needs of various learners while teaching the entire group.
- The second section addresses adults in the group-piano class. This section is divided into chapters exploring college-age music majors, non-music majors, leisure adult students outside of the college setting, life-span development of adults, special concerns of older adults, and methods and materials that are effective for adults in a variety of group-piano settings.
- The third section explores teaching children in groups. It explores general music programs for children, addressing techniques that can be applied to the piano class, and looks at teaching children from the perspective of the independent studio teacher, the community music school instructor, and the K–12 educator. Methods, materials, and resources for children engaged in group piano are explored.
- The final section considers group piano from the perspective of the instructor. Topics include advantages and disadvantages of group-piano teaching, characteristics of effective teachers, common pitfalls of novice group-piano teachers

and how to avoid these, establishing trust within each group, logistics of teaching group piano, and technology that can be useful in the studio.

## How to Use This Book

Depending on your level of experience with teaching group piano, and your current teaching realities, you may choose to use the book in different ways. Following is a suggested order of study for various types of novice group-piano teachers.

### To the Student

*Students learning to teach piano* could use this book as the required text for the group-teaching portion of the semester. I teach a graduate class devoted to the topic of teaching group piano, and this text serves as our textbook and sourcebook for further readings and discussions. The evaluation forms and other resources in the appendices can be used by students long after the class has ended.

Suggested order of study for the piano pedagogy class in group-piano teaching:

• It is recommended that the class read and discuss topics in the order in which they appear in this text. Your instructor may choose several pedagogy-in-action questions for you to complete from each unit.

### To the Teacher

*Preservice and novice professional teachers of group piano* can use the book as a resource. As you prepare to teach your first group-piano classes, you will want to refer to the sections and chapters that are relevant to your immediate teaching needs. Once you have begun teaching, you may use some of the evaluation forms to assess your teaching, reflect on topics such as group dynamics, specific groups or types of classes, and assessment. Once the semester has ended and you contemplate how to improve your teaching for future semesters, it can be helpful to review portions of the book that are relevant to your specific situation and needs.

Suggested order of study for the group-piano graduate teaching assistant:

• Chapter 1
• Chapter 5
• Chapter 6 (if teaching non-music-major classes)
• Chapters 11–13 and Chapter 15

- Chapters 2–4
- Chapters 7–9
- Chapters 10 and 14

Suggested order of study for the independent studio teacher:

- Chapter 1
- Chapter 10
- Chapter 7 (if teaching adults)
- Chapters 8–9 (if teaching children)
- Chapters 11–15
- Chapters 2–4

Suggested order of study for the K–12 group-piano educator:

- Chapters 1, and 8–9
- Chapters 2–4
- Chapters 10–15

I believe that there is no substitute for guidance and mentoring as we embark upon group teaching. I encourage you to read the sections that pertain to your current or future group-teaching needs, discuss these readings with peers, colleagues, or trusted mentors, observe good group teaching when possible (there are video resources on my web site), reflect on your own teaching, and continue the evaluative and reflective cycle throughout your career. The group-piano environment can bring great joy and satisfaction to both the students and the instructor. I invite you to read on and discover the wonderful world of dynamic group-piano teaching!

# ACKNOWLEDGMENTS

I want to begin by acknowledging every student who has ever participated in one of my group-piano classes. Looking back, I have worked with thousands of students, from shortly after birth in Kindermusik classes to nonagenarians in my third-age piano classes, and all ages and stages in between. I have worked with college music majors who were stressed about passing the piano proficiency exam and groups of children having fun creating music and playing piano ensembles together. Each class has been unique. I honed my skills and teaching techniques because they committed themselves to making music with the group and trusted me to guide them. I thank my students for some of the most informative, influential, and memorable teaching experiences of my life.

Thank you, too, to all of my teachers. From my first piano lessons, I was blessed with learning from master piano teachers who provided me with solid piano technique, a grounding in our piano repertory, and a desire to engage others in playing the piano. The music educators with whom I have worked in the academy have helped me continue to build a strong, philosophical and practical foundation for my teaching, and colleagues with whom I interact now inspire me to continue refining my teaching skills.

Thank you to the reviewers who offered excellent insight into this manuscript during a busy time in the academic year, especially Thomas Parente of Rider University, Barbara Fast from the University of Oklahoma, and Jackie Edwards-Henry of Mississippi State University. The team at Routledge has been most helpful. My editor Constance Ditzel's guidance and support of this project have been invaluable. Finally, thank you to my family. To my parents, Vince and Florence, who were professionals in other fields but modeled outstanding leadership and teaching skill in so many of their pursuits. Even today, in retirement, they work with peers, teaching gently and collaborating on important projects. My grandmother, Mildred, who is approaching 100, has been a living example of how engaging with others in a shared community can enhance our well-being. Finally, my husband, Steve Binz, whose quiet support of my teaching passion has led us to countries and cities we could not have imagined! I've learned a lot as I've watched him write and teach during our time together; he is a source of inspiration for me.

Pamela D. Pike
Baton Rouge, LA
November 2016

# INTRODUCTION

Visit any music school or conservatory in North America on any given day, and you will find scores of undergraduates sitting in digital piano labs, headphones on, playing various exercises and repertoire with MIDI (musical instrument digital interface) accompaniments supporting their rehearsal and performance. One might also see computers at each keyboard, with students working independently, in small groups, or with the guidance of an instructor—in essence, exploring music through the piano. This experience of group-piano classes is common, and the majority of undergraduate music students study and hone their piano skills in the group setting, since it is the most efficient means of developing keyboard skills quickly with entire classes of music majors. Generally, at the end of four semesters of group piano, students are ready to pass a piano proficiency test, which requires students to assimilate piano skills and keyboard theory and confirms that students have attained a basic level of piano competency. One will find scores of graduate piano performance and pedagogy majors and full-time or adjunct music faculty instructing these piano classes.

Similarly, at any number of performing arts academies, independent studios, or K–12 schools throughout the world, one might observe precollege children studying piano in groups. A typical beginner class of eight children might include off-bench group activities such as singing, movement, and aural skills tasks interspersed with exploration on keyboards or acoustic pianos. The children might work independently before engaging with one another through music-making activities in pairs or small groups. Then the instructor might facilitate multiple-piano ensemble playing and outline goals for individual practice prior to the next class. Typically, children participating in well-designed piano classes display high levels of motivation, engagement, collaborative ability, and satisfaction.

Group-piano instruction has been common in the United States for decades, and it takes place in more than just the finest universities and conservatories. Group-piano classes are also effective in engaging the very young and the senior adult in group music making. Yet most group-piano teachers never benefit from experiencing a class from the student's perspective. While undergraduate non-piano music majors typically study piano in the group setting for about four semesters, the majority of piano majors are exempt from these keyboard classes. Although some teachers discover group teaching later in their careers, many young teachers first encounter group-piano teaching when they are thrust into the position of teaching the undergraduate piano class as part of their graduate teaching assistantship. Some novice instructors struggle with engaging all learners. Others struggle with the unfamiliar setting and teach the group much as they would a private lesson. However, many pianists fall in love with group teaching and make its pursuit their life's work.

Whether one plans on teaching group piano for four semesters or for forty years, teaching skills can always be honed and improved for the benefit of the students. Group instructors must convey concepts in meaningful ways to the entire class and facilitate group work among students. Teachers will notice that groups take on their own identity; no two classes are the same, which can be stimulating and invigorating. We must continue to grow and develop as teachers, honing our art and craft by keeping abreast of the latest musical materials and technology and by being aware of and applying principles from other disciplines such as general education, psychology, cognition and instruction, and even counseling and social work (which offer a wealth of knowledge about group dynamics and group work).

Magic can happen in the piano lab when musical material is perfectly sequenced, when students are purposefully prepared and receptive to stimulating instruction and problem-solving tasks, and when meaningful learning is taking place. The joy that envelops such a task-oriented and motivated class of students is akin to what we can experience in the concert hall when a gifted performer makes a real connection with the audience. There is a palpable energy between performer and audience members or, in the case of group piano, between the teacher and the students. The group-piano setting is a place where stimulation, learning, excitement, musical expression, and camaraderie merge to create a magical environment for piano study.

At its best, effective group-piano teaching is fast-paced, introducing carefully sequenced material through a variety of presentation modes, with the instructor availing of a broad range of music and keyboard technology throughout each class period. Successful teachers introduce new information through a spiraled curriculum, enabling students to experience these musical concepts in a variety of ways, both individually and in small-group combinations, throughout the class period. College-level group-piano curriculum incorporates technique, sight reading, harmonization, transposition, improvisation, basic accompaniment, and solo and ensemble repertoire. The curriculum for children tends to contain the same elements but may include more theory, aural skills, movement, games, and off-bench or small-group activities. Group-piano curricula for adult leisure students and for older adults can vary widely and tends to progress at a slower pace. But courses for adult piano groups tend to emphasize the skills essential for enjoyable music making at the piano: technique and coordination exercises, sight reading, and opportunities to make music through solo and ensemble repertoire.

While educationally valuable in many respects, the plethora of technological resources employed during group instruction can prove to be distracting for some students (and teachers) due to the massive quantity of simultaneous stimulation from several visual and auditory sources. Technology in the piano lab becomes invisible to students when it is used well. Yet it enhances their learning experience. A multi-pronged introduction of new material and well-designed lessons that address individual learning styles and individual learning preferences of the students enrolled in each particular class are more likely to meet the needs of all students participating than a one-size-fits-all approach to curriculum design. Social psychologists who work with clients in groups acknowledge certain predictable stages through which a group will progress. Similarly, the group-piano instructor must be aware of and encourage a healthy social structure and unique group dynamic that develops within each class, as these will impact student learning.

Although group teaching requires considerable skill and preparation, the rewards for teachers and students make it a worthwhile endeavor for instructors who are up for the educational challenge. The concepts, strategies, materials, and resources presented throughout this book are essential for effective group-piano instruction. As you explore each idea and chapter, consider how these concepts can be included in your group-teaching "instructor toolkit" and how they will impact student learning in your classes. Group-piano teaching can be a most rewarding and stimulating experience for the teacher. Each group of students develops its own personality and group dynamic. Classes offer the opportunity to integrate collaborative learning, to explore musical topics from multiple perspectives, and to avail oneself and one's students of music technology in a way that is not easily accessible to those studying piano privately. Every week, the group-piano teacher has an opportunity to hone teaching skills and delivery methods, to find creative ways to solve problems presented by each unique group, and to facilitate music making among peer groups of learners. We investigate these concepts in the following chapters.

# Section 1

# BACKGROUND OF GROUP PIANO AND WORKING WITH GROUPS

# 1

# GROUP PIANO 101

## Objectives

By the end of this chapter, you should be able to answer the following questions: What is group piano? What are the benefits? What technology is available to support it? Why should I consider it?

## Historical Overview of Group Piano and Its Context Today

When I ask teachers and piano pedagogy students if they've ever been a student in a group-piano class, invariably they shake their heads. Yet during the past decade, I have witnessed an increasing number of colleagues who teach outside of the academy incorporate group teaching into their studios. In the United States, the Music Teachers National Association (MTNA) even offers a group-piano specialist designation to teachers who complete a series of projects and teaching videos that are reviewed by experts. In reality, at present, many of the pedagogy students and teachers who will teach group piano have had little exposure to the kind of teaching that takes place in a piano lab. Many have only vague impressions of a room outfitted with several digital pianos where non-piano music majors learn to master basic keyboard skills.

Generally, piano majors are exempt from having to take the group-piano sequence in college since they develop their functional skills at the keyboard in their private lessons and presumably already read piano music with a certain amount of proficiency. Yet I contend that all piano majors have participated in group-piano classes. Group piano, as we know it today, is a highly organized means of teaching piano, and the advent of electronic keyboard laboratories has elevated group piano to a new level. However, teaching piano in groups has been around for much longer than one might imagine. Group-piano classes gained enormous popularity across the United States in the early 20th century in public schools. This was long before the dawn of digital piano labs. But group-piano teaching was popular in Europe in the late 19th century, and Franz Liszt was one of the great master group-piano pedagogues! This early form of group teaching was known as the master class, and Amy Fay (1965), the young American woman who traveled to Europe to study piano with the master pedagogues, did so primarily through such groups. She wrote about her experiences in her book of letters entitled *Music-Study in Germany*. Her thorough and engaging commentary on the experience offers insight into a student's persistence, anxiety, personal practice, preparation, and learning outcomes that are possible if students are prepared and willing to engage in group-learning activities.

Today, group-piano teaching encompasses everything from the piano master class to the sophisticated, highly sequenced and structured classes that take place in digital piano labs on college campuses, at arts academies, in K–12 schools, and in independent piano studios. In the United States, Raymond Burrows (at Teacher's College, Columbia University) laid the groundwork for teaching college-aged adults in piano labs during the 1930s and 1940s. Robert Pace succeeded him and brought his interest in educational psychology to the group-piano experience for children. Emergence of electronic teaching labs and technology in the late 1950s, along with a contingent of dedicated group-piano pioneers, elevated the field of group teaching to where it is today. Appropriate teaching materials were created, technology was (and continues to be) developed, and the benefits of integrating basic functional piano and theory skills at the keyboard for the college music major came to be understood during the latter part of the 20th century.

While there were isolated group-piano programs throughout the world in the late 20th century (most notably the worldwide Yamaha Music Education System initiative; see Chapter 8), educators in the United States were on the cutting edge of developing effective group teaching throughout the 20th century. As there are detailed synopses of the development of American group-piano teaching in other sources, further details will not be repeated here. However, readers are encouraged to explore the history of the group-piano teaching medium and to learn about the teaching philosophies and techniques of early experts. Noteworthy group-piano pioneers included Frances Clark, Louise Goss, Richard Chronister, Robert Pace, and Guy Duckworth. These pedagogues left extensive writings in pedagogy periodicals such as *Keyboard Arts*, *Piano and Keyboard*, and *Keyboard Companion*. Three of these group-piano pedagogues, Duckworth, Chronister, and Pace, each spoke on panels at MTNA Pedagogy Saturday in 1999. Pedagogy Saturday III, which took place in Los Angeles on March 20, 1999, was devoted to group teaching.[1] One of the primary items on the agenda that day was addressing the various configurations of student groupings that fit under the heading of group teaching and exploring why teachers should consider teaching piano in groups. So let's explore the different types of group-piano experiences that you might create for various age groups within your studio.

For clarification, it should be noted that the terms "group" and "class" are often used interchangeably. Technically, the term "class" is used if the number of students is higher than 10. "Groups" are made up of smaller groupings of students (generally from 3–10), and it implies that the teacher will be availing of group theory, group dynamics, and collaborative-learning strategies in which students share in an active and creative learning environment. This is a far cry from the large lecture class—which group piano is not! Because I have witnessed the benefits of students learning and making music in small groups, and I am encouraging all to explore collaborative learning in the piano setting, I will use the term "group piano" throughout this book.

## Categories of Group-Piano Lessons

Group lessons, then, may be the only mode of instruction for a student, or the group may take place in conjunction with private or partner lessons. The types of group-piano instruction that are most frequently encountered include the following categories:

- Occasional group classes
  - These might include performance classes, master classes, or group activity/history/ensemble classes periodically throughout the year.
- Regular group classes as adjunct to the private lesson
  - These occur regularly throughout the semester and can focus on topics such as history, performance, theory, keyboard skills/technique, sight reading, functional skills, or creative activities incorporating rhythm and movement.
- Occasional group camps
  - These can be done instead of private lessons during the summer, periodically throughout the year during school holidays, or as a "boot camp" prior to the beginning of the fall semester.
- Group lessons only

Now, let's explore each of these categories of group teaching in more detail:

## Occasional Group Classes

Occasional classes, particularly performance classes, are familiar to most musicians, as these are a common mode of group instruction for those who take weekly private lessons. Performance or master classes tend to only be offered to those students at late-intermediate to advanced levels of performance. Often performance classes only happen once or twice a year, prior to the annual studio recital. However, activities can be tailored to suit the age group and students who play at a beginning level. For example, if one has a group of elementary students, the teacher can prepare a simple worksheet that encourages students to listen for specific details in a peer's performance and to note these features on the worksheet while the performer is playing. The possibilities for creatively encouraging this type of active listening among young students in a performance class setting are endless. A sample set of worksheets that could be used with elementary and intermediate students may be found in Appendix A.1, A.2, and A.3.

Similarly, some teachers find it helpful to offer periodic classes on special topics for small groups of students throughout the semester. Music history and theory topics can serve as a focal point for each class, but such classes might also engage students in aural skills, technique, and other musical topics that serve as unifying themes for these gatherings. Over the years, I have offered many occasional classes featuring a specific composer. In preparation for these classes, students independently work on repertoire by the composer that they will share with the group, they engage in games and activities featuring the composer (and interacting with the music) during the class, and take away more knowledge about that composer than they could have through their individual study.

Ensemble classes are another effective type of occasional group class. There are several good sources of keyboard ensemble music on the market (for three to eight digital pianos). Rehearsing and performing these ensembles provides educational opportunities rarely available to students in the private lesson. Unlike students who play band or orchestral instruments, piano students often work in solitude. My students who have worked with others in piano ensembles tend to listen better, play more musically, and stay motivated to practice when they know that others are depending on them. Piano duets, duos, and trios also provide ensemble experiences, but using digital pianos and different musical sound settings can encourage attentive listening to phrasing, dynamics, and articulation nuances and result in increased technique at the instrument. Generally, I conduct these ensembles and lead rehearsals (with input from the students), so they learn to speak about music and collaborate with others. If students are working at the appropriate level, the ensemble music sounds more musically complex than their individual repertoire, which most find quite satisfying. Piano ensembles are perennial recital favorites in my studio with children and adults.

In my studio, the "Technique Olympics," in which students prepare various technical exercises, participate in solo and group "events," and serve as judges for their peers' events, is another popular group class during the spring semester as we prepare for annual piano examinations. The culmination of the Olympics includes a medal ceremony, complete with a group performance of the Olympic theme music. For my students who do not participate in regular group lessons, the occasional group class serves as a way to connect with peers in the studio, whom they would otherwise only see at recitals. Occasional group classes provide an opportunity for these students to engage in music making and musical activities in fun and diverse ways while sharing good music with others.

# Regular Group Classes

Regular group lessons that are *adjunct* to private lessons provide an intriguing and practical first foray into the group-teaching arena for teachers. There are several means of configuring group lessons which supplement the private lesson; these might include:

- 3 weeks of private lessons; group lesson only during the fourth week of each month
- 4 weeks of private lessons; group lesson also during fourth week of each month
- Weekly private (or partner) lessons and weekly group classes
- Alternating group and private lessons each week

## *Three Weeks of Private Lessons; Group Lesson Only During the Fourth Week*

Many teachers enjoy the flexibility of having fewer contact hours with students during the fourth week of each month, since they see their students in groups during that week. Groups are typically scheduled according to age or performance level so that activities planned for the class will be appropriate and engaging for all students who participate. Teachers who have success with this category of teaching usually offer several time options from which students can choose to attend during the group week. Students sign up for their class at the beginning of the semester so that the number of students in each group is manageable for the teacher to ensure that optimal learning for all students can take place and to enable students to grow together as a group. The size of the group may depend on the activities that will take place during the classes. Novice group-piano teachers often benefit from offering smaller classes until they develop successful group-teaching strategies and skills.

The regular monthly group lesson can be a musicianship class in which students focus on keyboard theory, creativity, or improvising. It could consist of repertoire sharing and performance, ensemble playing, or development of some other piano skill (such as sight reading or composition). If the teacher has access to a digital piano lab or to multiple keyboards, there are many options for the types of activities in which the students can be engaged, but activities will need to be planned based on the number of keyboards available to pupils. Other types of group classes such as a performance, music history, or music theory class are not necessarily dependent on having multiple keyboards for the students. However, teachers who do not have access to several keyboards should carefully plan activities that will engage all students at all times (more details are provided in Chapters 4, 11, and 12).

Teachers who have not tried this category of teaching may worry that students will not practice during the week of the group lesson. Successful teachers find creative ways to motivate their students to practice. If one is having a music history class, for example, all students could come prepared to play a preassigned piece that reflects the topic of the class. Several years ago, I had monthly music history classes that featured a "composer of the month." The students really enjoyed learning about, performing, and hearing lots of piano music by our featured composers. I actually found that motivation to practice during the group lesson week increased as a result of these classes. If you do not have time to hear every student perform during the class, you could choose performers via a "lottery" (there are some apps, such as You Decide, that increase the sense of excitement for children), and the pupils will be motivated to practice their repertoire in case they are chosen to perform for their peers.

## Four Weeks of Private Lessons; Group Lesson also During the Fourth Week

This category of group teaching can present scheduling challenges for teachers with very high studio enrollments, but it can provide an alternative for teachers who want to incorporate some group learning into their studio curricula without sacrificing individual time with students each week. These classes can be an effective learning opportunity in studios or academies where there are several teachers employed and where the group teaching can be shared among the instructors or where teaching assistants might be available to help with the groups. This monthly group option addresses the problem of students who are less motivated to continue practicing their assignments during weeks when the group class takes place. Offering both group and private lessons will ensure that students maintain their consistent practice in preparation for the private lesson while they benefit from group activities. This bonus lesson during the fourth week of each month can serve to reinforce concepts discussed at the private lesson and can prove to be extremely helpful for students. The group lesson could be similar to those listed earlier. Participating in both group and private lessons provides a stimulating fusion of music study for many students if the instructor can manage the increased teaching schedule for 1 week each month.

## A Private (or Partner) Lesson and a Group Class Every Week

While this may seem like a scheduling drawback for teachers wishing to earn a living, it is actually the model that has been used by many master piano pedagogues. Increased musical engagement and achievement among students provides immense rewards to the teacher. This paradigm is more likely to be used in community schools and performing arts academies that may be affiliated with

institutions of higher education, but independent teachers should consider implementing a similar lesson structure due to the positive effects experienced by both
student and teacher.

The benefits for the teacher include seeing and working with students twice each
week so that mistakes can be prevented or fixed before they have been practiced
incorrectly or become ingrained. Teachers also benefit from increased student motivation. Students tend to be motivated to keep up with practice assignments if they
have to see the teacher twice weekly, and parents generally exhibit more commitment to piano study if they agree to this schedule. Frequent teacher guidance allows
students to experience success in the studio and can increase motivation to practice
effectively outside of the class. Because there are fewer days between lessons, practice
assignments might be shorter and feel more manageable to students. Better retention
and mastery of material due to the frequency of lessons and motivational benefits
from learning with peers during group sessions are commonly noted by teachers
using this teaching format.

Teachers who choose to engage in this combination of group and private teaching will need to decide whether they will disseminate the majority of new information during the group or the private lesson. Many teachers (myself included)
prefer to introduce new information during the group time, when they can guide
students through new and creative experiences that encourage them to explore the
new material together and then follow up individually (or with a partner) later in
the week. The private or partner lesson tends to be shorter than the group lesson.
In general, an hour-long group lesson (or 45 minutes for younger students), followed by a half-hour private or partner lesson, is ideal. If one chooses to make the
private lesson the place new material is introduced, this can be done early in the
week (though 45 minutes may be necessary), and the hour-long group session will
be used to explore the new material through various supplemental activities later
in the week.

### A Note about Partner Lessons

The partner lesson is similar to a private lesson except that two students take the lesson together. Young students can share a piano bench at an acoustic piano and play
together, listen and evaluate one another, and learn how to speak about (as well as
play) music. Partner lessons or pairs of students work well for the beginning and the
intermediate student. Some teachers have even found success offering partner lessons to their more advanced students (see *MTNA Proceedings*, pp. 40–45), though one
could do some overlapping of lessons instead. For example, in a 45-minute lesson,
one advanced student could have a half-hour private lesson and then a 15-minute
partner lesson with a peer. The partner who came in for the last 15 minutes of the
lesson would then have his own 30-minute private lesson following the brief partner

tutorial. Many teachers schedule this type of overlapping lesson for technology or enrichment activities with their younger students. In general, these types of private/ partner combination lessons can be organized fairly easily.

## *A Private Lesson and a Group Lesson on Alternating Weeks*

This category of group and private lessons should not need much explanation. Although this is my least favorite group option, the students do benefit from the group experience a couple of times each month. The teacher who offers this type of lesson schedule may value having fewer contact hours with students during group-lesson weeks. This time could be used to pursue personal musical development or performance opportunities or to prepare for the group classes. The caveat with this type of schedule, however, is that the teacher needs to be extremely organized and should have the studio schedule prominently posted in several places to remind parents and students of the lesson schedule. For example, the schedule should be posted on the studio website for 24-hour access by students and parents. Additionally, weekly or bimonthly email newsletters might include reminders to students about which type of lesson they should prepare for in the coming week. An automated email or text message service might be used on Sunday to remind parents of the upcoming schedule.

Some busy parents may be attracted to this type of lesson structure for two reasons. First, group lessons generally cost less for the parent than private lessons, so the tuition for the semester would be lower than if they enrolled their child for private lessons only. Second, families that are overscheduled may perceive the idea of being able to drop the student off for a longer session every other week as being easier to accommodate. However, some families are extremely busy and may have trouble keeping on top of the weekly schedule change. This is why prominent posting of the schedule and frequent reminders through email, studio newsletters, even text messages are imperative if one engages in this category of group teaching.

## *Occasional Group Camps*

Group-piano camps can offer students the benefits of group-piano study at pivotal points throughout the year or semester. They also serve as a wonderful entry point into group teaching for the teacher who is new to the arena and may not be willing to commit to this type of teaching for an entire semester or academic year. Additionally, these camps can prime students to return to piano study after a hiatus or provide extra motivation at strategic times during the year.

Piano teachers might consider offering week-long piano camps during the summer. These camps keep students thinking about music and playing the piano for concentrated periods throughout the long stretch of time when many students might not find their way to the instrument on their own. Summer camps allow students to maintain and increase skills, since the teacher sees the students for several hours each day for a week. Also, summer camps can provide time to work on functional skills or composition or to explore creativity through the piano. These topics may get short shrift during the year as students focus on preparing repertoire for festivals, contests, and recitals. Parents tend to be fans of piano camps because they recognize the opportunity for their child to maintain piano skills, which can decline during the summer months, and they value being able to enroll their child in an educational and musical activity during the summer. Teachers reap these aforementioned benefits too, in the sense that there is often not the frustration of trying to regain lost ground with students during the first several weeks of the fall semester if students participated in piano camp. Some teachers value being able to earn additional income without having to teach for the entire summer.

Some piano teachers offer mandatory "boot camps" several weeks prior to the start of each semester for transfer students who are deficient in specific areas such as rhythm, sight reading, ear training, improvisation/composition/creativity, or some other musicianship skill. Such topics can be addressed effectively and efficiently in the group-piano setting and in a manner that most students find enjoyable and memorable. But the piano boot camp can be equally valuable for the returning piano students whose attention has been on travel, relaxation, and nonmusical play for several months during the summer. Additionally, piano camps can be useful for students at specific points during the semester when they need an additional motivational boost or some extra time to develop complex skills. Teachers may coordinate these piano camps to correspond with breaks in the school year, such as spring break or winter break, but it is also possible to offer a half-day "performance boot camp" for students several weeks before the studio recital or before a piano festival.

While themed piano camps might address various skills and techniques, ensemble camps permit students to discover and hone ensemble playing. June Montgomery (1998) lists several very good options for scheduling piano camps at the beginning of her series of activity books entitled *Piano Camp*. She summarizes activities for meeting every day for 1 week (Monday through Friday) and for meeting three times a week over a 2-week period. She also outlines how a typical 2-hour session might unfold. For example, for a 2-hour daily camp, students might begin with 15 minutes of flash cards and review from the previous session, then continue with note-reading, rhythm, music symbol, and keyboard activity pages (including at least one game) for 45 minutes. Following a 15-minute break, the students would engage in additional activities for reinforcement during the final 45 minutes, and awards and assignments for the following day could be presented (Montgomery, 1998).

I would suggest that the list implies that group activities and games, along with exploration of technique and repertoire, will be incorporated into each of the lesson segments. A list of additional resources for piano camps is provided in Appendix B. Although extensive, this list is not meant to be exhaustive. Exploration and use of these resources should provide grist for the creative teaching mill, and many variations and activities for piano camps are possible based on the available facilities, the strengths of the teacher, and the needs of the students.

## Group Piano Only and the Teaching Space

Teaching students only via the group piano class is becoming increasingly popular, and many teachers find personal fulfillment and student success in this arena. At the college level and for adults of all ages, a digital piano lab will be the heart of the ideal teaching space, as sharing pianos can be challenging for adult-sized students. Specifics about electronic laboratory setups can be found in Chapters 14 and 15, but college classrooms tend to house between 10 and 20 student keyboards, connected by a controller that permits the teacher and students to communicate with one another. Adult leisure classes, especially those offered outside of an academic setting might have fewer keyboards. Many teachers find four to eight keyboards, connected through a controller, to be ideal. The smaller class size for an adult studio lends itself to music making and sharing among all members of the group. When teaching both children and adults, easy access to a whiteboard and to some sort of visualizer (that displays both keys and pitches on the staff) is advisable. In the smartphone age, when everyone has a personal music playback and recording device in their pocket, teachers should be sure that they have the capability to record students and play high-quality music through Bluetooth speakers in the classroom. Listening to recorded music is important for students of all ages and levels.

If one chooses to use a digital piano lab for group teaching (which is my personal preference), the initial start-up costs can be significant. The teacher will need to purchase or rent several student keyboards, a teaching console, and a controller to link the keyboards together for optimal group work and student learning. Although the most basic studio setup requires minimal technology, a teacher who wishes to rely heavily on technology, due to the teaching strategies and opportunities it may offer, will need to invest more capital. Additionally, the size and space of the studio will need to safely support the number of students and the planned activities that will occur in the room (more discussion about this in Chapters 9 and 14). In addition to the classroom space, there should be a waiting area for students and parents, and there must be ample, unrestricted parking, since pick-up and drop-off times for classes tend to be busy. All piano instructors need to ensure that their studio is located in an area that is free of city or community restrictions on using the space for business purposes. However, group teachers must be especially cognizant of the congestion caused by groups of students entering and exiting the studio simultaneously and ensure that there is ample space both inside and outside of the premises.

Many successful group teachers work in a hybrid classroom, where they have several digital pianos and one or two acoustic instruments. When teaching small-group or partner lessons to younger children and beginners, these can take place on one or two acoustic instruments. Oftentimes, the bench is pulled away from the piano for certain activities, and students take turns (in pairs) at the piano completing assignments, performing musical examples, and playing musical-performance games. Regardless of the type of instruments used, ideally children will have room for movement and off-bench activities and a large table for theory and dictation work. Young children will benefit from working with educational manipulatives such as floor staves, keyboards, and flashcards.

These classes, like all group-piano lessons, must be carefully planned, sequenced, and undertaken with an awareness of the students' learning stages and individual learning styles (see Chapters 2 and 4) and of facilitating group activities (see Chapter 3). All group-piano teachers benefit from critical reflection on their teaching and student learning following each class. Novice teachers often find watching video of their own group teaching to be highly instructive (see Appendixes E.1–E.5 for evaluation forms). Additionally, inviting observation and critique by trusted, qualified colleagues and observing group classes taught by experienced professionals can be extremely helpful in stimulating ideas for one's own group teaching and for discovering new musical activities to employ with various groups of students. It can be invigorating and refreshing to see the exuberance of the children as they approach playing the piano with all of the pleasure and amusement of playing a great musical game.[2] Figure 1.1

*Figure 1.1* Children and Adults Working in Group-Piano Classes

highlights students working in six different group-piano settings. See Chapter 14 for additional details and ideas to consider.

## Benefits of Group Piano for Student and Teacher

By now it is hoped that you have some sense of the various guises under which group teaching can work in the piano studio and that you are beginning to generate ideas about how you might schedule and implement group lessons. Before moving into deeper discussion about important issues, such as lesson preparation and student assessment during group teaching, it might be helpful to discuss reported advantages for studying piano in groups. These benefits have been reported among participants in group piano at all levels and ages. (More thorough discussion of advantages and disadvantages of group teaching and learning may be found in Chapter 10.) Common benefits, cited by instructors and researchers, are worth considering. These include:

- Students progress more quickly than they do on their own (this phenomenon is especially notable at the beginning stages of piano study).
- Students learn from one another, and they learn to help each other (this includes having the opportunity to hear the questions and comments of other students).
- Students learn to listen carefully (to music and to others in general).
- Students learn to speak intelligently and thoughtfully about music.
- Students gain performance experience, poise, and composure from the outset of music study.
- Students hear a greater variety of repertoire (especially if students have individual repertoire assignments).
- Students have numerous and varied opportunities to explore functional skills (harmonizing, sight reading, technique, improvisation), rhythm, games, ear-training/aural skills activities.
- Students can use technology as a vehicle for learning music.
- Students learn to rehearse and perform ensemble music.
- Students tend to have a strong sense of rhythm (especially if the teacher is using MIDI accompaniments or other teaching technology and if the students rehearse ensemble music regularly).
- Students experience opportunities for greater creativity. Students who are naturally creative can encourage those who are more structured in their approach to the instrument.
- Students can benefit from positive peer pressure, which can be a great motivator and behavior shaper. It should be noted that the group dynamic is unique to each class, and each class's unique energy can be harnessed to benefit all students (see Chapter 3). In order for the group dynamic and peer pressure to be used to full,

positive advantage, however, the teacher must create a safe, caring space in which students can learn and explore together from the outset.

- Students will stimulate and energize each other, but the teacher needs to steer this creative energy!
- Students tend to have fun in groups! Practicing the piano can be a lonely endeavor, and the opportunity to make music with peers on a regular basis can make the journey much more enjoyable.

There are some notable benefits for the teacher who chooses to teach group piano too. Because teaching is an art involving great skill and passion, teachers should not underestimate the importance of acknowledging the benefits to oneself when choosing an appropriate career path. Benefits for the instructor of teaching piano in groups include:

- More efficient use of teaching time. This should not be the primary consideration when deciding to teach groups, however, because preparation for each class is considerable, and due to the uniqueness of each group, even similarly leveled classes will need slightly different class activities and teaching strategies.
- A stimulating challenge. Many teachers find it energizing to reach groups of students at once. Monitoring students and teaching technology can provide inspiration and variation from more traditional teaching routines. New teachers find that it can be challenging to maintain class integrity while employing the technology in a piano lab. At times, standing at the teaching console, instructing, and monitoring students can feel like manning mission control at NASA! However, once a teacher is on the path toward masterful teaching in group piano, it can become a true flow or optimal experience. Additionally, being able to teach more than one or two students per hour means that you will be able to work with more students in your community each week.
- Potentially more income. While teachers may make more money per hour when teaching groups, there are some caveats to this benefit, especially for new group teachers. There can be considerable start-up costs, difficulty attracting ample numbers of students for each class, and a large amount of planning time when one begins teaching group piano. Please see details under the list of considerations in what follows.

## Considerations Regarding Group Piano

Of course, there are a few considerations that one should contemplate when weighing whether group teaching is the best choice for one's studio. First, classes can have only as many students as space and equipment permit. Based on geography, city codes, and budgetary realities, it may not be economically viable for some teachers to offer group piano. Most teachers find that there is a minimum amount of technology required to make group-piano classes effective, and this technology can be expensive to purchase and to maintain. While classes cannot have more students than the space permits, classes do need to have enough students at the same level for them to be effective. Scheduling can be another challenge. Novice group piano teachers, with a smaller student pool from which to draw, may encounter difficulty finding enough students who are available for a particular class or level. Additionally, all students in the group will need to stay together in a basic method or else be reassigned to another group. There should be an understanding among the parents, the students, and the teacher that the group will remain together for a specified amount of time (i.e., a semester or an academic year) unless there are extenuating circumstances. It changes the group dynamic to lose or gain students midway through the semester; this can be very disconcerting and unfair to the class and should be avoided. I have known of many groups in which students and parents have been so pleased with the group dynamic that they make great effort to keep the group together for several years. When students in groups are performing at slightly different levels (but otherwise the group dynamic is positive), some teachers maintain the learning and musical integrity by assigning more or less challenging supplementary material to individuals within the group, in addition to the common group music.

Another aspect of scheduling has to do with group size. Classes for younger students should have fewer students, and economic implications of a smaller class size need to be considered when setting up a group-piano studio. Indeed, for some teachers, groups past the elementary level may not be economically viable, since there may not be enough older students to warrant a class. Other teachers only wish to teach beginners in a group setting because they may not want to figure out how to address technical and musical issues at the intermediate level in a group-piano class. If a teacher decides that she will only offer one or two years of group instruction, she then faces a moral obligation to know how she will direct these students once they have graduated from her group-piano program. Will she be able to take on these students for private lessons? Does she have another colleague in the region with whom arrangements have been made to transfer former group students? Is there a young teacher in the community who will be willing and able to accept these transfer students? Is there a music school in the area with competent piano pedagogy students whom she might be able to hire for a couple of days each week to teach the displaced group students? Does she have enough studio space to consider this option? These are just a few of the questions that group-piano teachers should consider before embarking upon enrolling students in group piano.

## Special Skills Required of an Effective
## Group-Piano Teacher

I have observed many successful and unsuccessful group-piano instructors. I have made identification of skills associated with expert group-piano teachers an important component of my research agenda. I will discuss some essential teaching skills in what follows. It has not gone unnoticed that skills that are imperative for successful group teaching are similar to those exhibited by successful private music teachers. While teachers should always prepare thoroughly and hold themselves to the highest standards regardless of the lesson setting, if group-piano instructors let any of the following techniques slide, the students will not be able to interact, learn, and achieve optimal musical expression during the instructional period. As noted previously, the ability for the teacher to multitask is imperative. Many novice group-piano teachers find it difficult to simultaneously operate the equipment, give verbal instructions to the group, keep each individual on task, and hear what the students are playing! Additionally, the sequencing and the pacing of each lesson is critical and only improves with careful preparation, observation of one's own teaching (through video, for example), and reflection prior to starting this process anew the following week. The teacher needs to be able to disseminate information effectively to all learners in the group, thus maintaining an awareness of the different learning styles of the students participating in each class. Informal assessment of individuals in the group is imperative to ensure proper student learning, though this skill is difficult for teachers accustomed to private teaching only. This assessment may be done visually with certain activities and through careful listening during group activities. Additionally, the instructor needs to have read and digested the most recent literature on individual learning preferences and on collaborative learning so that he is able to facilitate interactions between students. He must know which students to pair together for in-class work. The partner groupings may vary from one activity to another depending on the skill set required and the learning goals and outcomes for the activity.

Long-range planning is imperative and often difficult for the novice group teacher. Both long-term goals and measurable objectives for each class must be included in this planning. I recommend having just a few measurable objectives for each class and developing all activities around these. Good objectives will be expanded upon in subsequent classes, but music or activities that do not serve the stated goals or objectives may be better saved for a different lesson. The teacher must be comfortable with the fast pace of a well-sequenced lesson and be able to switch quickly from one activity to the next. This skill is part of the true art of teaching group classes. Properly sequenced and paced, the transitioning from one activity to the next can be masterful, allowing the class objectives and music making to develop innately (and providing little opportunity for disruptive or off-task behavior). If the teacher is unable to keep all of the students engaged throughout the lesson, chaos may erupt among children, and learning may become haphazard. It can be helpful to be able to spot potential disruptions and thwart them before problems arise; however, this is a skill that teachers develop over time.

While adhering to the objectives for each class, the teacher must possess the ability to guide student learning but to remain open for "teachable moments" when an unplanned topic or musical activity can be explored. After careful lesson planning and preparation, there can be a certain amount of fluidity to the instructional period. If the teacher has clarified the long-range goals for the group, she may see the potential benefits in exploring an unplanned topic upon which the students have stumbled at any given point in the lesson. The group-piano teacher must also be aware of each group's morale and be able to maintain it throughout the semester (especially midway through or toward the end of the semester).

Finally, it can be difficult to refine a student's technical development and artistic playing within the group environment, though some pedagogues have argued that this is not necessarily the case. While I urge teachers to do as much group work as possible, spending some class time listening to students individually over headphones or, better yet, having them perform for one another in pairs or for the entire group, provides time for reflection and thoughtful feedback from both students and teacher. These types of activities certainly engage students in active music listening and reflection while preparing them to present artistic and musical performances. I have heard beginning group-piano students exhibit far more musical playing and effortless technique than typical beginning private students. Likewise, some of the most musical solo performances that I have judged in competition have been from students who took only group-piano lessons. I am certain that these students honed their listening skills and technique during carefully sequenced activities designed by masterful group-piano teachers.

## Student Readiness for Group-Piano Lessons

Once one has decided to teach group piano, the next step is to group the students appropriately. As has been alluded to previously, age and ability levels matter. However, when assessing beginning students as potential group-piano candidates, teachers should be cognizant of an individual student's readiness for piano, maturity level, learning ability, physical development, rhythmic development, and aural skills.

These criteria are similar to those used to assess student readiness for private lessons. But group-piano students will need to be able to stay with the group, follow simple instructions without too much help from the teacher, maintain focus for the entire class, and be at the same approximate age with no more than two years in age difference between children in the group. Although it is important to maintain the integrity of the group, sometimes students may need to be moved into another class or into private lessons if they fall behind, outgrow their group, or simply cannot maintain focus on tasks with other students in the room.

## Teacher Readiness for Group-Piano Lessons

So, are you intrigued by and interested in group teaching? I believe that you must first ask yourself if you are well suited to it. I will tell you that I fell in love with it the first time I taught a group-piano class, but not everyone has that same experience. Despite the current trend toward teaching piano in groups, if you are not well suited to teaching in this environment, it is better not to do so. Frances Clark felt that for teachers to be successful at group piano, it was imperative that they:

- Believe that the group learning situation is best for every student in the group.
- Know how to keep every student learning for every second of the class. (I contend that this skill depends on teachers' abilities to use interactions between students to their advantage.)
- Know and avoid the pitfalls of group teaching . . . the group lesson is a music lesson with an emphasis on musical listening, musical thinking, and musical performance.
- Be aware that there may be a student who is unduly held back or who is experiencing undue pressure to keep up with the group [and have contingencies for accommodating that student].

(Goss, 1992)

Hopefully this chapter has helped you understand that while group piano can be extremely effective, there are some considerations. If a student is extremely advanced (considerably ahead of the group), he or she may need private lessons instead of simply assigning supplementary repertoire during the group class. Other students simply need individual attention in order to thrive.

Most educational activities are in groups. For example, school and sports activities tend to take place in group settings. Thus, the student may need one-on-one time with the piano teacher for optimal learning. However, some students with special needs may not be suited to the group setting. There is a lot of visual and auditory stimulation in the group-piano class, and this may be distracting for some students. Teachers should consider the age, intelligence, coordination ability, motivation, home support, and practice habits of each student when considering including them in a group-piano class. In most group-piano classes (with the exception of some recreational piano classes), independent practice outside of the lesson will be required in order for subsequent group activities to proceed as planned. If students won't be able to commit to practicing at home, they may impede the progress of the entire group. However, many students find the fact that they will contribute to the group's success to be motivational when it comes to individual practice; they don't want to let their group members or classmates down at the next lesson. Above all, group-piano teachers must remain cognizant of the fact that group teaching is about musical listening, musical thinking, and musical performance. Regardless of the group activity, the music making should always be musical and the technique as refined as possible.

There will be additional and specific discussion of effective group teacher characteristics and common pitfalls of novice group-piano teachers in Chapters 11 and 12. At this point, however, I would like to suggest that teachers might ease themselves into group teaching by providing a group-piano class with a colleague in the area. This team-teaching approach is used in many fields, the preparation and teaching can be shared, and the teachers will learn from one another both during class and in the postclass reflections and preparation

## A Final Note of Caution

While several pedagogy texts suggest that group-piano classes offer teachers an opportunity to make more income than they would in the same amount of time teaching private lessons, I would offer a word of caution about this notion. While all teachers should prepare thoroughly for piano lessons (whether private or group), every master group-piano teacher that I have met jokes that they don't teach group for the money. Preparation time and lesson planning will consume an inordinate amount of time when one is beginning to teach piano in groups. Even those who have been teaching group-piano for decades still prepare thoroughly and consider each individual in the class when planning, which takes time. While I have observed much excellent group teaching, I have also witnessed poor group-piano instruction. In addition to failing to engage all students or require the highest level of musicianship, often teachers of ineffective classes devote too little time or thought to lesson planning, sequencing, pacing, or teaching. For each concept that is taught, the instructor should have several ways to explain it, several activities to reinforce it, and contingencies beyond the plan. Following each class, time should be devoted to reflection of what worked well and what could be improved, and steps should be taken to make these improvements at the next lesson. Initially, it is advisable to video each lesson, as many student behaviors that had gone unnoticed during class will become obvious on video. The most successful group-piano teachers offer group instruction not because of the promise of more income but because they believe that students learn better in groups, the music making is more fulfilling for everyone, and they enjoy the challenges of teaching group piano.

## Pedagogy in Action (Questions to Answer)

1. Review your personal teaching philosophy. Do the tenets of group teaching explored in this chapter resound with your personal values? If so, add a paragraph incorporating group teaching into your teaching philosophy.
2. Share your thoughts and updated teaching philosophy with a trusted colleague who has been teaching group piano for several years. Ask your colleague to share his philosophy with you and inquire about how his personal philosophy evolved.
3. Choose one category of group teaching that you would like to experiment with. Write a detailed plan for how you will incorporate this group class into the cadre of lessons you offer. Conduct additional reading and discussions with group-piano teachers if you would like more information. (In subsequent chapters, you will learn more about lesson planning, course materials, teaching strategies, etc. For now, just consider and learn about the type of group class you can envision offering on a regular basis.)

## Notes

1 See the Music Teachers National Association (1999) *Proceedings from Pedagogy Saturday III* for a complete overview of all presentations, papers, and panel sessions presented during Pedagogy Saturday.
2 Please see my web site for video clips of successful group-piano classes with students of all ages at www.pameladpike.com. A video entitled *Conversation with Frances Clark: Her Life and Teachings* provides footage of Clark working with children in groups. The video is available from www.keyboardpedagogy.org. Additionally, many local teachers' organizations have teachers who are willing to have other teachers observe their group classes. The Music Teachers National Association (www.mtna.org) has resources for group-piano teachers online and at national conferences.

## References

Fay, A. (1965). *Music-Study in Germany from the Home Correspondence of Amy Fay*. New York: Dover Reprint.

Goss, L. (Ed.). (1992). *Questions and Answers by Frances Clark*. Northfield, IL: The Instrumentalist Company.

Montgomery, J. (1998). *Piano Camp, Books Primer-4*. Van Nuys, CA: Alfred Publishing Co., Inc.

*Proceedings from MTNA Pedagogy Saturday III*. (1999). Cincinnati: Music Teachers National Association.

# 2

# BRIEF OVERVIEW OF LEARNING THEORIES THAT TEACHERS SHOULD CONSIDER

## Objectives

By the end of this chapter, you should have a working knowledge of major learning theories and be able to apply key concepts from each to help students in your group piano classes learn more effectively.

## Introduction

As piano teachers, we are fortunate. There are many exceptional instruction books (or methods) available that can be used effectively with beginning piano students. If we teach private or one-on-one piano lessons, we might note that the pacing, sequencing, and presentation of materials seems appropriate for many students, and usually we figure out how to help individual students consolidate the information and new concepts. So why should we explore the complex psychological field that encompasses learning theories? It has been suggested that if our curriculum, daily instructional choices, and practice assignments are informed by learning theories, including understanding how students learn at any given time and how to help them place new concepts in their existing store of knowledge, our students will learn more effectively (Bigge, 1982).

In a group-piano setting, there are two additional considerations. While the popular and most widely available group-piano methods are educationally robust, the sequencing and reinforcement may not be as extensive as in multibook methods for individuals. Additionally, within each group of students, we are likely to have learners with different backgrounds, experiences, learning attributes, and learning preferences. Students tend to benefit from different types of activities to enhance learning at various ages. Thus, understanding learning theory should inform which students we group together for piano instruction and which materials we choose to use. Since each individual in the group may learn differently, we need to foster and facilitate various types of learning within the group. Therefore, the ability to understand how different people learn and knowledge of various strategies for enhancing learning and musical growth become extremely important for both efficient teaching and creating effective learning environments for all students in the group.

Generally, in pedagogy classes we look at psychologists who proposed and tested theories of learning as a way of studying those theories. Although we cannot learn about all of the theories in detail, we commonly review behaviorism, cognition, humanism, and constructivism. Pedagogy texts tend to highlight multiple intelligences, learning styles, learning modes, and developmental theories, though these are not specifically learning theories but rather differences in how individuals may acquire new information, process it, and thus learn. Finally, in music and general education, there is currently much discussion about communities of practice. We will briefly describe communities of practice, as these address how groups of students learn collectively, such as in a group-piano setting. What follows is a brief overview of features of learning theories and learning styles that are applicable to teaching and learning in a group-piano setting. Then we will apply some of the research to group-piano settings.

## Learning Theories

### *What Is Learning?*

Take a moment and think about how you would define learning. One way psychologists recognize that learning has taken place is when individuals exhibit a lasting change in their knowledge, skills, and even motivation. Merriam-Webster defines learning as "the activity or process of gaining knowledge or skill by studying, practicing, being taught, or experiencing something." As the definition suggests, knowledge may be acquired through somewhat passive means (such as being taught or listening to a lecture) or through more active experiences (such as practicing a skill or working with new ideas). In fact, learning piano is rather complex in that students must demonstrate learning through development of two types of knowledge: declarative and procedural. Declarative knowledge is understanding concepts and ideas about music. An example might be being able to explain how a major scale is created and even notating it on a staff. Procedural knowledge means demonstrating understanding by doing something, such as playing that major scale accurately, with the correct fingering.

### *Behaviorism*

Throughout the 19th and early 20th centuries, psychologists became interested in how they might get individuals to exhibit changes in their behavior. These psychologists did not consider how they might get people to think about their own behaviors; rather, they tended to elicit desired responses by applying strategies and stimuli over which the person (or animal) had no control. This field became known as behaviorism. Behaviorism was appealing during a time when scientists were seeking to maintain objectiveness and scientific rigor because changes in behavior could be easily observed and recorded. Many of the experiments led by behaviorists were actually conducted on animals.

Ivan Pavlov (1049–1936), who trained a dog to salivate at the sound of a bell (after teaching him that he would be fed following the ringing of the bell), is well known us un early behaviorist. Pavlov's system of training came to be known as operant conditioning. B. F. Skinner (1904–1990) and other Americans explored operant conditioning and expanded upon these concepts. Eventually, behavioral psychologists achieved changes in behavior by training animals and people to recognize a stimulus and respond to it in a specific way, through positive or negative reinforcement. This training is called stimulus-response (or S-R). Edward Thorndike (1874–1949) was one of the theory's first proponents and Robert M. Gagné (1916–2002) defended it more recently in his influential text *The Conditions of Learning*.

While many contemporary teachers do not espouse behaviorist theories, it could be argued that when we rely on extrinsic motivators, we are encouraging students to operate on a behavioral level. For example, if a student plays a piece well and we reward her with a sticker, she may be motivated to learn the next piece well. However, we must ensure that we are not setting up a simple stimulus-response reaction (in which the student plays well just to earn the prize) instead of encouraging the student to enjoy the intrinsic process of learning and playing music well.

## Psychosocial Development, Cognitive Development, and Human Learning

In the late 19th and early 20th centuries, a number of German scholars began exploring how people actively make their own associations and spot patterns that enable them to learn if provided with the appropriate environment and experiences. Kurt Lewin (1890–1947), for example, was influential in this break from the behaviorists because he highlighted how people perceive reality individually and that they could exhibit some control over their own learning. This more humanist approach paved the way for developmental psychologists, who recognized that at different stages in our lives, we are ready for different types of learning, and for pioneers in cognitive theory.

Unlike the behaviorists, these psychologists observed what subjects were doing without necessarily employing artificial stimuli. One of the first cognitive psychologists whose influence remains was Jean Piaget (1896–1980). It should be noted that while he was concerned with how children thought and processed information, Piaget's cognition was different from the cognitive psychology and human development field that has exploded in the decades since the advancement of brain-imaging technology. Piaget began formulating his ideas as he observed his own children playing. He learned more and fleshed out his theories through subsequent research studies with children in which he observed them experimenting with various mathematical and scientific principles such as categorization of objects, conservation of numbers, space, and substance, and problem solving. He noted that children are not miniature adults (in other words, they think and process information differently), and he suggested that they have different stages of development at which time different types of learning are possible. Piaget proposed four sequential stages of development that can be observed in children even today. As you read about these stages, think about the types of instructional activities that might be appropriate for a child at each stage.

1. Sensorimotor (birth–2 years). During this stage, infants develop schemes to represent the world they are experiencing around them.
2. Preoperational (2–7 years). Children at this stage, including preschoolers, develop mastery of symbols (such as words or musical notation) to enhance existing representations and form new schemes. They benefit from bodily movements and manipulation and generally cannot mentally reverse actions.
3. Concrete operational (7–11 years). Children at this stage can mentally reverse actions but generally only when the objects are present, or when they have experienced something concretely. Students may still need to manipulate objects to solve complex problems, but they are able to use past experiences to infer and explain results.
4. Formal operational (11 years and older). At this stage, children can mentally generalize and come up with hypotheses and deal with mental abstractions. However, subsequent researchers have suggested that these abstract mental manipulation skills must be practiced and may not develop fully until late adolescence.

(Snowman, McCown, & Biehler, 2012, pp. 36–48)

There is one more developmental theory that can be helpful when working with children, adolescents, and adults in the piano classroom. It was proposed by Erik Erikson (1902–1994), it covers the entire life span, and it considers not just cognitive abilities but psychosocial commonalities at each stage. Thus, it can be very useful when working with groups of students in the piano lab. Erikson, who worked with Sigmund Freud before emigrating to the United States at the outbreak of the Second World War, defined essential psychosocial characteristics that appear in children between certain ages or stages. See Figure 2.1 for an overview. Like Piaget, Erikson arrived at these stages based on personal observations. He wrote about them extensively in *Childhood and Society* (Erikson, 1963). Where Erikson differs from Piaget is the psycho-social aspect, or how the child and the person interact with others and how those interactions, both positive and negative, define the person during any given stage of development.

29

| Stage of Psychosocial Development | Age Range of Stage |
|---|---|
| Trust vs. Mistrust | Birth to 1 year |
| Autonomy vs. Shame and Doubt | 2 to 3 years |
| Initiative vs. Guilt | 4 to 5 years |
| Industry vs. Inferiority | 6 to 11 years |
| Identity vs. Role Confusion | 12 to 18 years |
| Intimacy vs. Isolation | Young adulthood |
| Generativity vs. Stagnation | Middle age |
| Integrity vs. Despair | Old age |

*Figure 2.1* Erikson's Stages of Psychosocial Development
Adapted from Snowman, McCown, & Biehler, 2012.

Between birth and 1 year of age, children are in the trust versus mistrust stage. During this time in their young lives, infants learn to trust the world around them. If parents adequately meet their child's needs consistently and with positive affection, the child develops a view of the world as a safe place. If parents inadequately or negatively meet these needs, the child will come to view the world with mistrust and suspicion. This uncertainty can manifest itself in poor social interactions and behavior problems when the child is older. Between the ages of 2 and 3, children begin to explore their world and develop a sense of autonomy. Erikson cautions that if parents are too eager to do too many things for their young child or if they grow impatient with his progress, the child may begin to doubt his autonomy. Using shame as a behavior modifier is unacceptable at this stage and will lead to self-doubt in the child. We might see children in a piano class who should be beyond this stage (based on their age) but who have yet to develop their autonomy.

At the ages of 4 to 5 years, children are able to participate in many physical activities and can use language to explore. Teachers and parents should provide children at this stage freedom to learn from exploration and experimentation. For these reasons, a small-group piano class can be an ideal place for 5-year-olds to explore music and movement. Although there is a push to get all children into preschool or early childhood education programs in the United States and other industrialized countries, Erikson's industry versus inferiority stage, which occurs between the ages of 6 and 11 years, coincides with the traditional first years of formal education. How a child is encouraged or dissuaded to complete an activity and how she is praised or discouraged will determine whether that child is able to be industrious or whether she feels inferior when attempting to learn. As anyone who has worked with teenagers knows, between the ages of 12 and 18, adolescents are involved in developing an ego identity. If young people at this age are permitted to succeed at integrating specific roles, especially those related to future career choices, they will be much more likely to forge a strong identity rather than suffer from role confusion.

The group-piano setting can be a wonderful environment for teenagers to display mastery and ownership of musical concepts while experiencing positive interactions with peers through music.

We will look more closely at adults in Chapter 7. However, we should note that Erikson speculated that in young adulthood, we each need to develop an intimate relationship with another person; otherwise, we will experience a sense of isolation. The generativity that is optimal in middle age refers to serving as a role model for the next generation and guiding children so that they can achieve their optimal psycho-social development at each childhood stage. The last stage that Erikson highlights is integrity versus despair. Integrity refers to accepting that how our life unfolded was the only possible outcome for our lives due to the influential forces of the parents, teachers, and people who shaped and nurtured us. If one realizes that the cycle of life is drawing to a close and that there is not enough time to experiment with another integrity path, despair may result.

In terms of adult development, in recent decades, some researchers have focused on life-span development, which accounts for the many phases and roles that adults experience throughout life. Life-span theories tend to break adult life into more stages than young adulthood and middle and old age. A theory that I have found particularly useful for framing adult needs in the group-piano class is Levinson's task-development stage theory (1978). Simply, Levinson defines ten stages through which most adults pass. These are early adult transition (ages 17–22), adulthood (22–29), age 30 transition (29–33), settling down (33–40), midlife transition (40–45), middle adulthood (45–50), age 50 transition (50–55), culmination of middle adult-hood (55–60), late-life transition (60–65), and late adulthood (65+). While you may disagree with the descriptions or number of stages that Levinson identified, when we work with adults in the group-piano setting, it is worth recognizing that their goals, objectives, and time commitment will vary depending on their stage of life. Please see Chapter 7 for further details on life-span theory as it applies to working with adults in the group-piano class.

The field of cognition has continued to evolve. Advances in computer and brain-imaging technology in the 1980s fueled a renewed interest in understanding learning through new kinds of advanced observation and extrapolation. Contemporary cog-nitive psychologists use modern medical imaging technology to understand specific processes that take place in the brain as we perceive information, attend to it, process it, and store it for future retrieval and use. This process is often referred to as encod-ing, storing, and retrieving. Some cognitive psychologists are pursuing such research in an effort to understand how teachers might help students learn more effectively. Others are actively exploring how the brain and subsequent learning change as we age. Thus, early in the 21st century, the field is often referred to as "cognition and learning." Cognition informs how we present material and encourage students to make meaning of concepts, information, and music notation, both during the piano class and when practicing at home. Ultimately, it is the aim of many practitioners and teachers to help students understand how they learn and to apply that knowledge to future learning tasks. This type of understanding about how we learn is known as metacognition.

## Other Theorists and Theories for Teachers to Consider and Explore

In the United States, Jerome Bruner (1915–2016) was influential in leading the exploration and development of cognitive theories so that they could be applied to education. He is remembered for having chaired or served on influential national committees that changed public school curricula and for numerous books, including *The Process of Education* (1960). In his obituary in *The New York Times*, psychologist Howard Gardiner noted that Bruner "was the most important contributor to educational thinking since John Dewey" (*NYT*, Benedict Carey, online 8 June 2016). Bruner wrote about and explored ideas that we use in the piano class today, including the nonspecific transfer of skills and the spiral curriculum, in which critical concepts are introduced (in an age-appropriate manner) early in a child's study. Then these topics are continuously revisited and expanded upon throughout the course of instruction.

Lev Vygotsky (1896–1934) supported the notion of using cognitive strategies to improve learning. In particular, he recognized the importance of the adult in helping children learn more than possible without intervention (or mediation through the zone of proximal development, as he called it). He is credited with the technique of scaffolding new concepts onto previously learned material to help students organize and understand material.

Abraham Maslow (1908–1970) was an existential psychologist. Although he studied with the behaviorist Edward Thorndike, he did not espouse behaviorist theories. One of his most influential books was *Toward a Psychology of Being* (1969). He believed that the purpose of education was to help each person reach their full potential, which he called self-actualization. He recognized, however, that if a person's basic needs (such as food, shelter, safety, love, belonging, etc.) were not met, he or she would not be able to focus on educational pursuits that would lead to self-actualization. Maslow's hierarchy of self-actualization is most often represented by a pyramid (Figure 2.2).

Although best known to musicians for his influential book *Developing Talent in Young People* (1985), Benjamin Bloom (1913–1999) was another educational psychologist whose work influences how we present material to students and encourage them to make meaning of these concepts. In 1956, Bloom and his colleagues defined mastery learning and introduced a hierarchical list of learning categories that could be assessed by teachers. These learning outcomes were usually represented in a pyramid and came to be known as Bloom's taxonomy (of educational objectives). At the base of the pyramid are activities that require less understanding or synthesis of concepts

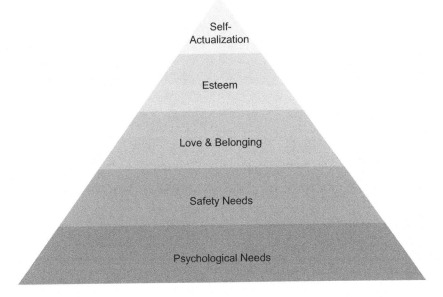

*Figure 2.2* Maslow's Hierarchy of Needs

than those at the top. In 2001, the pyramid categories were revised to be less static and more easily recognizable by teachers. The hierarchy still represents a progression from display of factual knowledge, conceptual knowledge, procedural knowledge through to metacognitive knowledge. See Figure 2.3 for a comparison of the 1956 and 2001 versions. Use whichever of the pyramids is more meaningful to you when you evaluate students' learning in your piano classes.

Finally, expanding upon the concepts of synthesis and creation, constructivism is a theory that reminds us that the most effective learning is active, not passive. If learners can apply new concepts in different and novel situations, evaluate their work, and create new work, they will have learned more effectively. In essence, this is what learning to play the piano should be about. When working with students individually, it is easy to get them to try new concepts and improvise and guide them through learning new repertoire. However, when first teaching piano in a group setting, some teachers revert to the more passive lecture-type teaching, in which they give students information and have them repeat and play, without engaging the mind. If we can use discovery learning, scaffold concepts, and spiral our curriculum to engage students in actively exploring new ideas, evaluating, synthesizing, and creating together, the learning can be extraordinary.

In music education, there is interest in communities of practice. This theory suggests that the shared knowledge created collectively by students, through cooperation and collaboration, is greater and more deeply learned than knowledge acquired individually. If we can create a safe environment in the piano lab in which students share

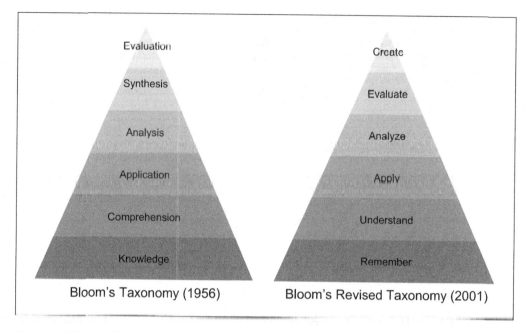

*Figure 2.3* Bloom's Taxonomy of Educational Objectives and a Taxonomy for Teaching, Learning, and Assessment

mutual respect, trust, and joy in learning together, we have created a community of practice. In the next chapter, we will explore how to use group dynamics to create meaningful learning communities in group-piano settings.

Although several of the aforementioned theories seem to be diametrically opposed, in truth, group-piano teachers use knowledge gleaned from each. While some of the theories appear to suggest that everyone learns the same way or at the same stage, we know that individuals each experience learning in unique ways. In Chapter 4, we will look at individual learning modes and individual learning styles or preferences and discuss how we can harness individual differences to enhance the learning of the group. In general, learning takes place when students are interested, engaged, and extended just beyond their current limits of knowledge and skill.

## Discussion and Implementation in the Piano Class

### *Reflection on the Use of Learning and Developmental Theories in the Group-Piano Setting*

So why do we need to learn about how learning theories evolved and know specifics about learning theory? As thinking about learning theories evolved, certain principles observed and explained in one generation informed how the next generation thought and experimented. Thus, small tenets of even some late-19th-century learning theory traditions are important for understanding the most recent theories of our day. Additionally, teachers of music still use helpful pieces from each of these traditions to facilitate learning. When one teaches groups of piano students, it is critical to have a broad understanding of how individuals within the group might learn. Then the instructor can present material to be learned in ways that will facilitate learning by each of the students in the class. Furthermore, when designing group activities for students in our group-piano communities of learning, providing pillars such as constructivism and scaffolding, while helping them evaluate, synthesize, and create music together will enable more enjoyable, meaningful, and deeper learning experiences.

As group-piano teachers, we must design and build the curriculum to suit the learners in each class we teach. We must remain cognizant of developmental and cognitive learning theories. The curricula for beginning groups of 5-, 8-, or 20-year-olds will each look very different. The materials will vary, but so will the group activities. When designing the curriculum for the 8-year-olds, the teacher would need to be aware of the developmental stage of the children, their basic problem-solving abilities, their learning readiness, their mental processing abilities, and previous learning experiences that could affect their motivation. Finally, there must be some means of assessing what the child has learned based on their developmental stage, their motor-skill abilities, and on where they are within the larger sequence of learning a skill within the spiraled curriculum.

While many of these same issues will affect the curriculum design for adult students, the cognitive and developmental stages may not be as important as they were for children. Most adults, for example, can create a mental representation of the musical alphabet and say it backward without having to see the letters written in front of them. Five-year-olds in the preoperational stage cannot be expected to do this. However, instruction that is sensitive to the student's past learning experiences, motivation, and individual learning style will be critical to success within the adult group. Humanist, cognition, and learning theory may need to be relied upon to a greater extent when building curricula for adults than for children. Beyond curriculum design, when creating lesson plans and leading in-class activities, teachers must remain cognizant of the students' stage of learning, of how each learns, and of individual and group motivation.

### Two Sample Classes

When I observe piano teachers, I am often pleased to note that new material is presented with thought and care, in a systematic fashion. However, when teaching the same concept to another student, the teacher often proceeds to give the exact same presentation even though the age of the two students may differ. When I observe this teaching technique, I know that the teacher has clearly identified the learning objectives (a good thing) but has failed to take the child's developmental or cognitive abilities into account. In fact, I would argue that when we teach children, we should first think about the developmental stage and the learning characteristics of the student. Then the teacher should provide instruction that speaks to both the learning objective for the task and the specific group of students. How might this look if one were planning a lesson on harmonization of a simple folk tune during a piano class? Let's assume that we are preparing to teach this activity to two different beginning groups: a group of 8-year-old students and a group of high school students, aged 16. Our lesson plans are reflected in the Figure 2.4 charts.

**Sample Lesson Plan:** Harmonization of Happy Birthday (8-year-old group)

**Learning Theory/Developmental Premise:**
- ☐ Concrete operational (solve problems by generalizing from concrete experiences; may be able to work backwards)
- ☐ 3rd grade
- ☐ Difficulty dealing with abstractions
- ☐ Are they used to dealing with rewards in school? (behaviorism)

| Phases of Learning | Ways to Meet Learning Objectives | Measurement of Success |
|---|---|---|
| Create structure for solving the musical problem<br>☐ Row, Row, Row Your Boat (harm example 1)<br>☐ Sing melody together<br>☐ Play 3 chords/root notes needed (provided by teacher)<br>☐ Put in groups, let them try to discover which chords work (ear; based on prior knowledge of the song)<br>☐ Write these in and practice with group (theory & performance)<br>☐ Listen to group performances & choose correct/best examples (evaluation)<br>☐ Recap steps we took to find the chords (synthesis) | ☐ Look at lyrics and score<br>☐ Show these LH chords (on staff & Visualizer)<br>☐ Facilitate the learning with each group, as needed<br><br>☐ Apply the theory<br>☐ Practice & evaluate their small-group performances<br>☐ Evaluate other performances<br>☐ Demonstrate skills<br>☐ Systematize the steps needed to solve this problem | ☐ Small groups engaged & enjoying (intrinsic) experience<br>☐ Everyone sings correctly<br>☐ Everyone plays chords<br>☐ Groups figure out which chords are appropriate; correct choices are made<br>☐ Students write in correct chord symbols or Roman numerals (theory applied correctly)<br>☐ Students perform sufficiently (competent performance)<br>☐ Listening & evaluating each other appropriately; Build confidence in perf skills<br>☐ Can list steps taken to harmonize the melody |
| *Happy Birthday* (harm example 2 – in same key)<br>☐ Put in pairs, have them follow same steps | ☐ Facilitate learning, as needed. They will help each other & any incorrect attributions or problems in the understanding will be visible to the teacher<br>☐ More advanced groups are encouraged to try an alternate accompaniment pattern | ☐ They complete similar steps, in the same key, with a different example<br><br>☐ More advanced groups perform with alternate accompaniment pattern |

*Figure 2.4* Sample Lesson Plans for a Small-Group In-Class Harmonization Exercise for 8- and 16-Year-Olds

**Sample Lesson Plan:** Harmonization of Happy Birthday (16-year old group)

**Learning Theory/Developmental Premise:**
- ☐  High school students
- ☐  Focus on possibilities vs. reality (Erickson: trying to avoid role confusion; provide successful experiences; peer groups important)
- ☐  Should be able to generalize from the experience of in another key to this one
- ☐  Apply knowledge of theory from other contexts to this one

| Phases of Learning | Ways to Meet Learning Objectives | Measurement of Success |
|---|---|---|
| Create structure for solving the musical problem<br>☐ *Row, Row, Row Your Boat* (harm example 1; D Major)<br>☐ Sing melody together<br>☐ In small groups, figure out melody by ear & notate<br>☐ Play/review primary chord progression<br>☐ Choose chords (ear; theory; other?)<br>☐ Write these in and practice with group (theory & performance)<br>☐ Listen to group performances & choose correct/best examples (evaluation)<br>☐ Recap steps we took to find the chords (synthesis) | ☐ Provide effective feedback to peers<br>☐ Transferring knowledge to new situation (harm)<br>☐ Recall melody<br>☐ Use aural skills to play it on piano<br>☐ Review progression<br>☐ Choose appropriate chords using one or several skills (aural, theoretical)<br>☐ Notate melody & chords<br>☐ Perform, listen & evaluate their playing<br>☐ Provide feedback (to small & larger group)<br>☐ Systematize and synthesize the process for harmonizing melodies | ☐ Providing framework for learning but allowing them to help each other, gain confidence in their abilities & transfer skills and knowledge<br>☐ Using broad skills (chords, aural, theory) and applying to specific example<br>☐ Some may consider other possibilities for chords too (alternate harm)<br>☐ Less reliance on teacher; becoming more independent as they help each other<br>☐ Create strategies for future harmonization examples |
| Transpose *Row, Row, Row Your Boat* (both hands) to A Major in pairs, different group leader | ☐ Transfer learning & apply skills in another key | ☐ Completion of the exercise with minimal input from teacher |
| Happy Birthday (harm example 2; E Major)<br>☐ Keep in same pairs, they may choose to follow same steps; different group leader<br>☐ More advanced groups can switch group leader and try in a different key with an alternate accompaniment | ☐ Continue to develop feedback & listening skills with peers<br>☐ Transfer harmonization skills to a different context<br>☐ Hone all skills needed to harmonize melodies | ☐ Confident taking on new roles within the partnership<br>☐ Listening & responding to each other & the music<br>☐ Effective performance of the example with minimal input from the teacher |

*Figure 2.4* (Continued)

# Pedagogy in Action

1.  Imagine that you will be teaching a sight-reading activity that involves only seconds and thirds, ascending and descending, with each hand playing separately, to three different groups of beginning piano students. The groups are comprised of the following aged students: Group 1: six children (aged 6); Group 2: six children (aged 12); Group 3: eight adults (aged 35–45). Create and notate two exercises

for each group and write out a detailed lesson plan for how you will introduce, work on, and evaluate this sight-reading activity with each group. Remember, your plan should consider the student characteristics (developmental stage theory, age-level characteristics, and metacognitive abilities) and encourage exploration through different theories of learning (behavioral, developmental, cognitive) while meeting the instructional objective(s). You could put your plan in a chart (see Figure 2.4). At your next pedagogy class, be prepared to share your answers by giving a peer demonstration of your lessons. After working with your peers, be ready to discuss how your plan addresses the students' developmental and psychosocial abilities.

2. Read more about one of the theories highlighted in this chapter. You might start with a learning theory text such as Bigge and Shermis (2003) or Snowman, McCown, and Biehler (2012) and seek out further references from your library later. Use this opportunity to learn a little more about a theory that you think will be important to be aware of when you plan future teaching. For example, if you know that you will teach only children, you may wish to explore the theories of Piaget and Erikson in more detail. If you plan on teaching more advanced students, high-school aged and adults, you may choose to focus more on life-span development or cognition and human learning strategies that have emerged in recent years. Write an overview of important aspects of the theory and identify at least three ways you will implement the theory when you work with groups of piano students.

# References

Bigge, M. L. (1982). *Learning Theories for Teachers*, 4th edition. New York: Harper & Row, Publishers, Inc.

Bigge, M. L., & Shermis, S. S. (2003). *Learning Theories for Teachers*, 6th edition. Boston: Allyn & Bacon.

Erikson, E. (1963). *Childhood and Society*, 2nd edition. New York: Norton.

Levinson, D. (1978). *The Seasons of a Man's Life*. New York: Knopf.

Snowman, J., McCown, R., & Biehler, R. (2012). *Psychology Applied to Teaching*, 13th edition. Belmont, CA: Wadsworth, Cengage Learning.

3

# GROUP THEORY AND GROUP DYNAMICS IN THE PIANO CLASS

## Objectives

By the end of this chapter, you should be able to discuss the typical stages of group growth, know how to facilitate growth of groups of piano students at all ages, and have ideas about using the group to keep individuals motivated and accountable to one another.

## Two Vignettes of Group-Piano Students

### *Vignette One: First-Year Group Piano*

It is a Monday morning during the first week of classes and 16 nervous freshmen enter the piano lab at Typical State University. They have just come from theory and, already feeling overwhelmed about the expectations of being music majors, they sit down at the keyboards and wonder why they have to take this piano class. After all, they each came to music school to study their respective instruments, not to learn the piano! The instructor enters the room, introduces herself, and asks each student to give a brief introduction, which includes his or her goals for piano this semester. Her experience has taught her that the act of having each student articulate a goal for piano study (even if it was made up on the spot) is useful for framing the group-piano study within the context of the undergraduate experience. The teacher provides an overview of her goals for the semester. She begins with a brief introduction of notes on the keyboard, of whole steps and half steps, and of the pentascale patterns. After this succinct introduction, she puts the students in pairs and gives them 3 minutes to figure out several major five-finger patterns over their headphones. Following the short but focused exploration at the keyboard, she solicits pairs to volunteer to play specific pentascales out loud for the group. She reminds the students who are not playing to take their headphones off and listen for correct notes and for steadiness of rhythm and invites comments following each performance, calling on students who may need encouragement.

It is now 3 weeks later, and after just six class meetings, the students enter the class-room, again on a Monday morning. They excitedly chat with one another, and as the instructor is setting up, they review their practice assignment (individually over headphones), anxious to work on the harmonization that they have rehearsed prior to class. The instructor begins with a quick review of the harmonization example, which the students play together but over headphones with a MIDI accompaniment. Most have successfully performed the example, so the instructor puts the group into pairs and asks them to spend 4 minutes coming up with alternative accompaniment patterns and transposing the example to a different key. The students quickly get down to work, experimenting with various left-hand accompaniments and helping each other with coordination and balance between the hands. Several of the groups quickly move on to transposing and try the example together in the new key. The more advanced students begin challenging one another by choosing harder keys for transposition and providing feedback to one another. Other groups who find the transposition exercise more challenging decide to split up the example (with one person playing the melody and the other playing the accompaniment) until they become comfortable with the motor skills. Splitting up the parts between them, they have discovered, allows them to listen and perform more effectively at this stage. As the instructor circulates through the room, she hears laughter and engaged discussion about musical and technical aspects of the example. The students are engaged and comfortable working with each other. They do not rely on the instructor for their learning, though they ask questions if they need help during the group work. This is but one group activity in which students engage during the class. It becomes clear that throughout the group session, the students are listening to one another and providing feedback. In short, they are functioning as musicians and communicating as musicians via their secondary instrument.

### *Vignette Two: Beginning 7-Year-Old Group Piano*

On a Wednesday afternoon, eight 7-year-old beginners excitedly enter the piano lab 5 minutes before their fourth weekly piano class. They each go to their assigned keyboard and take out their books and materials. The teacher circulates, checking assignments and inquiring about any practice issues they encountered during the week. At the assigned time for class to begin, the instructor calls all of the children to the whiteboard, where they form a semicircle and begin a call-and-response chant with their teacher. They step and swing their arms, listening to and learning a new rhythmic chant. After several repetitions, the students know the chant (stepping on each beat and clapping the rhythm while intoning the words). Then they take turns notating it, one measure at a time, on the whiteboard. When Becky makes a mistake, Susan raises her hand and says, "Becky, this is what you wrote [she claps], but this is what we chanted [she claps the correct rhythm.] Susan looks a little puzzled, "We held the second note longer," Becky offers. Susan claps and chants again and, seeing her error, fixes her mistake on the board. The children clap for her. Once the dictation is complete, they chant the example together one more time.

"Excellent work," the teacher says. "Now, I challenge you to quickly move to your keyboards, open your book to pages 25 and 26, and find the piece that contains the rhythm we just notated." The children quickly but orderly proceed to their keyboards, put on their headphones, open their books, locate the piece, and indicate through a raised hand that they have completed the challenge. Meanwhile, the teacher has moved to her piano, and they proceed to sight read through the example together. The teacher asks the students to point to the most important note in the first phrase, and all correctly identify it. Now, "how might we lead toward and away from that important note?" the teacher asks. Jane raises her hand and says, "We could sneak into and out of the phrase." The teacher nods. "Do you think you could pencil in something on the page to remember to do these dynamics?" The children each pick up their pencils and mark crescendos and diminuendos on their score. After giving them just 2 minutes to practice the example individually, the teacher has the students unplug their headphones and take turns trying the first phrases with these dynamics. The children listen carefully to one another and respond honestly but tactfully about what they hear. Finally, the group plays the piece aloud while singing the words. It has only taken a few minutes, but the students perform a musical rendition of the new piece.

## The Power of the Group

An outsider to group-piano teaching might be surprised to learn that both of these groups had only been working together for a month. A private piano teacher might be amazed at the level of independence and problem solving exhibited by the students after just 4 weeks of instruction. Perhaps the outsider would be surprised at how effective the novice piano students were at evaluating their peers' work, offering suggestions, or working through problems together. With carefully prepared lesson plans and through reflective practice, a group-piano teacher can get most groups to this high level of cohesiveness within just a few classes.

When my pedagogy students observe videos of children working in groups, they often comment on how far they appear to have progressed and how musically they seem to play compared with their own private students who are at the same age and level. They marvel at how quickly the children studying in groups progress. Indeed, much of the progress experienced by those studying piano in groups (under the supervision of a masterful teacher) is due to the fact that they become good listeners, problem solvers, and independent learners, even though much of their class work occurs with little individual instruction. Group-piano students are motivated by each other to work hard, both in and outside of class.

However, in order for instructors to harness the power of the group, they must be aware of the typical stages through which a group will pass and purposefully develop and use strategies that quickly move students into the more productive phases of group work. Simply placing students in groups for piano instruction will not automatically deliver positive learning outcomes. In fact, in groups in which teachers do not engage all members or harness the power of the group, musical results and motivation may be much less positive than if the student had been taking private lessons. If the teacher does not carefully plan lessons and respond to student cues during class, individual students may not progress as described, nor may they learn together or engage in music as a cohesive group. However, it is possible to acclimate all students to the expectations of group work during the very first class and to foster group cohesiveness, which can lead to individual motivation and successful musical performance at the piano.

## Group Dynamics and Group Growth: Background and Relevance to Group Piano

As we have discovered, teaching piano in groups has been prevalent in the United States since the turn of the 20th century. Indeed, at the university level, it has become the preferred means of efficiently facilitating development of keyboard competency among undergraduate music majors, as mandated by the National Association of Schools of Music (NASM).[1] Group piano has become a way of also teaching large numbers of non-music majors basic piano skills in a college or continuing-education setting. To date, a growing number of researchers have explored *skills* taught in college group-piano courses. Yet despite the hundreds of piano classes that take place throughout the country each year, surprisingly little formal research or written commentary exists about the group *process* as it unfolds in the piano lab.

If, as group-piano experts assert, the piano class is an effective way to engage students, improve motivation, and teach basic keyboard skills to groups of students in a relatively short period of time, several questions must be answered: what can we learn from groups working together effectively? How are musical skills acquired by people in the group setting? Is there more that we could do as educators to improve the quality of instruction and the learning environment for our group-piano students? And is there a more efficient way of grouping piano students that emphasizes learning outcomes rather than ease of scheduling? Furthermore, as more teachers outside of the university setting instruct all ages of beginners and intermediate students, answers to these questions could lead to more effective and efficient instruction of students in various types of group-piano settings.

I believe that many of our best group-piano teachers do not have time to write about their experiences. While some have shared their ideas at conferences, thus far we have had few reliable means of disseminating this information widely to those who are interested in availing themselves of the best group-teaching techniques. While scholars have researched the efficacy of educating groups of students in the general music setting, researchers have just begun to unpack the wealth of anecdotal data that we have accumulated about effective group-piano instruction.[2] Although most non-musical instruction occurs in classrooms, one should not assume that simply because students are accustomed to learning (or listening to lectures) in groups efficient learning or group work will occur naturally in the group-piano lab. In fact, I have observed many piano classes in which students do not seem to be engaged (with one another or the music), in which there is little interaction among students, or in which meaningful learning does not seem to be occurring. It is not unusual to see novice instructors teaching group piano much as they would a one-on-one lesson or to see students using individualized technology to guide their learning in the lab. In such situations, even though students occupy the same educational space, they do not reap the problem-solving or musical benefits of learning together. I have also observed classes in which the expectations for group work or in-class engagement were neither made clear nor reinforced from the outset. In such cases, even teachers who tried to employ group work encountered more student resistance than necessary. However, if teachers are aware of typical stages through which groups pass, they can steer the group toward the most effective learning stages quickly and avoid student resistance.

Since most instructors who teach group piano received their own formal training via private lessons, they may not always avail themselves of efficient teaching techniques or even be aware of how the members of the group can learn from and motivate one another. Learning to play the piano, like any acquisition of new knowledge, requires the students to understand and assimilate both declarative and procedural knowledge. When students work together and help each other fill in gaps in both types of knowledge, they tend to make more meaningful connections between new and old concepts, store the new knowledge effectively, and retrieve it more successfully when it is needed to perform repertoire and demonstrate musical concepts. Each of these steps does not necessarily occur during the private lesson. Thus, as we consider the group-piano setting, it may be instructive to step away from the fields of piano pedagogy and music education and preview findings from research in general education, leadership studies, psychotherapy, and psychology to learn more about group processes. Educators and psychologists have done extensive work with children and adults learning in groups. Likewise, management and educational leadership experts have explored how adults learn to work effectively in teams, which are small groups. In the fields of psychotherapy and social work, where practitioners work with adults in group settings, much has been written about group dynamics and the process of group growth. If we can learn important lessons from experts who work with children and adults in groups and apply these in meaningful ways in the group-piano context, we may be able to add to our pedagogical content knowledge and optimize teaching and learning in the piano lab.

The idea of group dynamics was of interest to early philosophers throughout Europe from the Renaissance onward due to the potential implications for a democratic society. Democracies, after all, rely on humankind to work in groups to achieve common goals. However, as a field of research in the United States, group dynamics became popular following the Second World War (Cartwright & Zander, 1960). A definition of "group dynamics" that will be useful for our discussion of teaching group piano comes from Cartwright & Zander (1960). According to the authors, "group dynamics . . . refers to a field of inquiry dedicated to achieving knowledge about the nature of groups, the laws of their development, and their interrelations with individuals, other groups, and larger institutions" (p. 5). Gestalt theorist Kurt Lewin is credited with establishing a research tradition devoted to studying group dynamics, where initially researchers were interested in identifying specific conditions which might produce certain, predictable effects within groups.

I have always been intrigued by the vast differences between various group-piano classes that I teach. At certain points in my career, I have had the opportunity to teach three sections of the same class, one after the other. Never have two of these groups been the same. Indeed, in any given semester when I am teaching several sections of the same class, where the students are drawn from a relatively homogeneous student population, the "personality" of each class gradually reveals itself. Even though I have the same instructional objectives and general lesson plan for each class, no two instructional periods ever unfold in exactly the same fashion, especially if the students are engaging with one another and the course content in meaningful ways during the class. Although the eventual outcomes are similar and I cover the same topics, I may need to introduce them differently depending on the particular group that I happen to be teaching, as student responses to the concepts can vary considerably. I must be cognizant of the individuals within the group and present concepts to meet individual needs. But I must also be aware of how these individuals interact with one another and make small-group assignments that avail of individual strengths and weaknesses while maintaining an awareness of the overall dynamic of the larger group.

## Stages of Group Growth

Although many novice group-piano teachers fail to recognize the importance of facilitating group growth, shaping and reinforcing positive group dynamics are critical for truly effective learning in group-piano classes. While group-piano teachers must pay particular attention to the learning objectives, outcomes, and needs of individual students within the group when planning lessons, we must not ignore the group as its own entity. In fact, if we plan for the stages through which most groups pass, we can facilitate the healthy growth of each group with which we work so that all members glean as much as possible from weekly group classes. Over the years, there have been several viable stages of group growth put forth. The stages identified by Bruce Tuckman align well with group stages encountered in the piano lab and will be discussed with respect to group piano teaching in what follows. In 1965, Bruce Tuckman identified four stages of typical group process: forming, storming, norming, and performing. Twelve years later, he added a fifth stage, adjourning.

## *Forming*

The forming, or the initial phase of the group's formation, is when members test the waters (with one another and with the instructor). During the first class or two, they are learning about their classmates, testing the boundaries, trying to find their place within the context of the larger group, and learning the "ground rules" (Friend & Cook, 2003; Tuckman, 1965; University of Vermont, 2008). In the piano class, the forming stage occurs during the first few class meetings, and every effort should be made to move the group through this stage expeditiously. Group-piano teachers should make sure that expectations are made clear and reinforced through in-class activities during the forming stage. If students are in a university setting and have not been briefed about the expectations and the parameters of the class, they will need to learn them during the first group meeting. Independent studio teachers of precollege students are advised to provide group-piano orientations for parents and students prior to the first lesson so that the expectations for comportment during the class and practice requirements or other assignments to be prepared outside of class can be outlined and agreed upon by all participants. Noncredit adult groups also benefit from a group-orientation session or individual interviews in which the teacher can ascertain the adults' receptivity to studying piano in a group setting and outline expectations.

In the typical college group-piano class, most students are told during student advising that they must take piano courses and may arrive at these classes feeling resentful about having to learn an instrument for which they did not come to university to study. Additionally, many wonder how one can learn an instrument with a group of other music students, since much precollege instrumental instruction occurs one on one with an independent teacher. In fact, it is during these initial class meetings that some students will jockey for individual attention, and if teachers aren't careful, they will find themselves devoting extra time and energy to particular students during group sessions. This is why setting forth the rules of engagement and explaining expectations for good "citizenship" in the classroom is important for success of the group during the forming stage. Helping students understand that they share a certain amount of the responsibility in assessing their own individual progress on a daily basis is critical.[3] In a group of music majors, it may not be unreasonable to ask students to perform music aloud for the class, either solo or in small ensembles. Music majors might also be expected to reflect upon performances, discuss musical concepts, transfer knowledge to new contexts, and direct musical learning among peers during short in-class small-group work. On the other hand, such expectations may not be reasonable for adults in a recreational group-piano setting. Thus, activities undertaken during the first classes must be tailored to include the types of group work in which students will engage for the remainder of the semester. If group work is not undertaken from the very first class, students may resist participating fully later on.

During this initial forming stage, the piano instructor must ensure that everyone in the class is grouped appropriately, according to level. If a student has been misplaced (either in a group that is below or above his or her level of keyboard or musical competency), frustration may be experienced by the student, the classmates, and the teacher. It should be noted, too, that so-called "problem students" who tend to surface partway through the semester are often just seeking attention because they are unable to achieve optimal learning if the class material is either too difficult or too easy for them. Often it is "misplaced" students that exhibit disruptive behavior, so proper group placement is critical both for optimal learning of individuals in the class and for optimal participation and learning during group activities. Improperly placed students should be transferred to an appropriate group by the second class so that the group can progress to the second stage of group growth.

### *Storming*

The second stage of group development is storming and may be characterized by some disagreement between group members (Tuckman, 1965). During this phase, group members get to know each other better, learn how to navigate conflict, and build consensus. The instructor will need to facilitate student interactions and musical activities so they can get to know one another and become comfortable collaborating, which they will do throughout the remainder of the semester. I always find that early on, students learn which of their classmates will emerge as risk takers (within the context of the class), who will be comfortable leading the group, who will ask questions, who will volunteer to play out loud, and who will provide comic relief. When one of the class "leaders" is absent, it can completely shift the dynamic of the group, often empowering other students to take on leadership roles. Therefore, instructors must be aware of creating ample opportunities for all students to participate during class. It is during this storming stage that the group-piano teacher should assess individual student learning preferences (see Chapters 2 and 4) so that successful partnerships for collaborative work can be made throughout the semester. Students should also be exposed to collaborative activities and group work in various combinations (i.e., groups of 2, 3, or 4 students) at this stage so that they get to know one another and become accustomed to the expectations involved in various group endeavors during class.

Group-piano instructors will likely find it necessary to assign groups for specific activities, provide clear guidelines of objectives for each activity, give timelines for completion of the group work, and facilitate group interactions during the early part of the storming stage (Pike, 2014a). Since much group work will take place in small groups over headphones, the instructor will need to monitor group work closely, offer suggestions when groups struggle to work effectively, and provide clarity about each group member's responsibilities for the activity. Students should become accustomed to taking on various roles during group work in the storming stage. That is to say that for one activity, a student may be given a leadership role (such as guiding the rehearsal), while he might take on a different role for the next group challenge (perhaps listening for balance between parts and reporting on this to the group throughout the activity). Also, instructors must provide precise time limits for each activity, and like Goldilocks, the timing has to be "just right"—not too long and not too short. If the timeframe for the small group work provides too much time, off-task behavior might be exhibited. However, it must allow for enough time to complete the assignment, especially if the group is expected to share their work with the entire class.

### *Norming and Performing*

Norming is the third stage in Tuckman's group development scheme. By the time a group reaches this stage, it is beginning to function as a group, students or group members understand their role within the group, and the members are learning how to work with one another. Inevitably, as students become more comfortable in the group-piano setting, there will be questioning of both classmates and the instructor, and they will struggle with finding the balance between asserting their independence and learning how to solve musical problems within the framework of the group. This stage should be reached as quickly as possible so that the group can move toward the highly productive fourth stage. Although these stages appear to be linear, there may be some oscillating between the third and fourth stages as membership of small groups within the class shifts and as new musical activities and concepts are encountered. For example, although a group may be completing harmonization activities successfully, the first time a group is expected to transpose an exercise during small-group work, members may question their abilities to problem solve and complete the task. In such an instance, the teacher might provide cues or suggestions for the students until they regain their composure and confidence. So teachers should be aware that at any given point in the semester, students might exhibit norming behaviors and need help in moving into the fourth stage again.

The fourth stage, aptly categorized as performing, finds group members focused on learning, problem solving, and finding creative strategies, both within the group and individually, in order to contribute to the group's success. In the piano class, instructors will recognize that a group is "performing" when students take ideas from previous group work and incorporate them into problem solving outside the class. In effective group work, individual problem solving will be necessary, with each student bringing his or her strengths and ideas forward during the group music making, which occurs during class time. Motivation to practice in preparation for each group-piano class peaks when students recognize how their individual contributions affect the large or small group's progress. While the transition between norming and performing can be tricky to spot, ideally the group will spend the majority of the semester working in the "performing" stage.

Like the students discussed in the opening vignettes of this chapter, group-piano students who are working in the performing phase generally enter the lab or studio prepared for the class and knowing what the expectations will be for music making and peer interaction throughout the class. Skilled group-piano teachers move groups toward the performing stage within just a few weeks of the initial class. Students operating in this stage tend to describe optimal learning experiences, they enjoy the class time with their peers, they are motivated to prepare for upcoming classes, and they exhibit high levels of understanding and music making during the lesson, while the teachers report high levels of satisfaction with the teaching experience.

## *Adjourning*

In 1977, Tuckman added a fifth stage to his group growth phases: adjourning. As the label indicates, as the regular meetings of a group come to an end, participants must prepare for the loss of these regular group meetings and activities. At the college level, there is a predictable pattern of beginning and ending based on the semester schedule, so it might be easy to dismiss this final stage. Yet I have found that many groups of my undergraduates try to avoid this phase and stay together from one semester to the next because they enjoy working together and have become accustomed to the particular group structure in which they have been learning piano. However, if piano groups are unable to remain intact for subsequent semesters, any fears that individual students have about joining another group are usually allayed through activities during the forming stage in the following semester. A group performance that features newly acquired skills can be an effective capstone to the adjourning phase.

In my university groups, my students typically work through the forming stage much more quickly during their second, third, and fourth semesters of group piano because they are aware of expectations. Independent studio teachers who offer group classes can maintain the group relationships for longer periods of time, presumably for an academic year at a minimum. I have had ongoing groups of adult leisure students remain together for years, with relatively stable membership. Parents of children studying piano in groups often recognize the benefits of group instruction and the unique dynamics of groups that learn well together and attempt to schedule other activities around the group piano lesson so that the group can remain intact for several years (Pike, 2013).

## Discussion of the Stages of Group Growth and Cohesiveness

Since the introduction of Tuckman's influential theory of group process, group therapists in the fields of psychology and social work have described group evolution in great detail. Some of these findings can be useful for group-piano teachers to consider. Many different identifiers have been put forth to describe typical stages of group development. Common terms found in the literature include "induction," "experimental development," "cohesive engagement," and "disengagement." In fact, between 1956 and 1997, group therapists posited that there are anywhere from two to five stages in group development (Kottler, 2001). Regardless of the descriptor (or label) given to each stage or to the actual number of stages espoused by a theorist, a cursory review of the literature reveals that there is a consistency with how group development unfolds.

So if one expert purports that there are only three stages, one of his stages may include developmental processes that have been separated into several more discrete stages by another expert. Some scholars have argued that Tuckman's theory is too linear and that there may be a certain amount of movement back and forth between the storming, norming, and performing phases as the group grows and develops (Smith, 2005). I would agree with this assertion due to both observation of and personal experience with hundreds of piano groups and because developmental or learning processes rarely progress in a completely linear fashion. During MTNA Pedagogy Saturday III, piano pedagogue Guy Duckworth discussed dimensions of group growth that he had experienced in piano classes. Duckworth highlighted membership, individual influence, feelings, individual differences, and productivity and claimed that all groups passed through these dimensions regardless of age. While Duckworth's ideas have not been fleshed out as extensively as Tuckman's in the literature, they point to a similar idea of moving the group toward productive large- and small-group interactions as quickly as possible.

Thus, I believe that for our purposes as group-piano teachers, Tuckman's group growth theory can serve as a starting point, helping alert us to potential phases of growth that we might witness, encourage, and experience with our piano groups. Even though any kind of educational growth, personal development, or evolution of the piano group is rarely linear, such a model reminds us to remain cognizant of the overarching goal of using the group's dynamics to facilitate learning, problem solving, and music making as we pursue our daily class objectives.

An important concept to emerge from the literature about group work is the notion of cohesiveness. Irvin D. Yalom, a leader in group theory and practice of group psychotherapy writes:

[C]ohesiveness is a widely researched basic property of groups. Several hundred research articles exploring cohesiveness have been written. . . . Those [in the group] with a greater sense of solidarity, or "we-ness," value the group more highly, and will defend it against external threats. Such groups have a higher rate of attendance, participation, and mutual support, and will defend the group standards much more, than groups with less esprit de corps.

(Yalom, 1995, p. 48)

This sentiment about what cohesiveness can do for a group must be underscored for group-piano teachers. Initially, facilitating a group's growth may seem challenging or time consuming, especially if one is new to teaching piano in groups. In the long run, encouraging students to form and storm efficiently will lead to more effective learning and music making and more enjoyable weekly in-class encounters for both teacher and students. My experience with piano classes in which students value one another and where they are committed to problem solving together echoes Yalom's sentiment. If students feel a sense of belonging, they will be more likely to continue with classes. If students feel the responsibility to prepare for class so that they can participate fully with their peers, they will be more likely to practice outside of class. If students believe that they are making a difference in terms of the group's success and can help another individual learn a musical concept that they have just mastered, they will be more likely to share what they have learned with peers during the class. If students become engaged in the process of learning in the class, they will be much more likely to experience optimal learning and describe group piano as a positive experience, even if they are music majors who had no choice about taking the course.

## Priming the Group for Success and Considerations for Group-Piano Instructors

Much of the student attrition, dissatisfaction, and inability to succeed in group-piano programs is due to students being "misplaced" in an inappropriate group. One aspect that psychologists and educators have covered well is defining how groups should be set up. They have outlined how members are chosen for the group, how they are prepared to participate in the group, how parameters for participation within the group meetings are set, and so forth.

In terms of university-level group-piano curricula, placement auditions, and piano proficiency requirements that are mandated for all NASM accredited institutions, university group-piano teachers in the United States have an opportunity to meet and discuss ideas during the summer of odd-numbered years at the National Group Piano—Piano Pedagogy Forum (GP3) (details can be found at www.mtna.org). Furthermore, GP3 participants can dialogue throughout the year on discussion boards about specific piano competency topics such as harmonization, improvisation, and the like. Whether you are a first-time or experienced university group-piano teacher, I would encourage you to reflect on your experience of teaching group piano with regard to a group class that you have taught recently. If you are new to teaching group piano or have not taught music classes yet, you might consider your own experience of working within the confines of a small group in another discipline. Once you have explored university-level group-piano curricula for music majors and the NASM standards (in Chapter 5), you should be able to begin to develop a checklist for appropriate placement in each level of a four-semester sequence of piano classes for music majors at the typical accredited university offering Bachelor of Music or Bachelor of Arts in Music degrees. Articulating and assessing the keyboard skills required to begin each semester and to be successful throughout the semester is critical for proper student placement and thus for success in the group-piano sequence.

One issue that surfaces frequently with music majors in the university setting is that while some students may be able to play piano or sight read fairly well, they have not developed the specialized skills in harmonizing at sight, improvising, or ensemble playing that might be critical components of the piano proficiency exam. Therefore, proper framing by the piano instructor about what students can expect to gain from the class is also important. Instructors should feel free to supplement more challenging repertoire, accompaniments, or score-reading exercises for those students who might be a little more advanced than their classmates in those areas so that they feel challenged in all components of the group-piano program.

University group-piano instructors should also think about how they establish and enforce expectations for all students in the class in terms of class preparation and participation. They might think about how to help students understand the objectives for group piano from one semester to the next as they prepare for the ultimate goal of passing the piano proficiency examination. Students engaged in a group-piano class with the goal of facilitating learning and performance through group work among students will come to class with assignments prepared; otherwise they will not be able to participate in the group music-making activities and problems. This type of group-piano environment is not a lab class, in which students enter and work independently on a new assignment presented by the instructor that day. The group work discussed here involves active participation in activities that would not be possible individually.

In some respects, instructors of children's and adult leisure classes (either on a university or community-college campus or in the independent piano studio) may have more control over preparing students for participation in the group. They definitely have more flexibility in terms of the curriculum. Certainly, placement auditions and interviews are necessary, and care should be taken when preparing placement tests. Piano pedagogy texts have some wonderful resources for independent studio teachers to help with interviewing prospective students, creating suitable placement auditions, and establishing a proactive studio policy that acclimates new (and returning) students to study within one's private studio, particularly for children or recreational adults (see, for example, Baker-Jordan, 2004; Blanchard, 2007; Jacobson, 2015). However, instructors must remember to prime students (and parents) for anticipated outcomes from group-piano study and for individual responsibilities for class preparation and participation. These students will often have a choice between studying privately with a teacher or learning piano with a group of peers. I would recommend having a written list of group-piano expectations and rules for acceptable behavior that students will take away following the placement audition.

Not all children or adults will work well in groups, and the audition process should be designed to funnel such students into private lessons. On the other hand, I have encountered many adults who inquire about private lessons but, following an interview in which expectations and benefits of group work are explained, ultimately register for and enjoy group piano enormously. The accountability to group members keeps many students motivated to practice throughout the week and to show up for class when life becomes busy. I have even witnessed members of adult leisure groups maintain accountability (and compassion) for each other by checking up with group members who miss a class or by using carpooling to and from class as an opportunity to reflect upon in-class activities and common learning struggles or accomplishments.

Finally, part of what we have the opportunity to instill in our group-piano students is what it means to be a musician, either professional or amateur. Since much meaningful music making takes place with others during group piano, our students learn responsible behaviors with respect to practicing and rehearsing together; this ensures success for everyone involved. Just as orchestra players learn to rehearse their parts throughout the week, arrive early to rehearsals in order to warm up, tune their instruments in a certain order, and follow the direction of their section leader as well as the conductor, so too must our group-piano students learn acceptable behaviors in the piano lab and in preparation for weekly group experiences. The results of students working successfully together in the group-piano setting reveal engagement, enjoyment, and high-level music making, regardless of students' ages or levels.

## Pedagogy in Action

1. University Group-Piano Questions

    *Novice university group-piano teachers:* With a classmate, list the learning objectives and outcomes that you will measure at the end of this semester. Then review your textbook and lesson plans and identify two or three small-group or partner activities that you can implement in your classes during the next 3 weeks. Plan group work so that students have clear guidelines for assessment and timelines for completion and presentation of group work. Observe your classmates and video yourself teaching these classes. After each class, with your classmate, reflect upon what went well, what could be improved, and how you will improve implementation of the small-group work at the next class. At the end of the 3 weeks, devise ways to implement similar group work earlier in the semester (during the forming stage) and decide how you will continue to create opportunities for small-group work.

*More experienced university group-piano teachers:* Take a moment to think about and review the competencies required for each semester of a typical four-semester sequence of group-piano instruction for undergraduate music majors (see Figure 5.1 for suggestions). Working with a classmate, list those competencies that a student would need to demonstrate in order to meet with success for each semester of group piano. Now, imagine that you have a transfer student or a student who has some piano background but is not fully prepared to take the piano proficiency examination. It is your job to place that student in the proper section of group piano at your institution. Describe how you will evaluate proper group-piano placement. You may wish to list the competencies and then note materials and/or examples that you would use when evaluating a student during a placement exam. Then describe how you will use specific group activities to encourage forming, storming, norming, and group cohesiveness to develop within that level of group piano at the beginning of the semester. Be sure to consult your textbook and lesson plans to note specific techniques and strategies that you will use.

2.  Children and/or Leisure Adult Group-Piano Questions

*Less experienced teachers of children/leisure adult group piano:* Explore *The Music Tree* (children's method book) or *Group Piano 101* (adult group method) and design an 8-week curriculum that supports the five stages of group growth. Create detailed lesson plans that incorporate activities that engage both the entire group and small groups or pairs during each class. Share and compare your plans with a classmate and discuss feasibility of implementing these plans. Which activities promote forming, storming, and norming? Be sure to discuss how you will move students into the norming and performing stages as quickly as possible (and remember that you should include off-bench activities for children).

*More experienced teachers of children/leisure adult group piano:* Make some notes about what you would expect students at the conclusion of a first-year group-piano class and a second year group-piano class to be able to accomplish at the keyboard. Be sure you know which age group you will be teaching when identifying these broad competencies. Now, with a partner, discuss how you will assess learning and musical readiness for each of the classes and identify materials (or make up exercises and musical examples) that you will use in your placement interviews. Compose a one-page handout (policy statement) that you will give students to take home following the interview that outlines expectations for members (and parents if you will be teaching children) of the group. Think of this handout as preparation for the norming stage. It should establish the expectations and guidelines for participation in the group-piano class.

## Additional Reading and Exploration

Read Pike, P.D. (2014a). "An exploration of the effect of cognitive and collaborative strategies on keyboard skills of music education students." *Journal of Music Teacher Education*, 23(2), 79–91. doi: 10.1177/1057083713487214

- List some of the small-group activities in which the students engaged and report benefits experienced by those students. With your classmates, discuss how you could implement similar activities in your current group-piano classes and how you might expand upon these as students move into the performing stage to promote cohesiveness.

Read pp. 78–89 in *Proceedings from Pedagogy Saturday III* (1999) for next week.

- The readings cover group dynamics and use of language when teaching groups.

Read chapters 10 and 12 ("Group Growth" and "Group Dynamics") in Sylvia Coats (2006), *Thinking as You Play*.

- Explore some of the thoughts and concepts presented with your classmates and review some of the additional readings suggested by the author.

## Notes

1 See Chapter 5 for suggested piano standards for the university music major pursuing BM degrees at 4-year comprehensive universities, for BA degrees in music, and the NASM Handbook for specific requirements http://nasm.arts-accredit.org.

2 See chapter reference list for articles in peer-reviewed music education journals that explore strategies used by effective group-piano teachers. Primers include Pike (2013, 2014b).

3 As an aside, even though many instrumental and vocal music majors have been involved in band, orchestral, or choir activities throughout middle and high school, large-ensemble experiences tend to be autocratic in nature, with the conductor making all the decisions. Therefore, students may initially find the active-participation expectations in group-piano to be disconcerting.

## References

Baker-Jordan, M. (2004). *Practical Piano Pedagogy: The Definitive Text for Piano Teachers and Pedagogy Students*. Miami: Warner Brothers, Inc.

Blanchard, B. (2007). *Making Music and Enriching Lives: A Guide for All Music Teachers*. Bloomington: Indiana University Press.

Cartwright, D., & Zander, A. (Eds.). (1960). *Group Dynamics: Research and Theory*, 2nd edition. Evanston, IL: Row, Peterson.

Coats, S. (2006). *Thinking as You Play*. Bloomington: Indiana University Press.

Friend, M. P., & Cook, L. (2003). *Interactions: Collaboration Skills for School Professionals*, 4th edition. Boston: Allyn and Bacon.

Jacobson, J. M. (2015). *Professional Piano Teaching*, 2nd edition. Edited by E. L. Lancaster. Van Nuys, CA: Alfred Music Publishing, Inc.

Kottler, J. A. (2001). *Learning Group Leadership: An Experiential Approach*. Boston: Allyn and Bacon.

Pike, P. D. (2013). Profiles in Successful Group Piano: A Case Study of Children's Group Piano Lessons. *Music Education Research*, *15*(1), 92–106. doi: 10.1080/14613808.2012.754416

Pike, P. D. (2014a). An Exploration of the Effect of Cognitive and Collaborative Strategies on Keyboard Skills of Music Education Students. *Journal of Music Teacher Education*, *23*(2), 79–91. doi: 10.1177/1057083713487214

Pike, P. D. (2014b). The Difference between Novice and Expert Group-Piano Teaching Strategies: A Case Study and Comparison of Beginning Group Piano Classes. *International Journal of Music Education*, *32*(2), 213–227. doi: 10.1177/0255761413508065

*Proceedings from Pedagogy Saturday III*. (1999). Cincinnati: Music Teachers National Association, Inc.

Smith, M. K. (2005). "Bruce W. Tuckman—Forming, Storming, Norming and Performing in Groups, *The Encyclopaedia of Informal Education*." http://infed.org/mobi/bruce-w-tuckman-forming-storming-norming-and-performing-in-groups/. Retrieved: 10 October 2010.

Tuckman, Bruce W. (1965). "Developmental Sequence in Small Groups." *Psychological Bulletin*, *63*(6), 384–399.

University of Vermont and PACER Center. (2008). "Stages of group development." Online module www.uvm.edu/~pcl/Module4. Accessed 1 March 2016.

Yalom, I. D. (1995). *The Theory and Practice of Group Psychotherapy*, 4th edition. New York: Basic Books.

4

# ADDRESSING INDIVIDUAL LEARNING STYLES WITHIN THE GROUP-PIANO CLASS

## Objectives

By the end of this chapter, you should be able to list three learning modes, different personality types, and various learning styles of individuals that you might encounter in your classes. You will discover cognitive strategies that can help different students within the group learn and process information. You should be able to identify several ways to teach concepts that will appeal to the varied individuals within your group-piano classes.

## Preferred Learning Modes

In Chapter 2, we reviewed and discussed learning and developmental theories that should inform the way we structure our group-piano curricula and teach our students. Chapter 3 previewed group dynamics that we may encounter when working with students in groups. In this chapter, we will explore learning modes and individual learning styles and discover how we might pair or group various types of individuals for optimal learning during collaborative activities.

Though often discussed in relation to learning theory, learning modes refer to how an individual gathers and processes information. There are three main modes: visual, auditory, and kinesthetic. When learning, we use all three of these modes to some extent. However, we tend to prefer learning and processing new material in one way more than the others. Think about how you process information most effectively. Is it with visual aids, such as PowerPoints or video? Is it primarily through the spoken word such as in a lecture, without any visual aids? Or do you prefer to move around or manipulate objects as you learn? It has been said that the majority of the population prefers to learn via visual stimuli. Indeed, in today's world, where much of our information is consumed via online sources, tablets, and mobile phones, we seem to be receiving more information visually, regardless of our preferred learning mode. However, remember that task requirements for texting, playing video games, and playing the piano include a kinesthetic element. So be aware of "hidden" modes that might impact our learning when planning lessons.

In the piano class, it is good practice to introduce new topics and concepts using all three learning modes in order to capture the attention of all learners. Let's say that I am introducing a harmonization exercise to a college group-piano class. We might first look at the melody together on the projector, then hum it or play it together. Doing this engages not just the visual learners but the auditory and kinesthetic learners too. Then we might talk through appropriate chord choices together and notate chord symbols or Roman numerals on the score. At this stage, I have all students use their headphones, and I encourage those who would like to hear the harmonies to play them as we work through the exercise. To process the information effectively, kinesthetic learners may need to play and feel the chords too. Then I give students a brief (but appropriate) amount of time to work on the exercise individually before they work with another student or small group to check chord choices or inversions or refine technique in preparation for performance of the exercise.

Often, I notice that my pedagogy students have carefully prepared their lesson plans and considered both the logical sequence of activities and how they will explain new concepts clearly. But they tend to present material in a way that would be helpful for a learner who shares their preferred learning mode. When a student who relies on a different learning mode needs extra help or a more detailed explanation, the pedagogy student may find it difficult to explain the concept using another mode. Therefore, I recommend having several ways of explaining concepts that you will use in your group-piano classes. Be sure that you consider the differences in how a visual, auditory, or kinesthetic learner might need to process new information. In my pedagogy classes, my students practice teaching peers. This can help highlight where there might be misunderstandings between the "teacher" and "learner" before they work with actual students.

## Individual Personality Types and Learning Styles

Another topic that we should be aware of when working with students in groups is differences in personality types. There are several ways of categorizing students' personalities that are popular with educators. These include the Myers-Briggs Type Indicator (MBTI®), Keirsey's Temperament Sorter, Golay's Learning Pattern Assessments, and Kolb's learning-style preferences. We will first take a brief look at the Myers-Briggs, as this has informed both Keirsey's and Golay's work. At the end of the chapter, we will explore Kolb's learning styles, because these can be easy to spot in the piano lab without having to use complicated assessment instruments. Using knowledge about Kolb's learning styles, we can accommodate individuals through their specific partner and group assignments. For some activities, it may be helpful to pair similar types of learners, while for other exercises, learners with different styles can learn from and complement one another. Regardless of which theory you use in your teaching, it is helpful to recognize that individuals are inclined to rely on a preferred style when processing information. And the manner in which the material is presented will have more or less urgency for learners depending upon their preferred style.

### Myers-Briggs Type Indicator

In the 1940s and 1950s, Katharine Briggs (1875–1968) devised an in-depth assessment tool to help define the personality types that had been described as four archetypes (Jung, 1972) by the psychologist Carl Jung (1875–1961). Although these personality types were popularized through the Myers-Briggs assessment tool, they have actually been documented in writing since the time of Plato. Isabel Briggs Myers (1897–1980), her daughter, continued the work. They identified 16 distinct personality types, each with clear personality preferences and identified by a four-letter combination. A detailed questionnaire (MBTI®) is used to assess type. Each letter in a personality type indicates one's preference on a spectrum between: introversion (I) and extraversion (E), sensing (S) and intuition (N), thinking (T) and feeling (F), and judging (J) and perceiving (P). While Myers-Briggs experts stress that all types are equal, knowledge of how one might prefer to process information can inform instruction and creation of work groups.

As you read more about these personality types, please remember that there are no negative connotations associated with the type indicators. For example, I score very high on the judgment indicator. This does not mean that I am negatively judgmental toward other people but rather that I prefer order and structure, that I plan carefully, and that I can be focused and task-oriented. However, a person with a high perceiving preference (on the opposite end of the scale) can be just as organized, though they may exhibit more flexibility and respond to upcoming deadlines differently than I do.

There is generally a fee associated with the test, though it can often be taken at university career placement centers. A better option for teachers of adult students is to take the shorter Keirsey temperament sorter.

### Keirsey and Golay Personality Types

David Keirsey's (1921–2013) highly accessible book entitled *Please Understand Me II* (1998) is based on the Myers-Briggs type indicator even though he did not agree with all aspects of his predecessors' theory. For example, based on his observations of the actions and attitudes of people with ESTJ, ENTJ, ISFP, and INFP labels, he disagreed with the Myers-Briggs descriptions. Myers described intellectual predispositions and functions of people that can be difficult to perceive, whereas Keirsey was interested in identifying types through observable behaviors. Although he subdivided his types into 16 subsets, his categories are easier to remember, as there are only four main types: Artisans (SP type), Guardians (SJ), Idealists (NF), and, Rationals (NT). Basic observable descriptions of each type follow (Keirsey, 1998, p. 62).

*Artisans* communicate in concrete terms. They are tactical, optimistic about the future (though perhaps cynical about past events), artistic, excitable, impulsive, and good negotiators, and they seek stimulation. *Guardians* are also concrete communicators. They tend to be stoic, pessimistic about the future, dependable, trusting of authority, helpful, and they yearn to belong. Idealists and Rationals both tend to be abstract communicators. *Idealists* enjoy building morale. They are altruistic, empathic, they prize recognition, and they seek to build unique identities. *Rationals* are pragmatic, even skeptical about the future (thus they plan for contingencies). They are autonomous, seek knowledge, yearn to achieve, and are visionary leaders.

Keirsey's book includes a straightforward self-assessment, the Keirsey Type Sorter (KTS), that you can take or that you can use with your students to help identify their personality type. However, the KTS is only valid for adults. One of Keirsey's students, Keith Golay, developed his own test for adults, the Adult Learning Pattern Assessment (LPA), and created an LPA for children. Golay was interested in helping teachers adapt their teaching styles to meet the needs of each type of learner and outlined useful strategies in his 1982 book *Learning Patterns and Temperament Styles*. Golay's LPA became popular with American piano teachers in the early 2000s. While Golay kept Keirsey's temperament descriptors, some teachers remember the types better because he uses animals to personify each type. While the LPA can be used to assess a child's temperament, Golay suggests that teachers can ask open-ended questions of parents (and listen carefully to their answers) to discover the learning pattern best suited to each child. He refers to Artisan children as Apes, Guardian children as Bears, Rational children as Owls, and Idealist children as Dolphins. The four basic children types follow (Golay, 2003, p. 154):

- Apes or Artisans—impulsive and spontaneous
- Bears or Guardians—responsible and governed by rules
- Owls or Rationals—analytic and theoretical
- Dolphins or Idealists—diplomatic with romantic ideals

### Kolb's Learning-Style Preferences

There is another learning-style theory that I find useful when assigning groups of college-aged students to partner work. David A. Kolb (b. 1939) proposed his theory in 1984. It has since been used to explain how business people perceive and process information when they collaborate in the workplace. He views adult learners as operating along two continua: a perceiving continuum and a processing continuum. He suggests that when people perceive information, they have some degree of preference for either thinking about or intuitively feeling it. When processing information,

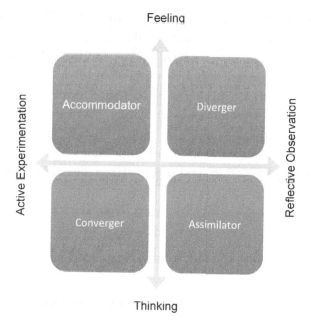

*Figure 4.1* Kolb's Learning Style Continua and Learner Types
Adapted from Kolb (2015).

we prefer using active experimentation or reflective observation. Based on one's pref-erences for perceiving and processing information, individuals fall into one of four types of learning styles: Accommodator, Diverger, Converger, or Assimilator. See Figure 4.1.

I find that considering each learner's style when assigning partners to work on harmonization, improvisation, and sight reading during group-piano class can have a positive effect on the learning outcomes of both students (Pike, 2006, 2014).

The following highlights each of Kolb's four types of learners.

## Accommodators (Doers and Feelers)

- Thrive on active experimentation
- Thrive on feedback from peers
- Learn by doing and applying through hands-on activities
- Rely on intuition
- Prefer to use analysis of others (rather than figure out for themselves)
- Find teamwork rewarding (independent work may be less effective)

## Divergers (Feelers and Observers)

- View concepts from various perspectives
- Enjoy observing and gathering information

- Use imagination and intuition to solve problems
- Enjoy brainstorming

### Convergers (Doers and Thinkers)

- Prefer concrete experiences
- Enjoy finding practical solutions to problems
- Enjoy experimenting with new ideas
- Rely on tactile stimulation
- Are not dependent upon others for learning to occur

### Assimilators (Observers and Thinkers)

- Find concise, logical, systematic approaches
- Able to assemble widely diverging information and organize it concisely
- Prefer to think things through (prior to active experimentation)
- Independent and need not work with others to reach conclusions

## Reinforcing Cognitive Strategies and Learning Styles in the Piano Lab

### *Useful Cognitive Strategies*

Regardless of personality type or learning preference, there are basic cognitive processes that are common to all human learners. Recall, in Chapter 2, we noted that in order for humans to learn new information, there are three basic cognitive processes involved: encoding, storage, and retrieval. It turns out that there are some things we can do during the encoding and storage processes that can reinforce understanding and subsequent retrieval. I like to think of what the brain does during the encoding process as analogous to what happens on our computer desktops when we deal with materials. In the brain, we work with new materials in "working memory" (WM). Working memory is like the desktop when we type, edit, copy, paste, and organize our thoughts in a document. In WM, once we recognize patterns and file information, we need to store that new information in close proximity to "like" information in long-term memory, just as we might file similar documents in a folder on the computer desktop. Previously learned material is placed in schemata (which are structures in long-term memory that are similar to the 20th-century filing cabinet or our electronic cloud storage or external hard drives). If we do not label the files appropriately or place the folders in a logical place or if we do not retrieve them regularly, we risk forgetting where we filed the documents. Similarly, if new information is not understood and stored with like information into our brain's schemata or if we do not practice retrieving and working with the information for long periods of time, that information is likely to be forgotten! In short, new information must be rehearsed and recalled frequently if subsequent retrieval is to be effective. And if the period of time between rehearsal and retrieval is too long, retrieval will be inefficient or impossible.

Cognitive psychologists have identified ways that we can make meaning of and rehearse new information for effective encoding and efficient storage. Five cognitive strategies are particularly beneficial for musicians, and these work well in group-piano settings:

1. **Chunking:** Refers to taking smaller, discrete pieces of information and linking these in meaningful ways so that the pieces can be processed as a whole. This is critical, because humans can only hold about seven pieces of discrete information in WM. If a piano student processes F#, A#, and C# as three separate adjacent pitches on a staff rather than as a single F# major chord, he will use up almost half of working memory, leaving room for little other processing.

2. **Elaboration:** Refers to connecting new information with material that already has meaning for the learner, thus making sense of the new data. We do this when we spiral the curriculum and scaffold new material onto previously learned concepts. An example from group piano might be asking students to create a left-hand accompaniment based on a previously learned waltz-style pattern. They have to figure out which chords fit best with the new melody, but they are using both chords and a waltz-style pattern that they have mastered in another context.

3. **Generation:** Refers to using new material in a meaningful way. As music educators have long known, things that we create are remembered more readily than things we hear only. An example might be having students improvise their own melodies based on a given chord progression. Almost any time we have students rehearse new techniques or use them in novel ways, they are generating. Structured feedback is important at this time so that students do not ingrain poor habits or create incorrect attributions.

4. **Distributed practice:** Includes breaking down complex information into smaller components that can be rehearsed without overloading WM. Automating individual visual cues with rehearsed and automated motor skills and integrating discrete parts back into the whole are critical parts of this process. Distributed practice should be a part of all effective music practice.

5. **Primacy–recency effect:** Refers to the fact that information must be rehearsed and recalled often and that data will be more dependably retrieved if there were optimal attention levels during encoding and storage. In educational settings, we tend to remember best what happened at the beginning of class and second best what happened at the end. The middle period (sometimes called downtime) is an ideal time to avail ourselves of off-bench or group activities in the piano lab. Sousa (2011) proposed that optimal learning occurs in 20-minute segments.

Many educators divide this time into 10-, 3-, and 7-minute segments in which the most important or challenging material is worked on for the first 10 minutes, there is a related but distinctive 3-minute downtime activity, and the last 7 minutes of the teaching segment contain another activity that requires focused attention.

## Using Cognitive Strategies and Kolb's Learning Styles in the Group-Piano Class

At this point, it may be helpful to consider some specific examples of how availing oneself of learning preferences and cognitive strategies can increase student engagement and learning in the piano class. These examples are drawn from my own experience. If you are currently teaching group piano at the college level, try to identify your student Accommodators, Divergers, Assimilators, and Convergers, and thoughtfully assign them to groups for optimal results with collaborative work. With experience, you may be able to identify which type of learning style each student prefers. In Appendix C.2, there is a short learning-style survey that your students complete and a key to quickly assess their preferred style in group-piano.

### Engaging Active Experimenters and Reflective Observers in Technical Exercises

When I introduce seventh-chord arpeggios (a common technical exercise), I avail myself of the technology in the piano lab to enhance the experience for each learner. During this brief 5-minute activity, students rehearse the five types of seventh chords. These chords will be encountered in subsequent harmonization, improvisation, sight reading, and repertoire. There, they will be reinforced through elaboration, generation, and distributed practice. However, the ability to perform proficiently depends on mastery of the seventh-chord arpeggio, so each student must attend to it during the initial introduction.

I begin with a brief visual explanation designed to refresh students' memory of seventh chords already encountered in theory class. This activity, which establishes the context for the new piano technique, is essential for engaging Divergers and Assimilators who thrive on reflective observation. The next logical step, which engages the remainder of the students, is to have them play some of the chords at the piano. The Accommodators and Convergers, who prefer active experimentation, become fully engaged at this point. By using a MIDI accompaniment track that can be slowed to an appropriate practice tempo without altering the pitch, the Convergers and Assimilators (who are likely thinking about the theory underlying the harmony they are hearing) continue to process the chords in a way that is meaningful for them. The Accommodators and Divergers, who use more emotional feelings and enjoy the aural and kinesthetic feedback as they process new information, will benefit from the tactile rehearsal of the new chords, coupled with the motivation of keeping up with the accompaniment.

## Engaging Thinkers and Feelers in Improvisation

When we work on improvisation in the group-piano class, I recognize that these exercises may be more challenging for students who reside on the thinking side of the perception continuum and on the reflective observation side of the processing continuum. I might first give the students a list of the chords that are required to be played by the left hand and provide a specific accompaniment pattern above which the melody will be improvised. Initially, the students are reinforcing and elaborating on concepts that have been practiced as technical exercises and in harmonization examples. At this point, if the curriculum has been spiraled and paced appropriately, identifying and practicing the left-hand chord progression is familiar and should be retrieved easily from students' schematic store of information.

The new information that requires generation and problem solving in this exercise is the realization of an improvised melody. By setting guidelines that remind students to choose the majority of their melody notes from chord tones, I am encouraging elaboration of harmonic material. Setting parameters enables Assimilators to feel more comfortable with the experimentation part of the exercise. If students are new to improvising or suffer from coordination issues between the hands (which is not uncommon during the first several semesters of group piano), pairing students to take turns playing the accompaniment and improvising a melody can be a valuable learning experience.

Due to the experimental nature of this exercise and differing individual comfort levels with active experimentation, I have found certain combinations to be more effective than others. Since the process of improvising a new melody is a creative one, I like to pair the feelers who are on similar sides of the processing continuum. If the pairs of students are encouraged to pool the strengths of their individual learning styles during a structured in-class activity (in this case in pairs over headphones with a clearly defined set of guidelines), the outcome of the exercise for both students will be more successful than if they had worked independently. In this instance, if the instructor pairs an Assimilator with a Diverger and a Converger with an Accommodator, the assignment success rate will be better than if students were paired in other ways.

To illustrate, I will share an example from one of my recent classes. Susan, an Accommodator, intuitively came up with creative melodies in class but struggled when she had to operate under time constraints and perform for her peers. Meanwhile, Scott, a Converger who liked to think about new ways of applying what he was learning, also enjoyed active experimentation with melodies. He struggled with settling on just one melody within the time constraints of in-class assignments. For one exercise, I paired them and asked them to take turns playing four measures of accompaniment and improvised melody. I asked them to listen to one another and respond with subsequent phrases based on what the other had just played. Because they were comfortable experimenting, they each processed within their comfort zones, but they learned from the other because of the active listening and experimentation. The result was more creative than anything either had previously performed individually, and they made good progress in a short amount of class time. Had I paired Susan with a Diverger or an Assimilator who preferred observation and reflection, they might have been less comfortable with the active experimentation and improvised melodic responses and, thus, made less progress. During the same class, I paired a Diverger and an Assimilator and suggested that they briefly outline their ideas about how the melody might unfold and then take turns playing it and commenting upon strengths and weaknesses. They, too, ended up creating a lovely improvisation within the allotted class time by drawing upon their similar processing strengths. You will note that I facilitated the learning differently for each group, depending on the strengths of each pair.

## Conclusion

Many of the basic cognitive processes required for understanding new material and executing specific, refined motor skills at the piano are similar for all learners. These include chunking, elaboration, generation, and distributed practice. However, only information that learners recognize as relevant will capture their attention and be processed. Due to the primacy–recency effect, teachers should plan to introduce important material at the beginning and end of class. Students should engage in active learning between teaching segments requiring focused attention. Additionally, if learners are not attentive to new information that must be processed in working memory soon after it becomes available to consciousness, they will not learn it, understand it, or store it for future retrieval from long-term memory.

Differing learning styles affect both attention to new information and how it is processed. While the group-piano instructor can present new material in ways that are conducive to efficient cognitive processing and long-term storage and retrieval, if students do not process the new information according to their individual learning styles from the outset, piano skills and musical learning will be less effective. In order to produce the best possible results for each learner within the group, the instructor must understand how Divergers, Assimilators, Convergers, and Accommodators perceive and process information and then address each of those four needs during in-class collaborative activities and through varied presentation methods.

## Pedagogy in Action

1. Imagine that you are teaching a small group of 8 year old beginners. Based on your informal assessment using Golay's personality types, most of the group members are Bears and Owls. However, there is one little boy who displays Ape-like characteristics. Describe how you would structure learning (1) a four-measure rhythmic exercise and (2) a new ensemble piece to accommodate his needs and those of the others in the group. Be specific in describing the sequence of activities. Remember that students do not need to sit at their keyboards for the entirety of each activity, and try to engage the entire group in working together.

2. Based on the descriptions of Kolb's learning styles, identify your preferred style. Choose a learner whose learning style is on the opposite side of the experimentation continuum from you (i.e., if you are a Converger, you would choose a Diverger). Imagine that you are working on a joint eight-measure composition project with that person. The parameters of the project include playing the piece in 3/4 meter, using the key of A major, and you must both perform your composition together. You are in charge of leading the partnership. What steps would you take to accommodate both of your learning styles? Write a script for your interaction.

3. Take the short Keirsey type sorter (KTS) test (found in his 1998 book). After scoring yourself, identify and read about your type. Write a brief paragraph about how this personality type affects your learning preferences.

## References

Golay, K. (1982). *Learning Patterns and Temperament Styles.* Currently out of print.

Golay, K. (2003). "Staying in Tune with Learning Styles: Matching Your Teaching to Learners." In M. Baker-Jordan (Ed.). *Practical Piano Pedagogy* (pp. 149–166). Miami, FL: Warner Bros. Publications.

Jung, C. G. (1972). *Four Archetypes: Mother, Rebirth, Spirit, Trickster.* Translated by R.F.C. Hull. London: Routledge.

Keirsey, D. (1998). *Please Understand Me II: Temperament, Character, Intelligence.* Del Mar, CA: Prometheus Nemesis Book Company.

Kolb, D. A. (2015). *Experiential Learning: Experience as the Source of Learning and Development,* 2nd edition. Upper Saddle River, NJ: Pearson Education, Inc.

Pike, P. D. (2006). "Addressing Individual Learning Styles in the Group-Piano Class." *Proceedings from the 27th World Conference of the International Society for Music Education* (pp. 932–947). ISBN: 0-9752063-6-2.

Pike, P. D. (2014). An Exploration of the Effect of Cognitive and Collaborative Strategies on Keyboard Skills of Music Education Students. *Journal of Music Teacher Education, 23*(2), 79–91. doi: 10.1177/1057083713487214

Sousa, D. A. (2011). *How the Brain Learns,* 4th edition. Thousand Oaks, CA: Corwin.

# Section 2

# GROUP-PIANO STUDENTS
## Adults

# 5

# THE MUSIC MAJOR
## College-Level Group Piano

## Objectives

By the end of this chapter, you should understand the purpose of including group piano in the undergraduate music curriculum, typical skills addressed in undergraduate group-piano programs, and useful textbooks. Resources for networking with other group-piano faculty, grading, and accreditation are provided for further exploration.

## Introduction

### *Philosophy for Including Piano Proficiency in the Undergraduate Music Curriculum*

Regardless of their primary instrument, undergraduate music majors throughout much of the world must display a minimum level of competency at the piano. The reasons for requiring proficiency with piano skills are not always clearly articulated to students. Even some faculty members might find it difficult to justify this requirement. I have found that if music students understand why they are required to take a class and develop skills that appear to be only tangentially related to their primary instrument, they are more likely to attend and prepare for class. Therefore, we must be able to articulate why piano proficiency is necessary for professional musicians.

For many educators, the keyboard is a logical instrument through which students can explore various facets of music including rhythm, melody and harmony, theory and analytic skills, musical form, aural skills, coordination, listening and evaluation, and even improvisation. Most students play instruments that can only produce a single note and rhythm at a time. The piano provides a platform that allows them to create complex rhythms, melody, and harmony by themselves on a single instrument. And the piano can serve as a tool to assist musical understanding of theoretical concepts if one has basic keyboard skills. When deciding how to frame the piano experience for students, including which skills they need to develop, we should also consider how they will use the piano in their future professional lives.

Even though undergraduate students may not realize it, after graduation, they can be called upon to use basic keyboard skills. For example, in preparation for a solo or chamber performance, many musicians find it helpful to play the basic harmonic structure of an accompaniment, parts, or open score to get a sense of how the final product will sound or to make interpretative choices. Most musicians, even those who were performance majors, will do some teaching during their career. A flute (or any instrumental) teacher will undoubtedly need to provide basic accompaniment during a lesson, since beginning and intermediate students typically do not attend lessons with professional accompanists. Voice teachers and choir directors may need to harmonize vocal warm-ups or provide basic accompaniment during rehearsals. Musicians who will be involved in formal music education in schools will need to draw on keyboard skills including harmonization, transposition, improvising, sight reading, and performing simple accompaniments (Baker, 2017; Christensen, 2000; Young, 2013). Thus, the acquisition of keyboard skills has become a common requirement for music degree programs, and we need to help students understand why they should develop basic piano proficiency.

The National Association of Schools of Music (NASM), the music accrediting agency for the United States and Canada, asserts that a basic keyboard competency is required for the Bachelor of Arts in Music and the Bachelor of Music degrees (NASM, 2016). Typically, at the end of the sophomore year, students demonstrate competency by taking a formal piano proficiency exam. However, individual institutions and educators have freedom to interpret which skills and what level of achievement their students should meet. College group-piano teachers who gather at the MTNA–sponsored GP3 Forum every other year discuss piano competencies and other issues related to teaching piano pedagogy and group piano at the college level. Thus, there is some consistency of piano skills and competencies required of students pursuing either the BA, BM, or BME degrees regardless of institution. However, requirements and standards still vary from one school to another, and keyboard proficiency does not transfer between universities. Generally, when students pass the piano proficiency exam, their advisor checks a box on their degree audit ensuring that the requirement was met. If they transfer to another university before graduation, they will need to demonstrate their piano proficiency at the new institution.

### Suggested and Required Skills

At most universities, the piano skills that are tested on the proficiency include technique (scales, chords, etc.), sight reading, harmonization, transposition, improvisation, and basic performance ability (usually displayed by playing solo repertoire). While some schools provide private piano lessons to help students develop these skills, the majority of institutions in North America offer a sequence of group-piano classes. Group piano is the most efficient way for a large number of students to acquire the requisite piano skills. The group-piano sequence typically lasts from two to six semesters. Most universities that offer the BM degree provide three to four semesters of group-piano instruction. Schools that offer the BA degree may only require two or three semesters of group piano, as these students do not need to achieve the same level of proficiency as BM majors.

There is a trend toward offering an additional semester or two of group piano for music education and music therapy students, as they will need to be able to accompany, harmonize, transpose, and sight read at an even higher level upon graduation. In addition to the basic keyboard competency, NASM guidelines recommend that undergraduate music majors learn about composition, improvisation, and demonstrate synthesis of musical knowledge (NASM, 2016, p. 107). Sometimes the only place that improvisation happens is in the group-piano class, and the piano lab provides an ideal setting for musical synthesis. Additionally, music therapy students must display advanced keyboard skills including sight reading, transposition, and improvisation (p. 114), and music education students must display functional performance at the keyboard (p. 117). Many music therapy and music education students benefit from additional courses devoted to developing these specific piano skills.

### Placement Tests

Because some students arrive at university with previous piano experience and because occasionally students will transfer to another institution prior to degree completion, the group-piano instructor will need to provide placement tests for these individuals. I offer placement tests at the beginning of each semester, but the majority of students will take their placements before the beginning of the fall semester or during their undergraduate orientation. Some group-piano coordinators at large schools prepare guidelines for the undergraduate advisor about where students with past experience can expect to be placed. They can share information with students and tentatively register them for a piano class (reserving the student's spot) until the student takes the actual placement test.

Teachers can only prepare appropriate placement tests if they understand which skills are required at their institution, how much competency must be displayed by the end of each semester, and which skills tend not to be taught in private precollege piano lessons. For example, I do not have students perform solo repertoire at piano placements, because performance of a piece that a student has worked on for months does not necessarily tell me much about that student's sight-reading or harmonization abilities, which are core skills in the piano proficiency. In my piano placement folder, I have a set of examples for sight reading, harmonization, and score reading (when applicable) that a student should be able to play at the conclusion of each semester. I also list basic technical skills such as scales and chord progressions that a student should know for each level. Then, at the placement test, I work through each skill component with the student until he or she cannot complete the task. This lets me know which level of group piano is appropriate for that student.

One final reason we must remain cognizant of specific requirements for each level in our group-piano sequence is that our curriculum will dictate which book and materials we adopt for our classes. When we choose the textbook we will use, we must be sure it will enable our students to develop the specific skills that are required on the piano proficiency test at our institution. Next, we will explore specific skills that are most often required. A brief review of textbooks and online resources that are most often adapted for college classes will follow.

## NASM Requirements and Recommendations

### Overview of Piano Skills Required of Music Majors

As noted, while there is some flexibility regarding standard keyboard skills required at the end of each semester and on the piano proficiency test, average expectations at each stage of group-piano study are illustrated in Figure 5.1.

This model assumes that first-year students have few, if any, piano skills. During the course of their group-piano studies, they will develop the requisite piano technique to play increasingly difficult sight reading, harmonization, score reading, transposition, improvisation, and solos, duets, accompaniment and ensemble music. If fifth and

| Skill / Level | Technique | Sight-Reading/ Score Reading | Harmonization/ Transposition/ Improvisation | Repertoire/ Ensemble |
|---|---|---|---|---|
| Piano 1 | • Pentascales (Major & minor) <br> • 2-octave scales (Major) separate hands <br> • Primary chord progressions (Major keys) | • Simple treble & bass reading <br> • Melody mainly within 5-finger pattern <br> • Transpose some sight reading (SR) | • Harmonize melody with primary chords (Major keys) <br> • Some alternate accompaniment patterns <br> • Harmonize w/ 2-hand accompaniments (prep for accompanying) <br> • Transpose harmonization <br> • Beginning improvisation (w/ prepared progressions) | • Elementary repertoire (level 1) <br> • Single-line ensemble repertoire |
| Piano 2 | • 2-octave scale (separate hands) Major & harmonic minor keys <br> • Minor primary chord progressions <br> • More facility with hand expansion/ contraction; finger crossings, etc. <br> • Pedal | • Octave (or more) melodic range <br> • Major & minor keys <br> • Introduce alto & tenor clef <br> • Transpose many SR | • Harmonize in minor keys <br> • Use secondary chords (particularly V/V) <br> • 2-hand accompanying <br> • Transpose most harmonization examples <br> • Improvisation (related to harmonic progressions) | • Level 2 repertoire <br> • Duets/ multi-part ensemble repertoire |

*Figure 5.1* Typical Keyboard Skills Categories for Music Major Group-Piano Levels

| | Some BA Programs End Here; Others Include a Third Semester & Modify Skills Listed Below | | | |
|---|---|---|---|---|
| Piano 3 | • Facility with scales<br>• Chord progressions incorporating primary & secondary chords<br>• Chord progressions with secondary dominants<br>• Seventh chords (various types) | • More complex SR; could be in modes<br>• Begin working on chorale-style SR<br>• 3-part score reading<br>• Transposition<br>• SR will incorporate harmonic progressions being studied elsewhere<br>*Assess BA student needs* | • Harmonization w/ secondary dominants (V/ii; V/iii; V/V; V/vi)<br>• Improvisation using these chord progressions<br>• Transpose many harmonization exercises | • Level 3<br>• Accompany peers on their instrument (learn how to communicate as musicians)<br>• Duets |
| Piano 4 | • Scales (HT if required on proficiency)<br>• Chord progressions with modulations<br>• Facility and hand independence (for level 3-4 rep) | • SR that modulates<br>• More complex LH accomp patterns<br>• Chorale-style<br>• 4-part score reading (w/ transposing instruments for band/instrumental students) | • Harmonizations that modulate<br>• LH accompaniment patterns should become more automatic as melodies get more complex (rhythmically)<br>• Hand independence and quick theory is essential | • Level 4<br>• Duets, peer accompanying, etc. |
| | Optional Levels for Music Therapy & Music Education Students | | | |
| Piano 5 | • Plug in modules that work on critical skills specific to the major | • SR 2 & 3-pt open score<br>• Learn simple pieces & SCR quickly | • Play progressions while singing & cuing<br>• Improvise harms & accompaniments | • Play appropriate accompaniments |
| Piano 6 | • Plug in modules that work on critical skills specific to the major | • SR 3 & 4-pt open score<br>• Learn music quickly | • Play more complex progs while singing & cuing<br>• Improvise/transpose harms & accomps | • Play appropriate accompaniments |

*Figure 5.1* (Continued)

sixth semesters of group-piano are offered for music education and music therapy students, instructors can choose to work on all components throughout the semester or divide key skills into modules that can be explored intensely for several weeks at a time throughout the semester.

## Assessment

### *Syllabus*

If you are teaching group piano as a graduate assistant or if you are an adjunct instructor teaching one of several group-piano sections, your supervisor may have already supplied you and your students with a syllabus. If not, universities require that instructors create and share a syllabus with students for each course. At my university, we consider the syllabus to be a contract between the faculty member and the students. In it, we outline our expectations for the course, and students acknowledge that they understand their responsibilities for the semester. Some institutions offer models of syllabi or require that specific topics (such as grading, attendance, disability services, etc.) are addressed. At other schools, faculty have more flexibility in what they include. Just as independent studio teachers publish studio policies, in which they outline expectations for the group-piano class, syllabi for individual university group-piano classes provide students and instructors with a set of policies for the course.

I think that in addition to university-mandated guidelines that must be included, the syllabus for music-major group-piano classes should reflect your objectives for the course, expectations of in-class participation and outside practice for the students, how grades will be determined, and concepts that will be addressed each week. Your syllabus should include:

- the course title, rubric, and number
- instructor's name, office number, contact information, and office hours (virtual and in-person)
- course objectives
- required text(s)
- expectations for minimum work/practice outside of class
- expectations for in-class participation and attendance
- grading scheme
- specifics about individual graded assignments (i.e., practice-log assignments, collaborative assignments, or anything beyond a typical individual performance assessment)
- tentative dates of exams
- links to university statements regarding the student code of conduct, outside work expectations, disability services and support, attendance, and accommodations for excused absences
- anticipated class schedule (including weekly concepts, skills, and text page numbers that will be covered)

Be sure to post a copy of your syllabus on the learning management system for your course so that students have access to it at any time. While few students enjoy having the syllabus read to them at the first class, I recommend highlighting important components of the syllabus (including practice expectations, in-class participation, and grading) so that students know what to expect and begin practicing immediately. As the instructor, you set the standard for the class by clearly describing your expectations and then by holding students accountable. From the very first class, I have students participate in group work, and I give skills quizzes (from the practice assignments) within the first 2 weeks to ensure that students establish the habit of practicing piano. Also, give some thought to the formatting of your syllabus. If it is easy to read and students can easily locate pertinent information, they will be more likely to consult it throughout the semester. For example, I put the class schedule information into a table so that students can easily see which pages we will be working on each week if they would like to get ahead during weeks when the workload is lighter or if they need to catch up after missing a class.

## *Purpose and Materials*

Even though you will be teaching students in a group setting and employing various group strategies to facilitate student learning and understanding, college music majors should be assessed individually. Assessments should be formal and frequent so the students know how they are doing and you have a record of improvement and know what you need to focus on during instructional periods. Feedback to students should be immediate and specific. Researchers and teachers have found that when students receive verbal and written feedback shortly after taking a test, they are better able to make adjustments and improve. If you give small tests and quizzes frequently throughout the semester, the stakes are lower than for exams, and students will be able to identify mistakes before bad habits become ingrained, adjust their practice strategies, and improve specific skills. Since they will have to perform a high-stakes piano proficiency, the more practice they have performing under pressure for you in quizzes, tests, and exams, the better they will be able to cope during the proficiency. I try to give my students specific written feedback at the class immediately following the quiz. Some of my graduate assistants provide feedback next to each student's grade in our online learning management system. The caveat with this type of feedback is that you want to be sure your students read it in order to benefit from it.

I also like to have a snapshot of what my students are doing at the midpoint and end of each semester. This can be useful if external evaluators from accrediting agencies visit campus and want to know what students in a specific piano class are learning. For this reason, and because I like my students to maintain a digital portfolio of their piano skills, my students record all of their quizzes, tests, and exams on a USB drive. I grade the performances immediately following class. The result is that I can evaluate students frequently but spend more class time teaching and having them explore concepts. Instead of me grading individual students during the class, they all record the quiz at the same time, and I grade the quizzes outside of class. If they have questions about a specific grade, we can play back the performance and listen together, which helps students develop self-evaluation skills. Sometimes, I have them evaluate their performances and reflect on positive and negative aspects. Along with their USB, they turn in a brief written reflection about the performance and include two or three specific practice steps that they will take to improve a self-identified problem. I still award the grade for the actual quiz, but they also receive a separate small grade (perhaps out of 5 points) on the quality of their reflective evaluation.

This is an example of how the technology in the piano lab enhances student learning and engagement and allows me to give frequent evaluations without losing valuable instructional time.

An efficient and effective tool to use when evaluating student performances is a rubric. In most of my music-major group-piano classes, the students and I develop the rubric (which contains the grading criteria) together. Grading performances is viewed as a subjective experience by many outside of the musical field. However, if we consider concepts and skills that students must display to receive a grade of C, B, or A, we can usually define these quite clearly. Students generally know what is expected of them, but it is helpful to have them articulate these thoughts and contribute to the decision about what will be evaluated. This exercise will help them more accurately evaluate their group work and their individual playing, too. A simple but useful rubric that I use contains four or five columns. The column on the left lists the attributes that I am grading (such as technique, dynamics, balance between the hands, group work, etc.), and there will be a separate row for each attribute. Then I have columns that correspond to grades A through D, with criteria for each grade. Rather than using letter grades or numbers in the headings, I use terms such as "exemplary," "competent," "developing," and "not there yet!" Stevens and Levi (2005) provide many helpful suggestions for designing rubrics in a short and accessible book on the topic. See Figure 5.2 for a sample rubric that I use with my 5th-semester vocal music

Rubric for Piano 5 Collaborative Project: (Accompaniment & Singing) **10 points possible**

Composition & Date:_____ Pianist's Name_____

| | 4.5-5 points | 3.5-4.4 points | 3.4 points & less |
|---|---|---|---|
| | **Exemplary** | **Competent** | **Developing** |
| **Performance Skills (5 pts)** Additional Comments: | o Musical performance<br>o Captured character of the piece<br>o Appropriate expression<br>o Observed all dynamic markings<br>o Maintained appropriate tempo<br>o Body language was appropriate (for collaboration) | o Mostly musical performance<br>o Character of the piece was evident much of the time, but lapsed during tricky spots<br>o Some expression<br>o Some dynamic markings observed<br>o Tempo was a little slow/too fast in spots or wasn't steady | o Performance lacked important musical elements<br>o Character of the piece was not completely captured<br>o Musical expression lacked finesse<br>o Few dynamic markings observed<br>o Tempo was too fast/too slow<br>o Body language was inappropriate (making faces, talking after mistakes) |
| **Group Work (5 pts)** Additional Comments: | o Evidence of collaborative musicianship<br>o Non-verbal communication<br>o Continuity throughout<br>o Appropriate musical choices | o Some evidence of collaborative musicianship<br>o Some non-verbal communication<br>o Continuity was maintained most of the time, with just a few minor lapses<br>o Most musical choices were appropriate | o Little evidence of collaborative musicianship<br>o Little non-verbal communication<br>o Overall lack of continuity throughout<br>o Musical choices appear to have been governed by limited technique or preparation |

*Figure 5.2* Sample Collaborative Rubric (used in group-piano 5 for vocal music education majors)

education students on their collaborative assignments. You will note that I expect that they will attain a minimum level of competency, so there is no column for a grade below 70% (though I could theoretically still award a lower grade).

I recommend having a set of exam materials for each level of group piano. You might have several examples you can cycle through so that you are not giving identical tests each year. If you do use the same or similar examples, especially for sight reading or other quick-study components, be sure that students do not remove copies from the piano lab or take photos that can be posted online for others to see. In my piano lab, cell phones must be turned off at all times (to prevent leaking of test materials and to maintain the integrity of the learning environment). I teach multiple sections of the same level each semester, and students do communicate about tests between classes. So I try to give similar examples but in different keys so that students who take the test later in the day do not have an advantage. Recall that I use a similar set of final exam examples during the piano placements, so I guard all materials closely.

### Piano Proficiency Exam

At my school currently, the piano proficiency exam is a separate assessment from the other tests and exams in the group-piano sequence. It takes place during exam week, and students sign up for specific times. Because we have tested many technical skills previously and have records of these scores, on the day of the exam, we hear the following items: an arrangement of the national anthem, sight reading, prepared harmonization and transposition, accompaniment, prepared four-part open score, and solo repertoire. We have at least two instructors evaluate the exams, and each makes written notes on an evaluation form. There is at least one music education faculty member present when music education students take the test. If we offered a music therapy degree, it would be essential for a faculty member from that department to be present during exams of those majors.

We record all exams on our acoustic Yamaha Disklavier piano, so we have both written and auditory records of piano proficiencies. At the end of each semester, as the group-piano coordinator, I report general proficiency statistics to our assessment committee. For example, I list the number of students who performed with basic competency (equivalent to a score of 70–79.9%), developed proficiency (80–89.8%), and mastery (90–100%). I break these numbers down for performance and music education majors, since that is how we have to report these statistics to administrators on our campus. Each school may define piano competency a little differently, based on degrees offered and perceived needs of students. The important thing is that you understand what the standards are at your school and that you have a common rubric to assess all students. Having at least two faculty members or instructors grade the exam ensures that the assessment is fair. It is recommended that you keep basic assessment data (such as what I send our assessment chair) for several years, until your regular university and/or NASM review has taken place.

At my university, we ask students to learn and prepare an arrangement of the "Star-Spangled Banner," because we believe that musicians may be called upon to play this at any time, and the performance displays the student's ability to lead through music. The national anthem of any country would serve this purpose. I have heard from many former students who report using this arrangement after graduation, and I occasionally get requests from music educators for a copy of the arrangement so they can play it during their school assemblies! While they have some time (from a few minutes to several days) to prepare each of the components of the exam, the material is challenging enough that if students are not proficient, they will not have enough time to prepare and perform each component well. My students have 8 minutes to prepare a sight-reading example that requires balance between the hands, coordination of motor skills, and good reading ability. They have 1 week to prepare a harmonization example that modulates, but they will be asked to transpose it at the exam to another key. They also have 7 days to prepare the accompaniment and score-reading examples. Each of these are related to their instrument type. For example, singers would prepare a simple vocal accompaniment and their score reading would include a tenor line, whereas string players would be required to read an open score that used the alto clef, and brass or wind players would need to transpose two of the instrumental parts. Actual requirements of the proficiency test will vary depending on the school and standards agreed upon by the faculty. However, if you find yourself in a position to revamp your proficiency test, consider skills that will be of value to students after graduation and how you can best assess and record each student's competency.

## After the Proficiency and Supplemental Resources

As noted, many schools require music education, music therapy, or other students to develop more piano proficiency and specific skills once they have completed the proficiency test. Some schools accomplish this through private secondary piano lessons, while others offer one or two additional semesters of group-piano classes. At my school, vocal music education students are expected to develop more advanced sight-reading, harmonization, accompanying, and score-reading skills. I use a combination of materials from harmonization texts, folk-song books, actual choral method books that they may use upon graduation, choral arrangements, and score-reading texts. The texts listed in what follows can also be used in preparation for the proficiency, either as textbooks or as a source of supplementary materials for students. Although not comprehensive, several books that you might explore include:

### Harmonization

- *Harmonization at the Piano* by Arthur Frackenpohl
- *Harmonization-Transposition at the Keyboard* by Alice M. Kern
- *Melodies to Harmonize With* by Frank D. Mainous

### Harmonization from Lead Lines and Improvising Simple Accompaniments

- *Folk Songs for Schools and Camps* by Jerry Silverman
- *Lead Lines and Chord Changes* by Ann Collins
- *Piano for Singers* by Jeffrey Deutsch

### Score Reading

- *Keyboard Skills for Music Educators: Score Reading* by Shellie Gregorich and Benjamin Moritz
- *Music for Score Reading* by Robert A. Melcher and Willard F. Warch

Even if you do not have to teach group piano beyond the proficiency, the materials listed can be helpful sources for supplementary materials that you may need when teaching any level of group piano to music majors.

## College Text Overviews

*Alfred's Group Piano for Adults*, 2nd Edition, Books 1 and 2
E. L. Lancaster & Kenon Renfrow, Alfred Publishing Co., Inc.
Contains CD and MIDI accompaniments.

There are 26 units in each book, plus supplemental repertoire sections that contain 17 and 18 solos, respectively. Each book works well for an entire year (two semesters), and together they provide ample material for a four-semester group-piano sequence. Each unit contains basic concepts, technique, sight reading, harmonization, improvisation, and solos. Many units have two-page worksheets and ensemble music. Objectives for each unit are clearly stated at the beginning of each chapter. Most units have about four sight-reading and four harmonization examples, so there are new examples at the correct level that students can work on throughout the week. Many examples have suggestions for transposition. The MIDI accompaniments are attractive, and the multivoice tracks add to the in-class experience, beyond the teacher accompaniments. These tracks are on the practice CD that comes with each book.

The first book begins with off-staff reading and progresses sequentially. The materials correspond with concepts that students typically learn in theory classes during the first 2 years of a BM program. By the end of the first book, students have learned scales, primary chord progressions, and secondary and seventh chords in all major and minor keys. There is also a brief introduction to six modes. The second book briefly reviews concepts from Book 1 but reinforces concepts and progresses to more difficult chord progressions, modulations, secondary dominants, and augmented sixth chords. Score-reading with transposing instruments and alto clef is introduced, though more reinforcement through supplementary materials may be needed. A teacher handbook, with lesson planning suggestions, is available at the publisher's web site.

*Piano for the Developing Musician*, 6th Edition (2009 Media Update)
Other versions: Volume 2 (1992); Concise Edition (2010)
Martha Hilley & Lynn Freeman Olson, Schirmer, Cengage Learning
Access to online media resources.

The latest edition of *Piano for the Developing Musician* is designed to be used in a four-semester group-piano curriculum. This is a comprehensive, 400-page text that features numerous sight-reading, harmonization, improvisation, composition, playing-by-ear, and ensemble examples that students enjoy playing. Since the book is aimed at music majors who already read music, the book begins with minimal theoretical information and uses on-staff notation from the outset. There are minimal instructions, but important points are stressed. Units contain "topics to explore" sections, providing teachers and students suggestions for further explanation and exploration. Novice teachers will need extensive preparation to pace and supplement this text. It is pedagogically strong, but careful lesson planning and clear practice assignments are critical for student success.

The true strength of the book is the online content that students can use to play along with as they practice, reinforce rhythm, and get practice guidance from the tutorials. Teachers can avail of these MIDI files and drum tracks during class. The online resources guide students through rehearsal, so they benefit from having a tutor as they practice. There are many creative activities, and students are encouraged to develop the ear alongside the keyboard and theory skills. There is ample material for group work during class, including ensemble music such as duets, multipart rhythm ensembles, improvised ensembles based on the rhythm ensembles, and multiple-keyboard ensembles. Because this book can be used for four semesters and is packed with examples, the pages are clean and easy to read but may be a little cluttered for some students. The author of this book has designed it so that the examples and online resources are attainable with just 20 minutes of practice (6 days per week). Clear assignment guidelines should help students not to be overwhelmed.

*Keyboard Musicianship*, Book 1, 10th Edition (2014) and Book 2, 10th Edition (2015)
James Lyke, Tony Caramia, Reid Alexander, Geoffrey Haydon, & Ronald Chioldi, Stipes Publishing
Contains CD accompaniments.

Each book is designed to cover 1 year of undergraduate group-piano for the college music major. Each unit contains an introduction to important concepts, technique, sight reading, accompaniments, harmonization, improvisation, suggested transposition activities, solo repertoire, American song repertoire, and ensemble repertoire. Students read on staff from the outset. Intervallic reading is encouraged, and there are about four pages per chapter of reading examples in various keys. While chords are introduced using Roman numerals and figured bass, the harmonization examples encourage students to write in and apply the chord symbols (lead line style). There are eight chapters per book, so students would spend more than 1 week in a chapter. Book 2 builds on core concepts including more complex chord progressions and score-reading examples. Appendices include additional solo and duet literature, as well as holiday music in solo (grand staff) and lead line format. There is ample white space on each page (pages are not cluttered); thus, the music is easy to read for many students. Some instructors find that they need to use supplementary materials if their course requires a substantial amount of practice outside of class.

*Contemporary Class Piano*, 8th Edition (2015)
Elise Mach, Oxford University Press
Contains online supplementary content.

Unlike the previous books, which were written for music-major group-piano classes, this text claims to be for either music majors or non-majors. Units feature specific topics and include technique and rhythm exercises, sight reading, harmonization, improvisation, solos, ensemble music, and written worksheets. The content is sequenced well, and it is pedagogically sound. Students learn five-finger patterns in many keys early on and are encouraged to explore these keys in numerous contexts. Various teacher accompaniments encourage musical performances in various meters. Harmonization is introduced using both Roman numeral and chord symbols. Due to the way the book is organized, it would work well in a class that is organized into modules. It could easily be used as a source of supplementary materials. There is enough material for several semesters of work, even if this were the only text to be used.

*Piano Lab*, 7th Edition (2011)
Carolynn A. Lindemann, Wadsworth Publishing
Premium web site access.

This book is also not specifically designed for music majors, though it could be used with majors. This book is packed with technique, exercises, reading, harmonizing, repertoire, ideas for ensemble playing, and composition projects. The book could easily be used over the course of two semesters. The materials are sequenced well. Like all adult books, the pace is quick, but the beginning examples and repertoire require more hand independence and coordination than some of the other texts listed earlier. Because important historical information about the piano, general music appreciation details, and appendices with extensive reference materials are included, this book could possibly be used as a text for piano classes that are classified as general education classes for non-music majors. It should be noted that there is a lot more material than could likely be used in one semester with typical undergraduate students. This book would be an excellent source of supplemental materials.

## Pedagogy in Action

1. If you are a graduate teaching assistant in group piano, consult the shared group-piano test documents or ask your advisor for sample exams for each of the group-piano classes offered at your school. From these and the group-piano text, create a list of concepts and skills required at each level. If your advisor provides you with such a list, compare it with your list. Create sample placement tests for each level of your group-piano sequence (either on your own using Finale, Sibelius, MuseScore, or another notation software or from exercises you've assembled from various sources).

2. Assume that you will be teaching group piano at a school that requires students to master the skills listed in Figure 5.1. Using the method evaluation form in Appendix D.2, review two of the college texts previewed in this chapter and note how they correspond to the list. Point out specifically where skill preparation is lacking or would need to be reinforced and identify a source for supplementary materials. Compare your notes with those of a classmate. (Note: If you are teaching college group piano for the first time, be sure to review the text you are using in your teaching. If you have some experience with group teaching, you may choose to review two texts you have not used.)

3. Choose one of the group-piano texts from this unit. Assume your class meets twice weekly. Create lesson plans for the first month of classes (eight classes). Be sure to cover technique, sight reading, harmonization, transposition, and repertoire (solo and ensemble) regularly and to sequence activities so you are scaffolding

upon familiar concepts. Consider what you will do with the entire group, what can be done through small-group work, and when you will use accompaniments, and be sure to note these details on your plans.

# References

Baker, V. A. (2017). Teachers' Perceptions on Current Piano Use in the Elementary General Music Classroom. *Update: Applications of Research in Music Education, 35*(2), 23–29. doi: 10.1177/8755123315598558

Christensen, L. (2000). *A Survey of the Importance of Functional Piano Skills as Reported by Band, Choral, Orchestra and General Music Teachers.* (Doctoral Dissertation, University of Oklahoma, 2000). *Dissertation Abstracts International, 61*(6), 2229.

National Association of Schools of Music. (2016). *Standards for Baccalaureate and Graduate Degree-Granting Institutions: NASM Handbook.* Reston, VA: National Association of Schools of Music. https://nasm.arts-accredit.org/accreditation/standards-guidelines/handbook/

Stevens, D. D., & Levi, A. J. (2005). *Introduction to Rubrics: An Assessment Tool to Save Grading Time, Convey Effective Feedback and Promote Student Learning.* Sterling, VA: Stylus Publishing, LLC.

Young, M. M. (2013). University-Level Group Piano Instruction and Professional Musicians. *Music Education Research, 15*(1), 59–73. doi: http://dx.doi.org/10.1080/14613808.2012.737773

# 6

# THE NON-MAJOR
## Adult Groups for College Credit

### Objectives

By the end of this chapter, you will understand the philosophy and purposes of college piano classes for non-music majors. You will learn about ways to assess individuals for proper placement in courses, texts that can be used, and how to assess individuals within the group throughout the semester.

## The Non-Music Major

### *Philosophy and Theory*

Many colleges and universities offer one or two group-piano classes for beginning non-music majors. For many students enrolled in non-major group-piano classes, the class period may be the only time the students enter the music building. Some instructors recognize that this is a chance to help non-majors develop understanding, appreciation, and a lifelong love of music. Musical seeds planted in the group-piano class may translate into future amateur music making for individual pleasure and advocacy for the music profession in general. Although we are helping students learn to play the piano in these classes, we may be cultivating future patrons of our profession.

Non-major piano classes offer a unique opportunity for instructors to work with mostly young adults who are interested in learning to play the piano but whose work at the end of the semester does not need to stand up to the scrutiny of outside music-assessment bodies. However, they are enrolled in the class for college credit, which implies that a certain amount of outside work (practice) is required and that they will need to meet specific performance benchmarks set by the individual instructor or program coordinator. These benchmarks likely remain fairly constant from one semester to the next. You will probably find that if you compared a group of young adults in a noncredit program (these are discussed in Chapter 7) and a similar group in a college-credit class, students in the latter may show more progress at the end of the semester because they are required to display skill acquisition and performance abilities throughout the semester.

Regardless, because the students will be learning in a group environment, group and partner work should be used during class to engage students, to enhance their learning, and so they experience music making with others. As instructors, we must be cognizant of the fact that non-majors' musical backgrounds are often quite different from our own. Although we grew up listening to recordings of masters and going to recitals, our non-majors may not share similar experiences. Therefore, group-piano students might even be prepared for and encouraged to attend accessible piano or music recitals presented by the music department.

When designing the curriculum for non-major classes, I try to think about student goals and my educational goals for the students. The two are often far apart. Then I create a curriculum that serves both of our needs. I find that I can help most non-majors redefine success by adjusting their goals and expectations. When I ask students in my non-major classes why they registered, they typically say that they always wanted to learn how to play the piano or that they played a little when they were young but remember little and want to regain skills. Of course, in a group-piano class, you may find as many goals as there are individuals! As instructors of non-major classes, we first need to help students (re)frame their goals and expectations for the course so we have common objectives.

Young adults who are not music majors will be interested in the final product—being able to play the piano (or a specific piece of music); instructors need to consider which skills are most important for students to achieve this goal. You may already have noted that learning to play the piano is a rather ill-defined and broad goal. One of the first items of business when teaching groups of non-majors is to define discrete skills that will lead toward being able to perform music on the piano. Then we must help students see how these skills lead toward the eventual goal and be realistic about what they can accomplish in a semester or two. We know that they will not be playing the original *Moonlight Sonata* by the end of the first semester, but we can help them to develop skills necessary to play similarly interesting music or a simplified arrangement of their favorite composition.

Sometimes the non-major classes are taught by college faculty; other times they are taught by graduate teaching assistants or part-time adjunct faculty. Unlike music-major group-piano programs, there can be more variation between individual classes from one campus to another and even between classes on one campus. On some campuses, the group-piano course is used for liberal arts or general education credit. If this is the case, there may be specific musical concepts (in addition to piano skills) that will need to be addressed and assessed throughout the course.

General education music classes typically develop listening skills and use diverse methods of delivery and varying content to help students develop personal connections with music so that it might become valued within our society (Enz, 2013). In this way, the music instructor is serving as an advocate and ambassador for music and, in our case, for piano in particular. If you are hired to teach a non-major group-piano class, be sure that you are aware of any department-wide requirements regarding the purpose and aims of the course, the text that is used, how students are assessed throughout the semester, specific materials used for assessment, and specific skills that should be tested. It is important to remember that most colleges have minimum expectations for outside work that students should expect to complete (based on the number of credits they receive for the course), so your practice assignments and testing should be commensurate with college-level work. See Chapter 5 for specifics about the course syllabus.

## Assessment

### *Individual Assessment*

As in other college-level classes, students should be assessed individually even if much of their work takes place in the group setting. You may find that giving regular quizzes on specific items from practice assignments (including technique, harmonization, and repertoire) can keep students working toward their goal of learning to play the piano. If feedback is consistent, students know where they are improving and which skills need additional practice. Rubrics help ensure that feedback is objective and clear for the student (Steven & Levi, 2005). In addition to regular playing quizzes, I like to give longer exams (such as a midterm and a final) on which they are asked to demonstrate declarative knowledge and procedural knowledge. They might answer a few short theory-type questions and play several compositions and a harmonization example that they have had several days to work on.

On the longer exams, I sometimes provide options for the repertoire from an approved list. Although the examples are at the same level, they are in different styles (such as classical, blues, or an arrangement of a familiar tune), and the students appreciate having some control over the experience. Many non-music majors get nervous when they have to play for a grade. The quizzes help them become accustomed to performing for the instructor and help them develop confidence alongside musical skills. As with all assessment, your feedback should be prompt and specific so that students know precisely what they did well and what needs work. If there are several negatives, prioritize those and offer suggestions for how students might work on improving the problem. Even if the testing, standard, or achievement level is not as rigorous as it is for music majors, students still need to know how they are improving and what needs additional practice.

Although all assessment is done individually, a benefit of adult beginners taking group piano is that the experience of learning complex skills is shared by many, and students realize that they are not the only ones struggling with unfamiliar concepts. When I notice several students struggling with similar issues, I address these with the entire group (without singling out students) and even solicit feedback from students about what they have found helpful during practice. The group camaraderie and shared musical experience is an important part of the learning process in non-major classes. Once they become accustomed to working on and playing piano ensembles, non-majors will benefit from playing more musically stimulating repertoire and making music with others in class.

### *Piano Placements*

If you teach a non-major class, you will likely receive inquiries from students who have some piano background regarding placement in your course. Sometimes students took many years of lessons; other times they studied only briefly and remember little. Either way, you will need to create a simple assessment tool to place students in the correct class. If students are too advanced for the first-semester group, they may be eligible to go directly into the second-semester class. If you do not have a class beyond the introductory level, these students may need private secondary lessons, or there may not be an appropriate course for them at your university. Other times, students do not remember as much as they think they do and benefit from taking the introductory class. Either way, you will need to place students appropriately and explain why you are making such recommendations.

Your thoughtful explanation of why you have placed a student who has some piano background in a first-semester beginning class will go a long way toward whether that student is content in that class or not. Often, students hold inaccurate beliefs about their own abilities. It is our job to help them understand how the appropriate course will fill in any gaps and to provide motivational supplementary material, as necessary, throughout the semester. We can also strategically pair and place students with some background with novices. When students have to explain or make meaning of knowledge with others, they discover how well they have learned it. In this way, the more experienced students can share some of their knowledge and learn where they may need additional assistance, while those with limited backgrounds learn from peers and develop confidence by contributing to the partnership.

## College Texts for Non-Majors

If you try to use a textbook designed for music majors in your non-major classes, you will find that the material tends to move too quickly, it may cover skills that non-majors will not use, theoretical concepts may be too complex, and you will likely need to find many supplementary materials so students can reinforce concepts and consolidate their learning. If you try to use an adult method book that is designed for recreational music making (see Chapter 7) or private instruction, you may find that there is not enough material or that the topics and skills are too limited for a college course. Thus, I recommend using a textbook designed for use in college classes with non-music majors.

Even with a reputable non-major group-piano text, you may still wish to supplement or create your own ancillary materials, as I do. But you will be using core materials that were developed by piano educators and honed through decades of experience working with classes of non-major college students. While I keep multiple copies of piano ensembles and sight-reading examples in my piano lab for supplemental work during class, typically I have my non-major students purchase an elementary repertoire book in addition to the main text. There are many fine pedagogical composers, such as Melody Bober, Robert Vandall, or Kevin Olson, who write music that is widely available through American music publishers such as Alfred, FJH, or Kjos. Their elementary compositions tend to sound attractive (so they are musically satisfying), they are highly patterned (thus relatively easy to learn and play), and they provide students with additional pieces they can play for pleasure, for family, or for friends. Many high-quality repertoire books that can be used as a second required text are at the $10 or less price point.

Brief overviews of three popular and widely available non-major group-piano textbooks follow. It is recommended that you use the group-piano college text evaluation form (see Appendix D.2) to complete in-depth reviews of at least two of the three books so you will be able to make an informed choice about which to adopt for your non-major classes when you have an opportunity to choose the text. Always remember to listen to any accompaniment CDs and online resources and play the student materials so you know how they feel under the fingers and how they sound.

*Piano 101*, Books 1 and 2
E. L. Lancaster & Kenon Renfrow, Alfred Publishing Co., Inc.
Contains CD and MIDI accompaniments.

Each book contains 15 units, allowing instructors to cover about one unit per week in a typical semester. Each unit contains new concepts, rhythmic exercises, ear training, technique, sight reading, solo repertoire, and brief "Did you know?" boxes highlighting a famous composer, musical form, or instrument. Most units also have harmonization examples using lead line–type chord symbols, ensemble repertoire and one-page written worksheets. There is a supplementary repertoire section at the end of each book that contains about a dozen pieces, mostly arrangements of American classics and classical favorites.

The first book focuses mainly on the keys of C, G, and F major, including primary chord progressions in these keys as well as major and minor five-finger patterns in numerous keys. There is an introduction to the blues and boogie styles toward the end of the book. The second book explores parallel major and minor keys and moves into B-flat major and G minor by the end. Augmented and diminished triads, as well as seventh chords, are explored. Rhythms become more complicated in Book 2, with various sixteenth-note patterns reinforced. In both books, the progression from beginning to end is sequential and well-paced. The MIDI accompaniments and CDs are attractive and inspire steady playing. These should be used by students when practicing and played in class from the teaching station.

*Piano for Pleasure:* Concise 4th Edition
Martha Hilley & Lynn Freeman Olson, Cengage Learning
Contains online access codes for accompaniments and supplemental materials.

Each unit contains listening, rhythm, technique, theory, reading, and improvisation exercises, in addition to performance repertoire. Much of the repertoire is original teaching music written by Olson, or it is traditional or classical standards arranged by the authors. The book includes a chapter with Jewish and Christian holiday repertoire along with a supplementary chapter with 12 additional classical pieces, such as the Bach *Prelude in C Major* and a Beethoven *German Dance.* There is ensemble music peppered throughout. Students learn to harmonize with chord symbols and Roman numerals and are introduced to alternate scales (such as the blues scale), compound meters, and dominant seventh chords by the end of the course.

The book is packed with useful exercises, many using off-staff notation and musical shorthand at first. There is an emphasis on listening, playing by ear, and improvising. The high-quality teacher accompaniments encourage musical performance. The online student resources include ear training, clap back, and theory drills that feature attractive musical accompaniments and drum tracks that reinforce steadiness and pulse. These supplemental activities are a strength of the book. This book contains more than enough music for two semesters of non-major group piano.

*Keyboard Fundamentals*, 6th Edition (2012)
James Lyke, Denise Edwards, Geoffrey Haydon, Ronald Chioldi, & Lee Evans, Stipes Publishing
Contains CD accompaniments.

The sixth edition of this book features six chapters (249 pages) of music and material. The book can be used with non-major classes for one or two semesters. After a few rhythm drills and three limited staff-reading examples, to get students recognizing seconds and thirds, students read primarily from the grand staff. Each chapter contains several concepts, basic theory, then sight reading, technique (often in the form of studies), composing, harmonization (from chord symbols and lead sheets), ensemble, and solo repertoire. There is an appendix of holiday music in the form of duets, lead sheets, and solo arrangements and an appendix listing some principles of composing that relate to each chapter. There are teacher duets throughout; these are also found on the CD. The CD contains 47 tracks. There are accompaniments for the solos and other exercises and performances of the ensemble music contained in the book.

## Pedagogy in Action

1.  Choose one of the texts discussed in this chapter. Use the evaluation form in Appendix D 2 to complete a survey of the book. Then figure out how many units you will cover in a first-semester non-major class. List all of the skills students will learn during the semester. If there are skills you believe are missing from the text, list these and find alternate sources for supplementary material. Make specific notes about sources, page numbers, and so on of the ancillary items so you will have them for future reference.

2.  Assume that you will meet with students for two 50-minute classes each week (for a 15 week semester). Write a detailed lesson plan for the first eight classes. Be sure to include ensemble and group activities as part of each class. If you need supplementary materials, list these on the plan.

3.  Look at the last couple of units of Book 1 and first few units of Book 2 of *Piano 101*. Make a list of skills that must be developed before a student begins Book 2. Now select several examples from the end of Book 1 (or create similar examples of your own using a music notation program) that you will use for a placement test to determine if students are eligible for the second-semester non-major group-piano class.

4.  Imagine that you have just completed a piano placement with a freshman non-music major who would like to enroll in the second-semester group-piano class at your university. During her placement, the student displayed poor coordination and reading, though her ear was fairly strong. She is lacking knowledge of some core concepts and really needs to take the first-semester non-major class. Write a brief script for how you will advise her of your decision.

## References for Chapter 6

Enz, N. J. (2013). Teaching Music to the Non-Major: A Review of the Literature. *Update: Applications of Research in Music Education, 32*(1), 34–42. doi: 10.1177/8755123313502344

Stevens, D. D., & Levi, A. J. (2005). *Introduction to Rubrics: An Assessment Tool to Save Grading Time, Convey Effective Feedback and Promote Student Learning.* Sterling, VA: Stylus Publishing, LLC.

7

# LEISURE ADULTS IN THE INDEPENDENT STUDIO, COMMUNITY SCHOOLS, AND OTHER LOCATIONS

## Objectives

By the end of this chapter, you should understand how the needs, objectives, and curriculum design of group piano for adults will be different than for children's classes. You should have an understanding of andragogy, life-span development, and specific needs of older, third-age learners, and design your adult classes accordingly. You will have an overview of materials that are available for working with groups of adults and be able to assess other materials based on specific criteria.

## Introduction

Teaching adult piano students is one of my true passions in life. In fact, my first paying student was a good friend's mother, a woman in her 40s. Since then, I have taught various groups of adults, from college-aged students in their late teens and early 20s through to retirees in their 80s and 90s. Whenever you have a group of adults with diverse experiences, expectations, and needs in a piano class, the dynamic and the environment is sure to be stimulating for both teacher and students.

In this chapter, we will explore various types of adult learners who fall into the category of leisure piano students. These are students who are not on the path to becoming professional musicians but people with or without a musical background who share one desire—to learn to play the piano. For some of these individuals, the group setting may not be the ideal way to undertake piano instruction. For others, the group-piano class can be an inspirational, motivational, enjoyable, and engaging way to develop musical and piano skills. Common locations for such adult leisure classes in which multiple keyboards or pianos are used include the large independent studio, community music schools, university piano labs (these classes are run through the campus extension and continuing education programs), or even music stores.

## Grouping Adults

When I was in graduate school, some pedagogy teachers (and textbooks) lumped all adult piano students into a single category, regardless of age or stage of life. This always struck me as odd, since a student in her late 20s, who might be focused on beginning her career or settling into family life, might have very different needs and time for piano study than a retiree in his 70s. I am a firm believer that when grouping adults into classes, we need to be aware of their life-span development stage (Levinson, 1978). Life-span development theories take into account the stage of life in which adults find themselves. As teachers, we are encouraged to remember that adults' life stages may impact their priorities, their ability to focus on piano, and their goals for music study. We must remain flexible, too, as goals are likely to change and evolve over time.

Additionally, there are important differences between the way that children and adults learn. In fact, there is an entire field devoted to adult learning called andragogy. Before discussing materials that can be used effectively with adult piano groups, let's briefly review core principles from andragogy and life-span development. Then we'll look at changes in human cognitive processing and physical functioning that accompany typical aging, as these may have an impact on student performance at the piano.

### *Andragogy*

We are familiar with the term "pedagogy." It stems from Greek roots that mean child (*paid* or *ped*) and leader (*agogus*), or literally the leader of children. While pedagogy has become synonymous with the art and science of teaching people of all ages, scholars in Europe have been using the term "andragogy" to differentiate between learning among children and adults since the early 20th century. It was first introduced in the United States by Malcolm Knowles (1913–1997) in a 1968 article, where he spelled it incorrectly! Knowles described andragogy as a theory of learning. His seminal book on the topic was first called *The Adult Learner: A Neglected Species*. It has since appeared in numerous editions, with various subtitles. Since his death in 1997, several editions have been printed with coauthors, and there has been some debate about whether or not andragogy is actually a theory of learning. Regardless, Knowles and other influential teachers of adults in general education and workforce development provide teachers with information that is useful for anyone who works regularly with adults.

Knowles, Houlton, and Swanson (2015) pointed to several key differences in the assumptions about children and adults as learners (see Figure 7.1). While some of the assumptions about children as learners have changed (for example, educators recommend more active, discovery learning experiences for children now), comparing the traditional pedagogical and andragogical models is helpful for teachers who work with both groups. In addition to the differences in the six assumptions about the learner, instructors of adults in groups should consider individual and situational diversity, as well as differences in goals and purposes for learning.

| Pedagogy | Assumptions About Learners | Andragogy |
|---|---|---|
| *Traditionally Teacher Centered* | | *Traditionally Learner Centered* |
| Learn what teacher presents; need not apply to life | **Need to Know** | Understand "why, what, how" information is related to own life before learning |
| Dependent on teacher | **Self-Concept** | Autonomous; self-directing |
| Past experiences hold little value; passive learning strategies employed | **Prior Experience** | Resources and mental models from prior experiences are valued; active learning |
| Learn to pass a class or satisfy an adult | **Readiness to Learn** | Learn to cope with life-related issues or when changing between developmental stages |
| Subject oriented; not contextual | **Orientation to Learning** | Problem centered; contextual |
| Extrinsic motivators | **Motivation to Learn** | Intrinsic motivators; personal satisfaction or payoff |

*Figure 7.1* Pedagogical versus Andragogical Models of Assumptions About Learners
Adapted from Knowles, Houlton, and Swanson (2015).

Some piano teachers find that there is more variability between adult students than between children, making it difficult to predict the learning trajectory. Many of the differences you will notice when teaching piano to leisure adults are related to one or several factors, including:

• A broader range of ages
• A lifetime of varied learning and/or musical experiences that each student brings to class
• Life-span development differences
• Cognitive declines associated with normal aging
• Physical differences and changes at different ages

As you might imagine, dealing with this variability among adults can be challenging, even in a private lesson (Magrath & Pike, 2002). It becomes more important to plan for it and adapt to students' needs in the group-piano class. Some of the factors listed may be viewed as negative; however, they need not be. Compensation can be made for losses, and positive attributes of adults include the fact that their desire to take piano lessons can increase their motivation to learn and practice. Remember, children usually take lessons because their parents want them to. Adults register, pay for, and make classes a priority because they have a desire to play the piano.

Adults are often self-directed and results oriented, which can improve learning outcomes in the group-piano setting. Regardless, Knowles reminded us that when working with adult students, the teacher is a facilitator. As such, we need to prepare learners

for the process of upcoming learning, establish learning environments that are conducive to effective learning, create mechanisms for mutual planning of goals, diagnose
learning needs of students, formulate objectives for the program of study and curriculum, conduct the weekly learning experience using suitable techniques and materials,
and evaluate learning outcomes and rediagnose needs and objectives. I see the process
as a cyclic and ongoing partnership with the adult students (see Figure 7.2).

You may notice, also, that adults in your group-piano classes favor one of three
learning orientations: goal oriented, activity oriented, or learning oriented (see Figure 7.3). As the instructor, you will want to address the needs of each type of learning

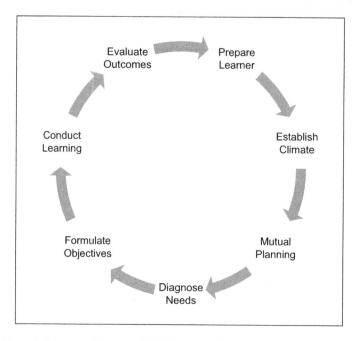

*Figure 7.2* Cyclic and Ongoing Process of Facilitating Adult Learning
Adapted from Knowles et al.

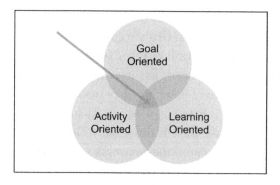

*Figure 7.3* Common Orientations of Adult Students in Group Piano. Arrow points to zone of
optimal learning for all adults in the group.
Adapted from Houle (1984) and Tough (1982).

94

orientation from introduction through learning and performance with each instructional activity within the class. There will likely be overlap between the types of learning, but the most effective teachers of adults find ways to meaningfully address all three types of learners, thus meeting them in the middle of the Venn diagram through activities, explanations, and repertoire.

Goal-oriented students may want to learn a specific piece of music. Activity-oriented students may enjoy working on specific activities, such as ensemble repertoire. Learning-oriented students enjoy the process of learning and may be less focused on the actual performance or outcome. It is possible to meet all learners where they are and include learning that optimally addresses all members of the group. For example, if you have several beginning students who want to learn the slow movement *Moonlight Sonata*, you could create technical exercises and situate learning around the skills necessary to perform the work (learning oriented), create an arrangement of the sonata for keyboard ensemble and rehearse it regularly (activity oriented), and perform the ensemble for family and friends at an informal performance (goal oriented).

### Life-Span Development

In 1978, Daniel Levinson (1920–1994) proposed the life-span development theory for adults. In Chapter 2, we explored Erikson's stages of learning with respect to children. Levinson fleshed out Erickson's three general stages of adulthood (young adult, middle age, and old age) by highlighting 10 stages through which most adults progress (see Figure 7.4). Levinson's work was popularized by Gail Sheehy in her book *New Passages: Mapping Your Life Across Time* (1995), and life-span development among professional musicians was studied extensively by Maria Manturzewska.

We should recognize that early in the 21st century, as we consider the life-span development theory of adults, the ages at which these stages of development occur

| Developmental Period | Age | Task |
|---|---|---|
| Early Adult Transition | 17–22 | Explore Possibilities |
| Adulthood | 22–29 | 1st Major Life Construct |
| Age 30 Transition | 29–33 | Reassess Life Construct |
| Settling Down | 33–40 | 2nd Life Construct |
| Midlife Transition | 40–45 | What Have I Done? |
| Mid-Adulthood | 45–50 | Create New Construct |
| Age 50 Transition | 50–55 | Minor Adjustments |
| Culmination Mid-Adulthood | 55–60 | 2nd Mid-Life Construct |
| Late-Life Transition | 60–65 | Prep for Retirement |
| Late Adulthood | 65+ | Create Late-Life Construct; Deal with Declines |

*Figure 7.4* Synopsis of Levinson's (1978) Lifespan Development Stages

may be slightly different from those suggested by Levinson. For example, the settling down phase may occur later now, as many Millennials delay marriage and starting families in order to pursue careers and financial stability. Similarly, late adulthood may be delayed due to people living more healthfully and longer and retiring beyond the age of 65.

Today researchers divide late adulthood into the third age (active retirement when adults engage in numerous leisure and personal-development activities) and the fourth age (which is defined by less mobility and physical and cognitive declines). Although Levison's life stages may have evolved since he proposed them in 1978, the theory is still valuable. It provides teachers with a framework that is useful for considering and identifying the priorities of students at different stages across the adult life span. Understanding where adult students are in terms of their life span can help us design classes that meet adults' needs, understand what they wish to learn, and know when they are most ready to learn, how they might learn, and how motivated they are to practice and learn.

## Characteristics of Adult Learners

### Common Characteristics of Adults and Considerations for Teachers

As we have noted, there can be a great deal of variability in adult learners. However, most adults vary from children in your piano classes in that they are likely successful in some other aspect of life (i.e., career or another hobby), they may be very articulate, and they likely have highly developed musical tastes or preferred musical styles. Thus, many expect to be able to execute complex motor skills at the piano immediately. Just because they understand what they need to do from an intellectual standpoint does not mean that they will be able to perform and learn motor skills any more quickly than children. Many adults are surprised when they encounter such difficulties in piano class.

Unlike children, adults tend to be farther removed from the experience of discovering new things daily and of having to make many attempts at new skills before they meet with success. Not only will you need to be patient as the instructor, you may need to remind your adult students that they are not unique in experiencing struggle when learning to play the piano. The benefit of learning to play piano in groups is that the students will experience these frustrating experiences together, and they can share learning and coping skills with each other. As teachers and professional pianists who spent years developing our skills, we cannot easily relate to how difficult learning basic piano skills can be for our students. But we can experience similar difficulties in other areas of our lives.

Personally, I regularly pursue new hobbies that involve complex and unfamiliar motor skills, in part to pursue leisure activities that interest me but also to remember what it is like to be a complete novice at an activity that I appreciate and understand intellectually. As an adult, I have taken figure skating and ballroom dance lessons and have pursued the practice of yoga. These activities remind me what it is like to be a novice in a group learning situation. As I age, they remind me of the limitations of an aging body, and I find that I am a better teacher of adult group-piano classes after I have reflected upon my own recent learning experiences.

## Cognitive Changes Associated with Age

Although there might be variability among adults with respect to their goals, motivation, learning orientation, and life-span stage, as we age, there are certain cognitive changes that affect all of us to some degree, and several of these will impact how we process music. As professional teachers and musicians, we need to be particularly aware of changes in cognitive and perceptual-motor abilities because we may not experience these ourselves. Research has shown that there is a weak correlation between age and peak performance in professional musicians. In other words, as professionals who have automated numerous complex skills over many years, we are not affected by typical cognitive and physical declines associated with playing the piano. Our adult piano students, however, will experience slower processing speed and physical responses with age.

In general, adults experience declines in fluid intelligence (involved with reasoning and memory often measured by IQ tests). However, crystallized intelligence (including knowledge that can be learned, stored, and retrieved, such as learning about music) tends to increase with age. This is sometimes referred to as plasticity, or the ability to create new neuronal pathways and connections in the brain that are associated with new learning. The increase in crystallized intelligence is particularly evident if the adult has attained a high level of formal education, where he or she would have developed strategies to enhance learning and may even be able to use these strategies to compensate for some cognitive losses. Adults will experience slower processing and cognition as they age, though when the slowing occurs is variable. In the group-piano lab, if we slow down our speaking, teach smaller discrete components, and give older adults time to process and work with the new material before moving on, they will process information more successfully.

For older adults, when multiple processing components are involved, the time that it takes to process that information slows even more. When we play the piano, we must process visual cues (interpret a symbolic score and recognize patterns), translate those cues to motor skills, execute these skills at the keyboard, listen to what we are doing, and respond to the aural cues by making adjustments in our playing and technique as we perform based on the aural feedback. When we break down music performance in this way, we recognize how complex playing the piano really is. We are processing visual and aural cues while completing complex motor tasks. The goal is to automate, through practice, several of these components. If certain motor skills and visual cues can be automated and linked to each other, our adult students will experience more learning and performance success. But we must recognize that as we age, it can take longer to process this information and perform the skills associated with these cues.

When older adults have not rehearsed enough or, are out of their routines, experiencing stress, tired, unfocused, or not concentrating, they are likely to experience more cognitive difficulties than younger adults under similar conditions. Because I know this, even informal conversations with students as they enter class can help me to get a sense of which students might experience unexpected difficulties with new material that day. I also try to remind my third-age students that these conditions, which are often beyond our control, simply make learning more challenging as we age. My third-age piano groups even form their own informal support groups (they chat before class, during carpool rides, and after class over coffee). In addition to the camaraderie, they remind each other of why learning is difficult at certain times, and they share strategies that they have discovered to be effective. They also celebrate together when they experience success.

## Physical Changes Associated with Age

As humans age, it is inevitable that we will experience declines in vision, hearing, and both fine and gross motor skills. Starting in our 40s, most adults begin to notice changes in vision, particularly when reading print and music. Some adults find that they need to acquire a separate set of piano glasses that are calibrated for a greater distance than their regular reading glasses. Others find that their computer glasses suffice for reading music at the piano. Regardless, you may need to remind students to discuss their piano hobby with their eye doctors. Even with piano glasses, many older adults find it increasingly difficult to read small-format music scores and notations made in pencil. I try to be aware of the size of the score and font for text or expression markings when choosing books for my middle-aged and third-aged piano groups. While my young students must mark their scores in pencil, I remind my older students that they may make notes using pens and markers.

Hearing may also begin to decline with age. It can be difficult for older adults to hear speech if there is a lot of background noise, say in a restaurant or a noisy piano lab, especially if they wear hearing aids. So if you speak to your students as they are playing or while you are playing, your middle-aged and older adults may have difficulty hearing what you are saying. In general, it is good pedagogical (or andragogical) practice to give important notes and information when no one is playing and when you have the full attention of all students in the group. It can become difficult or painful for older adults to hear high pitches, too. So keep range in mind when choosing music and ensemble repertoire.

Finally, as we age, we lose muscle mass, our strength decreases, and it can take longer to execute untrained fine-motor skills. In other words, amateur pianists simply may not be able to play as fast or with as much arm weight as they might have when they were younger. All of this does not mean that our adult students cannot achieve a high level of performance or learn complex skills. Over time, with appropriate training, they can develop or regain some lost strength and motor skills.

Even with the declines noted, older adults are still intelligent people who have likely developed learning strategies throughout their lives. It may take a little longer to learn new repertoire and, if your groups perform for each other or in informal settings, they may need more preparation and rehearsal time than groups of younger adults, but they can still achieve success at the piano. I find that keeping the focus on what the students can do and being patient as we work through the challenges creates a wonderful atmosphere for learning together during group-piano classes.

## *Other Implications of Age on Piano Study: The Importance of Clarity*

In a large study of adult music students whose average age was 71, the adults who had returned to music study following a 20-year break to pursue professional and family duties reported that their best performances happened either before the age of 30 or between the ages of 60 to 69 (Gembris, 2008). The perception that they were able to perform well into their 60s, once they had time to devote to practice, is important for instructors to remember. Just because our students get older, it does not mean that we should decrease expectations for them if their goal is to play well. We may, however, need to make important adjustments for the sake of clarity when we teach.

We have noted that large-format scores are easier for older adults to read. However, we must be sure not to use materials that were designed for children. It can be demeaning for adults to study from books that appear childish. Many publishers have printed books for adult piano students, and some of these feature less clutter on the page, larger font for the text, and scores that are reasonably sized. Ledger lines can also become more confusing to decipher as we age. For this reason, I look for scores that use octava signs above or below the treble and bass staves rather than ledger lines when choosing music for my adult classes. If I do find a score with excessive ledger lines, I will arrange it and reprint it in Finale for my students so they can paste an easier-to-read version into their scores. I encourage my students to use highlighters, pens, and colored markers to bring prominence to dynamics and other expressive details on the score.

From an aural standpoint, I ensure that everyone is looking at me and that there is no extraneous background noise when I give directions and instructions or introduce new material. I speak slowly, project my voice, and allow a brief silence to provide time for students to process verbal information at their own pace. When I ask questions,

I allow ample time (even if there is silence) for adults to formulate their answers and responses. Many of my adult students like to reinterpret what I have said. This helps them make meaning of new concepts, and it allows me the opportunity to address any misconceptions or incorrect attributions that students may have made. The other students in the group generally benefit and learn during such discussions, too. Using different MIDI sounds when rehearsing ensembles can make it easier for adults to identify their own part (and hopefully their own mistakes)! I also slow down many of the tempi so that we can learn and hear effectively. Some compositions may never reach optimal tempo, but most of my adult students report enjoying the process of learning and of hearing the composition, even at a slower pace.

## Needs of the Leisure Student and the Curriculum

### *Serious Music Study or RMM: Two Paths toward Musical Development*

As we noted, it is important to consider the goals, expectations, and needs of your adult students when designing your curriculum for group piano. While goals and expectations may remain constant for some throughout adulthood, the individual student needs and ways that we can compensate for cognitive and physical losses may change over time.

Music educators in the United Kingdom, Europe, and the United States have been exploring benefits of music participation throughout adulthood. Adults at all ages enjoy educational, musical, and social benefits of studying piano in group settings (Pike, 1999, 2001, 2011). Numerous psychosocial benefits for third- and fourth-age adults resulting from music participation have been identified (Gembris, 2012; Pike, 2015). For those making music in groups (such as piano classes, choirs, or bands), participants report that music contributes to their psychological and emotional well-being (Creech, Hallam, Varvarigou, & McQueen, 2014; Koga & Tims, 2001). Although there is little research to date (the field will likely grow) to corroborate students' perceptions, students believe that actively making music helps to maintain and improve their cognition and mental functioning (Perkins & Williamon, 2014; Pitts, 2012). Some research has shown that intense study of piano among older learners can decrease stress and enhance working memory for a period of time following practice (Bugos, Kochar, & Maxfield, 2016).

Because of the medical benefits of group-music participation identified by Karl Bruhn (1930–2010) and his colleagues in the late 1990s and early 2000s, recreational music making (RMM) has become popular in recent years. The program does not place musical performance at the center of the learning experience; rather, it seeks to engage adults in music participation in a group setting. Many of the purported benefits are social because there is less emphasis on developing specific technique and the curriculum is meant to be flexible (Chung & Dillon, 2008). Even though the curriculum is adaptable, there are specific materials on the mass market that were designed specifically for use in RMM piano classes. The creators recommend having the group vote on which book will be used at the beginning of each 8-week session. This gives adults some control over the music they will be playing. Each year at the MTNA Pedagogy Saturday preconference sessions, there is a specialized track for RMM that serves to introduce and informally train teachers to teach RMM classes. For adults who do not have time to practice or are involved in many hobbies, RMM can be an effective way to engage in music on a weekly basis.

But we should not underestimate the desire of many adult students to learn to play and to develop piano skills. Those who are devoting time to piano lessons and personal practice each week often wish to achieve serious goals. For these students, a longer-running and potentially more comprehensive curriculum may be desired. We should also consider the role of performance with each group of adults we teach. Most adults will insist that performance is not important to them and that they are not learning to play the piano for that purpose. Indeed, that is the case. Yet through extensive interviews and conversations with adult music students across the United States during the past 20 years, I have discovered that there are benefits to working toward certain kinds of performances. For example, I recently met a woman who had taken up a new instrument during retirement. She worked with other students in her community and went into nursing homes and hospitals to perform duets and trios with her peers. She saw sharing her music with those experiencing difficult times as a gift that she could give others. Another woman emphatically told me that performing was not even on her radar. Yet an hour into our conversation, I learned that when her grandson visited, they played duets together. Although this may not be how professional musicians would frame performance, sharing music with others is an authentic way that many adults do engage in playing piano for or with others.

I have also come to believe that if we prepare certain groups of serious adults for performances in safe spaces or where they feel that they are using music to serve others, their technical skill and ability improves in preparation for the performance. Concrete goals and deadlines tend to increase student focus and attention to detail. For 8 years, I worked with a group of third-age adults as part of an engagement program between the university and community. There were several levels and sub-groupings within the larger class, but group performances at retirement communities, nursing homes, retiree luncheons, and community festivals were undertaken every few months. We had a core set of pieces that we performed and, each semester, added one or two new pieces to the repertory. The ensembles were usually for four to six players, but we always doubled up on parts so that no one performer felt exposed during performance. During any given performance, students took turns performing and listening to peers when they were not playing. The group performed on portable keyboards, which they helped move to our off-campus locations. We sometimes added MIDI accompaniments to fill out the sound and provide backup in tricky spots, and I usually conducted, sometimes from one of the keyboards. The performances and classes always took place during the day so that students did not have to drive after dark.

A decade later, I am no longer teaching at that university, but the program has grown, and the students maintain their commitment to each other, to the piano, and to the program. In addition to participating in the piano class, they regularly attend recitals at the university, and they support music students. They have found a way, through the piano, to integrate into the intellectual and artistic university community. Over the years, the students have reported social and emotional benefits, but they also improved intellectually, musically and technically and developed listening skills. They appreciated being able to develop new neuronal connections in the brain as they developed new piano skills and learned about music together in the group-piano class.

As students get older, mobility may become impaired to the point that they have difficulty leaving the house or finding transportation to attend classes. With the prevalence of technology, our increased comfort level with using it, and our ability to communicate effectively over the Internet, some may turn to online music instruction (Pike, 2015). Unfortunately, many students will discontinue lessons altogether. However, if we have successfully taught adults skills that they can use to learn new music and play their favorite repertoire on their own, they may continue playing at home for their own enjoyment, even when they have ceased to take formal piano classes. For this reason, I believe that it is essential to thoughtfully consider the curriculum that is used with each group and choose materials that will enhance their musical experience and activities that will engage students and develop skills that they will need throughout the semester and beyond.

### Considerations when Designing Curriculum and Choosing Materials

Because there is an abundance of high-quality elementary and intermediate classical teaching literature, many teachers do not believe in teaching simplified arrangements or transcriptions of orchestral works. I have found that most adults appreciate working on familiar tunes, even in simplified form. Thus, you will find many adult methods and books contain such arrangements. I even create my own basic ensemble arrangements of famous classical works for my adult students because they enjoy the music so much. The music you choose for class may also depend on the group and its members. For example, if you have a group of younger adults that have little time for daily practice, you may need to work on several shorter compositions throughout the semester so they experience successful completion of musical tasks. On the other hand, some groups of students enjoy the challenge of working on one longer ensemble piece that pushes them to the edge of their abilities, and they are content to meet small weekly objectives, even if it takes all semester to learn the entire composition.

Other groups want to learn a little something each week, but their focus may be more on social engagement through music rather than developing extensive piano skills. These students may be better suited to recreational music making (RMM) programs in which little outside practice is required. As with all adult teaching, we must be cognizant of the needs of the learners in our piano classes, be sure that adults are placed in the appropriate group, and facilitate the overall musical learning experience. Regardless of the type of adult class you teach, remember to meet the learners where they are, acknowledge their past musical and educational experiences, respect their stage in life, be receptive to their desires and needs, help them reframe unrealistic expectations and timelines as needed, maintain flexibility, facilitate learning, accommodate for cognitive and physical declines, and prepare them well for any group performances in which they may engage. Above all, enjoy working with the wonderful people who will make up your adult piano groups!

## Adult Leisure Text and Music Review[1]

*Adult Piano Adventures*, Book 1 and Book 2
Nancy & Randall Faber, Faber Piano Adventures distributed by Hal Leonard
CD accompaniments available; general MIDI accompaniments available for the instructor.

This book is like several listed in this section; it was not created specifically for group-piano classes, but many teachers use it successfully with their groups of adults. This is a comprehensive piano course, or an all-in-one method. Technique, core musical concepts, theory, sight reading, and repertoire are all included in the text, which is divided into 16 units (about 180 pages total). Accompaniments are available on CD, and some adults enjoy practicing with these, but they are also notated so the teacher can play along with students during class. The duets are well written and encourage musical playing.

With many of my adult classes, we do not complete the entire first book in one semester, because we work on additional ensemble music and repertoire, but concepts are clearly presented, and there is adequate reinforcement, especially for the first half of the book. On-staff reading is introduced in unit 2, and the keys of C and G major are reinforced in the first book. F and D major and D and E minor are featured in the second book. Intervallic reading is encouraged, and tonic and dominant chords (and the sus4 chord) are introduced in Book 1, with all primary chords used in Book 2. The first book reinforces basic rhythmic concepts; the second uses sixteenth notes by the end. I like to introduce five-finger patterns for many keys and devise various practice patterns for students to develop finger independence and to explore more of the keyboard than they would if only using this book. I always use a supplemental ensemble book with this text to encourage ensemble music making from the very first class.

*Adult Piano Method,* Book 1 and Book 2 (Hal Leonard Student Library)
Fred Kern, Phillip Keveren, Barbara Kreader, & Mona Rejino, Hal Leonard
Enhanced CDs are included with the book.

Like most books written for adult beginners, this is an all-in-one adult book. Each book is about 100 pages and thus slightly shorter in length than the Faber or Alfred texts reviewed in this chapter. Each book contains five units that may be broken down into smaller sections each week. This method features technique, musical concepts, repertoire, and theory in each unit. Additionally, it contains effective creativity and improvisation exercises that are accessible to most adults. The accompaniments for both the solos and the improvisations are attractive, and the MIDI backing tracks are extremely well done. Adult students tend to appreciate the professional sound of these accompaniments. The Hal Leonard level 1 ensemble book integrates well with this method, as the themes used for the ensembles are explored in the text.

You may find that you need to supplement with additional materials if you are working with a group of adults that practices a lot or if some adults in your group are struggling with consolidation of new skills requiring reinforcement. The improvs, "quick licks," and "ad libs" are a unique and positive feature of this book for leisure adults. The pages are clean and uncluttered. Technique tips, music theory, quick licks, and style clips are clearly labeled in each unit. In general, this method moves quickly for typical adults, but it contains very attractive music. Instructors will need to assess each group of students and sequence, pace, and plan classes carefully to ensure students get the most out of this method. In addition to the ensemble books, there are popular hits, hymn tunes, and Christmas books for adults that correlate with this method.

*Piano Fun for Adult Beginners*
*Piano Fun* (Arrangements in Various Musical Styles Such as Pop, Romantic, etc.)
Brenda Dillon & Hal Leonard
CD included with each book.

This is a text designed specifically for recreational music-making (RMM) classes. The main book is 71 pages, with the correlated books in specific musical styles running between 40 and 60 pages. The supplemental books feature on-staff notation (with both lead lines and simple two-hand realizations). RMM classes typically run for

8-week sessions. In the main text, there are eight modules, with anywhere from three to five familiar tunes forming the core of each module. On-staff notation is introduced in module 4 (about halfway through the book), so the supplemental resources could not be used prior to this time. Many instructors use the supplemental books after the initial semester of instruction. Eighth notes are introduced early (compared with other methods) in module 6, but this is done through familiar tunes such as "Hush, Little Baby" and "Alouette," so students would be using their past musical experiences to feel the rhythm as they play. Then they learn to link the familiar rhythm with a recognizable pattern on the page.

There are short, simple explanations of basic concepts and visuals (such as keyboard hand placement and chord charts) for students to locate hand positions easily. Recall that the RMM approach is not necessarily a comprehensive curriculum; rather, it is meant to engage all students in the music-making experience. So text and multiple verses of songs are provided, and students are encouraged to chant and sing, even if they are not necessarily playing all of the notes with the group during class. The CDs feature high-quality recordings of accompaniments with which students can play along. Unlike most other method accompaniments, each track begins with a four-measure musical introduction rather than a click or drum track. Each song features a slower "practice" track and a faster track that is closer to the ideal tempo. It should be noted that even the faster tracks feature accompaniments that many would not consider to be up to tempo, but these are appropriate for older adults who may not be able to play at quick speeds. Even the performance tracks feature the solo, played on a piano, so students always have reinforcement when they play.

*Play Piano Now!* Book 1 and Book 2 (Alfred's Basic Piano Course)
Willard A. Palmer, Morton Manus, & E. L. Lancaster, Alfred Music Co., Inc.
Digital edition available for download; accompaniment CD included with print book; general MIDI accompaniments available for the instructor.

Although not specifically a group-piano book, the text was designed as an all-in-one method for busy adults of various ages. It expands upon the Alfred's Basic Piano Library method by providing additional examples for reinforcement of concepts, theory pages that can be done quickly and away from the keyboard, and arrangements of familiar classical themes and traditional American folk songs. Technique, sight reading, new concepts, and repertoire are integrated into each of the 11 units (about 150 pages total). The pace, which is slower than the older method, is ideal for many groups of adults. On-staff reading is introduced in unit 3 and by the end of the book, students are playing in 2/4, 3/4, and 4/4 meters that include eighth-note rhythms.

Through explanations and writing exercises, students are encouraged to read intervallically. When the staff is introduced, students spend two units playing in C position before middle C position is introduced. These positions are reinforced through unit 8, when G position is presented. Students learn the tonic and dominant chords in these keys. I usually introduce more pentascales early in the course and encourage some transposition of simple exercises and improvisation using these five-finger patterns in order to expand on the concept, develop finger independence, and provide opportunities for more keyboard exploration. The print and score size is not too small, which makes it easier to read for aging adults. There are brief composer and music facts scattered throughout. These can serve as learning links to additional topics for the group to explore. The solo student arrangements and the accompaniments are attractive.

## I Used to Play Piano: Refresher Course

*I Used to Play Piano: 20s and 30s Hits; 40s and 50s Hits; 60s and 70s Hits; 80s and 90s Hits*
E. L. Lancaster & Victoria McArthur, Alfred Music Co., Inc.
CDs included with each book; general MIDI available for the teacher.

The main text contains about 150 pages of repertoire and simple resources to fill in learning gaps for adults who are returning to the piano after taking time off from lessons. The supplemental books, which feature music from various eras, are ideal for groups of adults that are approximately the same age. For example, you might use the *20s and 30s Hits* with a group of octogenarians and nonagenarians, but the *80s and 90s Hits* would be more appropriate for a group of 40-year-olds. This book features more music than some other texts. The repertoire is at the late elementary/early intermediate level, which makes it suitable for some continuing piano groups too. If the teacher uses the MIDI accompaniments in class, they can be set to the exact tempo that will work for the group, providing extra flexibility for each learning situation.

*Returning to the Piano*: A Refresher Book for Adults
Wendy Stevens & Hal Leonard
2 CDs included with the book.

This 100-page book can be a useful when working with adult leisure groups in which everyone has some piano background but gaps in knowledge and skills exist and the group is not ready for only ensemble or more challenging repertoire. Divided into six units, it features familiar tunes from movies, the hit parade (that the older generation would appreciate), and classical themes. Students need to be able to play elementary-level repertoire with both hands, though technique, theory, reading from lead lines, and repertoire reinforce important concepts and skills. The CDs feature attractive orchestral accompaniments. The slower practice tracks include the piano solo, but the student part is omitted from the performance tracks, challenging students to supply the melody by themselves. Teachers can easily incorporate these accompaniments into the in-class group work, but they will not be able to alter the tempi from those provided.

## Handbooks for Teachers of Adults

*Making Music at the Piano: Learning Strategies for Adult Students*
Barbara English Maris, Oxford University Press

Although this insightful book was written for adult students, I have known many teaching colleagues who have pored over this book and used it to enhance their work with adults and to facilitate communication between teacher and student. Written in two sections, Maris thoughtfully and eloquently explores the topics of understanding learning, clarifying our goals, understanding the piano, moving efficiently at the piano, and playing musically in the first section. The second section deals specifically with productive practice through eight thought-provoking chapters that cover how to prepare for practice, how to listen and evaluate effectively, preparing for performance, and ways to engage in music making even when formal lessons have ceased. There are four appendices with useful resources that adult students can consult when sight reading, preparing a new piece, practicing, and performing. There is a helpful list of annotated resources, too. Throughout the book, there are activities for self-reflection and keyboard skills.

*Recreational Music Making Handbook for Piano Teachers*
Brian Chung & Brenda Dillon, Alfred Music Co., Inc.

This 51-page, nine-chapter book provides a brief overview of the philosophy of RMM, highlights the differences between traditional and RMM lessons, and gives seven principles of group teaching, tips for planning lessons, and suggestions for getting started in RMM teaching. It is easy to read and provides two pages of helpful resources for teachers interested in pursuing RMM. If you are curious about teaching RMM classes, this resource provides background and ideas for how to bring RMM into your portfolio of studio offerings.

## Pedagogy in Action

1.  Imagine that you are teaching a class of leisure adults in your studio or through the college extension courses. You will be teaching in a piano lab equipped with 10 keyboards. You have nine students registered for the class, which meets for one 60-minute class per week and lasts 12 weeks. There are no exams or tests required at the end of the semester. All of the students who have registered are

beginners. You do not know their exact ages but expect that they will range in age between 35 and 55 years of age. Choose the text or books that you will use,[2] justify your choice, create a weekly outline of your curriculum (you do not need precise lesson plans at this time, but include concepts addressed each week, units and pages covered in the book(s), and supplemental materials that you will use). Decide how you will assess, provide feedback, and maintain motivation for students to practice between classes.

2.  You have been hired by a local community music school to teach eight students for a 12-week semester. The class will take place in a keyboard lab once a week, and each class will last for 50 minutes. The students have studied together for two semesters already. They enjoy working on ensemble repertoire. Which books, ensemble repertoire, and materials will you use? Create lesson plans for the first three classes.

3.  You are preparing to teach a third-age piano class for the first time. Your group will meet at a local music store, where you will be renting the keyboard lab for 1 hour each week. You have determined that the class will run 10 weeks and hope to continue the class in future semesters. There are 10 student keyboards in the lab, and you have students between the ages of 65 and 80 registered. They all have some past experience with piano. During your interviews with the students, you determined that they play at about level 2, but many have gaps in knowledge. They all seem interested in working on duet, trio, and ensemble repertoire and mainly want to learn new pieces. Briefly describe your philosophy for this class. Which materials will you use? Write out your 10-week outline for the class.

4.  Choose one of the four-part keyboard ensembles from the Hal Leonard Piano Library, level 3, 4, or 5. Remember that there are Christmas ensemble books, too. Assume that you will devote 15 to 20 minutes of class to introducing and working on the piece with a group of adults. Write out a rehearsal plan for the first rehearsal of this composition. Consider where students might run into trouble, which parts may need to work together, and any other strategies you could use to promote effective music making.

# Notes

1  To complete your own more thorough assessments of these and other books, use the evaluation form found in Appendix D.2.
2  Evaluation forms for group-piano texts are located in Appendix D.2.

# References

Bugos, J., Kochar, S., & Maxfield, N. (2016). Intense Piano Training on Self-Efficacy and Psychological Stress in Aging. *Psychology of Music, 44*(4), 611–624. 10.1177/0305735615577250

Chung, B., & Dillon, B. (2008). Piano Teaching—Traditional or Recreational? What's the Difference? *American Music Teacher, 58*(2), 46–47.

Creech, A., Hallam, S., Varvarigou, M., & McQueen, H. (2014). *Active Ageing with Music: Supporting Wellbeing in the Third and Fourth Ages.* London: Institute of Education Press.

Gembris, H. (2008). "Musical Activities in the Third Age: An Empirical Study with Amateur Musicians." In A. Daubney, E. Longhi, A. Lamont, & D. J. Hargreaves (Eds.). *Musical Development and Learning Conference Proceedings, 2nd European Conference on Developmental Psychology of Music* (pp. 103–108). Hull: GK Publishing.

Gembris, H. (2012). "Music-Making as a Lifelong Development and Resource for Health." In R. MacDonald, G. Kreutz, & L. Mitchell (Eds.). *Music, Health, & Wellbeing* (pp. 367–382). Oxford: Oxford University Press.

Houle, C. O. (1984). *Patterns of Learning: New Perspectives on Life-Span Education.* San Francisco: Jossey-Bass.

Knowles, M. S., Houlton III, E. F., & Swanson, R. A. (2015). *The Adult Learner: The Definitive Classic in Adult Education and Human Resource Development.* New York: Routledge.

Koga, M., & Tims, F. (2001). The Music-Making and Wellness Project. *American Music Teacher, 51*(2), 18–22.

Levinson, D. (1978). *The Seasons of a Man's Life.* New York: Knopf.

Magrath, J., & Pike, P. (2002). Polyphony. *American Music Teacher, 52*(2), 83–86.

Perkins, R., & Williamon, A. (2014). Learning to Make Music in Older Adulthood: A Mixed-Methods Exploration of Impacts on Wellbeing. *Psychology of Music, 42*(4), 550–567. doi: 1 0.1177/0305735613483668

Pike, P. D. (1999). The Adult Leisure Student. *Keyboard Companion, 13*(2), 34–35.

Pike, P. D. (2001). *Leisure Piano Lessons: A Case Study in Lifelong Learning.* Unpublished doctoral dissertation. Norman, OK: University of Oklahoma.

Pike, P. D. (2011). Using Technology to Engage Third-Age (Retired) Leisure Learners: A Case Study of a Third-Age MIDI Piano Ensemble. *International Journal of Music Education, 29*(2), 116–123.

Pike, P. D. (2015). "Dismantling Barriers to Quality Music Instruction for Older Adults in Rural America: A Collective Case Study of Six Adults Taking Online Synchronous Music Lessons." *Paper presented at the Suncoast Music Education Symposium,* Tampa, FL. This paper has been adapted and will be included as a chapter in a forthcoming book entitled *The Handbook of Music Education,* edited by Bugos and Dege.

Pitts, S. (2012). *Chances and Choices: Exploring the Impact of Music Education.* Oxford: Oxford University Press.

Tough, A. (1982). *Intentional Changes: A Fresh Approach to Helping People Change.* Chicago: Follett.

# Section 3

# GROUP-PIANO STUDENTS
## Children

8

# OVERVIEW OF GROUP MUSIC PROGRAMS FOR CHILDREN

## Objectives

By the end of this chapter, you should have an overview of important group music programs for children throughout the world. You will have ideas for ways to apply important concepts from each program to children's group-piano classes that you teach.

## Introduction

In this section of the book, we will explore general group music programs for children. Some of these programs are suitable for young children and preschoolers. Others are often associated with preschoolers but, in fact, can be used with older children (and perhaps even adults). Rather than providing comprehensive information about each program, this chapter is meant to give a general overview of each program. The majority of the programs require specialized teacher training and certification before one can teach them. Many provide educational inspiration for the types of activities that we should be including in our children's group-piano courses. If we choose to incorporate best practices from children's programs discussed in what follows, we must beware of taking a piecemeal approach to highly sequenced curricula. If students do not engage in the entire curriculum, they might not experience the purported benefits. The strategies that we use must integrate into our own group-piano curricula and be scaffolded and reinforced weekly.

While a written description of the programs can give us a flavor of each, if you have the opportunity to observe master teachers in any of these programs, I would encourage you to avail of it. For example, during my doctoral studies, I observed several Kindermusik classes. Before I walked into the teaching environment, I couldn't imagine ever including preschool teaching in my professional teaching portfolio. After just a few observations, I was captivated. Following extensive research about similar childhood music programs, I became a licensed Kindermusik educator. Even when I am not teaching Kindermusik classes, my training influences all of my group-piano work with children, and my teaching is richer because of these experiences. Had I not been open to exploring a type of group teaching that was not on my radar in the 1990s, a rewarding segment of my teaching would be missing today. We will begin by looking at European and Asian music educators (in order of birth) that continue to influence music education and then explore popular contemporary music programs for children that were developed in North America.

## Historic Group Programs for Children—European Influences

### *Dalcroze Eurhythmics*

Emile Jaques-Dalcroze (1865–1950) was a Swiss music educator. Although piano pedagogues most often associate his work with pre-school music teaching, Dalcroze was a professor of harmony and solfège at the Conservatory of Music in Geneva (Conservatoire de musique de Genève) and developed his theories and approach while working with undergraduate music students. Although we are discussing Dalcroze in the chapter on teaching children in groups, I have colleagues who use these strategies with adult group-piano students, and my own experiences as a Dalcroze participant have occurred during adulthood. Throughout this section, I encourage you to be mindful of how you might transfer some of the techniques discussed to age-appropriate activities for adult group-piano students.

Jaques-Dalcroze noticed several issues among the students in his classes that concerned him. Although they could write complex harmonies and rhythms, they were not able to audiate, perform, or sing them with ease. The approach that he developed used eurythmics, solfège, and improvisation. As we will see, other educators have explored solfège and improvisation in their music programs. Dalcroze's legacy has been his rather unique use of eurythmics (Anderson, 2012). Activities employed in eurythmics classes include:

- free follow (in which students begin by simply stepping to the music but eventually adapt their movement to express changes in rhythm, dynamics, and tempo as the teacher plays the piano);
- quick-response activities (in which students quickly respond to the teacher's vocal command or musical variation at the piano by changing rhythm or movement);
- interrupted, semi-interrupted, or continuous canon (in which students move and clap based on the teacher's pattern, in canon);
- ball, balloon, and other exercises or activities (which explore anacrusis, crusis, and metacrusis).

Through eurythmic activities, students are encouraged to explore then refine musical expression, phrasing, and rhythm. This is first done intuitively through bodily expression before they have a chance to become mired in the mental processes

involved with writing and performing complex musical notation. Solfège and improvisation support the movement activities and the development of musical expression. In essence, the body becomes the first musical instrument for children who
learn using this approach. Dalcroze teachers are expected to be able to improvise
music at the piano.

There has been a lot of research, leading to useful suggestions about how Dalcroze
can be incorporated into music instruction (Caldwell, 1993; Mead, 1996). Music
educators have explored how eurythmic activities can be adapted for general music
instruction by creating eurythmic games based on follow, response, and canon activities (Aronoff, 1983). Others have explored similarities between eurythmic instruction and traditional ways of passing down folk music from one generation to the
next. Both eurythmics and traditional teaching often include singing and dancing.
Researchers have investigated how using Dalcroze eurythmics can facilitate learning
of complex rhythms found in multicultural music, such as that of Africa (Phuthego,
2005). Educators have also used eurythmics to increase musical awareness among
tertiary music-education majors. It is noteworthy that music students and teachers
who participate in classes run by experienced Dalcroze teachers report decreased
body tension, improved listening, better understanding, increased musical awareness,
and joyful music experiences (van der Merwe, 2015).

You will have a much better appreciation for the power of Dalcroze eurythmics
if you can observe a session in which you hear lovely piano music and see children moving to it. There are wonderful video clips of children involved in Dalcroze
classes in Geneva, published by the International Federation of Eurythmic Teachers
(FIER), on YouTube. I particularly like video clip number 5 because it shows various activities piano teachers could apply in their classes (https://www.youtube.com/
watch?v=TZwyX-jg12Y). I encourage you to watch this clip and others. Although
many are in French, you will get a sense of the types of activities and how teachers
introduce concepts during Dalcroze classes. The Dalcroze Society of America (www.
dalcrozeusa.org) has useful information for American teachers regarding workshops,
classes, training, and conferences for those who are interested in learning more about
the approach or working toward Dalcroze certification.

### *Applications to Group Piano*

Group-piano teachers can use one of Dalcroze's central ideas by having children
experience and move to music in different meters *before* they see it and learn about
theoretical underpinnings. Free-movement activities can help students learn how
to move through long notes or rests, how to move to various types of articulation,
and how to shape musical phrases, even before they are asked to do these things at
the piano. If we can help students internalize the pulse in simple and compound
meters, feel the beat, and clap various rhythmic patterns, their musical reading and

expression will have a strong foundation based on each student's personal experience. When students move to music in a group, they learn from one another, and they can collaborate in certain rhythmic canon games and activities.

## The Kodàly Method

Zoltàn Kodàly (1882–1967) was a Hungarian music educator whose work is familiar to many Western-educated musicians. Kodàly, along with pianist Béla Bartók, are remembered as conservators of folk music of their country, as they travelled the Hungarian countryside collecting and recording folk melodies on wax cylinders. However, Kodàly's most lasting contribution was to the music education system of Hungary.

He believed that all children should develop musical literacy as an integral part of their formal education. Using folk music, solfège (with movable *do*, so that intervallic relationships with reference to the tonic would be learned), Curwen hand signs, and Chevé syllables for rhythms (i.e., ti-ti for two eighth notes), Kodàly developed a systematic music curriculum for the Hungarian nation. In his system, children began learning music at the age of 3, primarily through singing folk melodies, and eventually learned other instruments. You will find that Kodàly educators use tuning forks and pitch pipes in the classroom (to give pitches for singing) rather than relying on a piano. The world learned of Kodàly's system, which was demonstrably successful in his homeland, at International Society for Music Education (ISME) conferences in the late 1950s and 1960s. As a result of Kodàly's success in Hungary and his presentations at prestigious music educator conferences, classroom music teachers adopted his approach throughout Asia, Australia, and much of the Western world, using folk melodies of their own cultures to develop musical literacy in children.

Many countries have Kodàly organizations, and teachers can work toward certification. The Organization of American Kodàly Educators (OAKE) states that its mission is "to support music education of the highest quality, promote universal music literacy and lifelong music making, and preserve the musical heritage of the people of the United States of America through education, artistic performance, advocacy and research" (www.oake.org).

## Applications to Group Piano

While Kodàly discouraged the use of the piano in teaching because he wanted children to use their natural instrument first, we can implement several of his strategies. Group-piano teachers should encourage children to sing before they play and as they are learning melodies and rhythms. When playing music on the piano, they can sing along with the words provided in the method book, or they can create their own lyrics. Singing promotes musical phrasing and expressiveness. If the children have learned the Kodàly approach to counting rhythm at school, using the same or similar syllabic approach in the group-piano class can reinforce what they have learned elsewhere. Just as Kodàly's method enabled children to experience the rhythm first through hearing, then clapping, recognizing, and writing the notation, we can engage students in similar activities in the group-piano setting (away from the keyboard at first). Aural skills activities could include singing solfège and using hand signs to reinforce intervals. Our goal should be to have students recognize patterns in the music (rhythmic, melodic, and even form). Incorporating some of Kodàly's methods can provide opportunities for deeper, more meaningful understanding and learning.

## Orff-Schulwerk

Carl Orff (1895–1982) was a German educator who was influenced by Dalcroze and other music educators in Europe at the time. He believed that free movement of the full body and dancing to music could help reinforce rhythmic and melodic concepts. Like Kodàly, Orff discouraged use of the piano during instruction of young children but employed mallet instruments for children to explore melody, harmony, and creativity. His approach, in collaboration with others, became known as the Orff-Schulwerk method and employs moving, dancing, singing, and playing percussion and Orff instruments. Performance and participation are central to becoming musically literate. Improvisation and composition are encouraged, and the method is popular among many music educators in public schools. Videos of children using the Orff approach are available on the American Orff-Schulwerk Association web site (www.aosa.org).

## Applications to Group Piano

Like the Orff-Schulwerk method, we recognize that learning to play the piano is about more than simply mastering terms and displaying declarative knowledge about music. Being a musically literate pianist involves being able to play the instrument with the correct technique. Learning about musical concepts through movement activities and singing before applying those at the keyboard is essential for children. Providing opportunities for children to improvise and work together to create music is a valuable educational activity. Likewise, there may be opportunities within the piano class to avail of Orff instruments with which children would use larger motor skills and arm movements to explore concepts, before applying those ideas at the piano. The more ways a child can experience new concepts and elaborate, generate, and create using those concepts, the more meaningful the learning will be. We must remember not to have children sitting at keyboards for the entire class but to permit a structured environment in which they can explore, improvise, and synthesize.

# Asian Influences

## *The Suzuki Method*

Shin'ichi Suzuki (1898–1996) designed his program to teach violin to very young children and their families using what he called the "mother-tongue approach." Although his formal training took place in Germany, Suzuki developed his method after working with a young violin student upon returning to Japan. He recognized that children learn language not by first learning to read specific letters and words but by listening to the spoken language, by copying what their families say, and by being corrected by caring adults. Once they have an aural model and can speak with some fluency, they learn to read and write that language. Thus, in the Suzuki method, initially music is taught to children by rote. They listen to high-quality recordings of the piece throughout the week, and parents facilitate and encourage repetition at home. In essence, Suzuki was training the parent alongside the child. Today, core principles of the program include parental involvement, encouragement, starting early, listening, repetition, learning with other children, playing carefully graded repertoire, and delaying reading until muscle coordination and technique have reached a certain level of development.

At first, Suzuki designed the program for individual instruction, but today group programs are typical. Surely you have seen video of dozens of young violinists lined up performing the *Twinkle Variations* together. Suzuki education began with stringed instruments. Today there are about a dozen instruments taught using the Suzuki method. In the Americas, 40.1% of Suzuki member teachers are violinists, while 15.1% are piano teachers. The Suzuki Association of the Americas (www. suzukiassociation.org) is an excellent source of information. To become a certified teacher, several courses and levels must be passed and an audition is required. Suzuki's most famous book on his approach is entitled *Nurtured by Love* (Suzuki, 2012). A valuable resource for those wanting to learn more about Suzuki piano is *Studying Suzuki Piano: More Than Music* (Bigler & Lloyd-Watts, 1998).

## *Applications to Group Piano*

As we have noted, we want to be cautious about applying just part of a well-rounded and carefully sequenced program in our group-piano classes. While the Suzuki method books are available (these contain only the music), the music is likely to be too difficult for most of your beginning piano classes. More important lessons from the Suzuki program include using the mother-tongue approach, using repetition, having students listen, enlisting parental support, and maintaining student motivation throughout the learning process. Many piano teachers choose to introduce reading and notation early in a child's musical development. Even if students learn to interpret music notation early, the group-piano environment provides ample opportunity to hear and experience music, to learn some examples by rote, to repeat and refine sections of music or exercises until technique and tone production are secure, and to include meaningful listening activities. If parents can be recruited to support students at home by providing a quiet practice environment, supporting daily practice, and encouraging musical development, student progress and motivation are likely to increase. Then each student's individual success will contribute to an engaging group environment.

## Yamaha Music Education Program

Unlike the aforementioned programs or methods, which were developed by a single musician (albeit several benefitted from state-sponsored support for teacher training and curriculum development), the Yamaha Music Education Program was designed by a group of unnamed music educators. The chair of the Nippon-Gakki Company, Ltd. (now the Yamaha Corporation) recognized that customers needed to learn how to play their instruments. He also believed that music education in Japan should be developed, promoted, and driven by local teachers (not European piano pedagogues). In the mid-1950s, he gathered top music educators from across the country to devise a suitable music curriculum, and by the mid-1960s, he had created the Yamaha Music Foundation to continue the work of research and music education. Today, the Yamaha Music Education program, which includes classical and popular music, is taught in more than 40 countries and is designed to cultivate lifelong music involvement.

Trained Yamaha Music Education System (YMES) teachers work in approved Yamaha Schools, which house Yamaha piano labs. The YMES certification program requires completion of a candidate exam, several seminars, and practice teaching. The exam is extensive and includes keyboard performance, keyboard harmony, improvisation, sight singing and accompaniment, transposition, aural skills, and music theory. The student courses include Music Wonderland (for 3-year-olds), Music Junior Course (4- to 5-year-olds), Young Musicians Course (6- to 8-year-olds), Junior Extension Course (6- to 7-year-olds), Junior Special Advanced (6- to 7-year-olds), and Junior Advanced Course (8- to 9-year-olds). Courses include listening, singing, moving, creating, and keyboard activities and contribute to social development and cultivation of the imagination. As students advance, they develop more specialized performance skills. The majority of the courses last for 2 to 4 years, and some include optional or required private lessons in addition to the weekly group class. Parental involvement is required for the courses for children under the age of 6. More information about the entire curriculum and about teacher training for the Yamaha Music Education Program can be found on the Yamaha web site. Be sure to consult the web site of your home country. In the United States, information about the courses is found at http://usa.yamaha.com/music_education/yms/courses/.

Yamaha also offers a Yamaha Graded Examination System, which is open to all teachers, students, and music professionals, not just YMES teachers and students.

### *Application to Group Piano*

The Yamaha Education Program is comprehensive and based on solid educational principles. But because the materials are proprietary, it is difficult for the non-YMES teacher to avail of best practices from the program. Based on what we know about the philosophy of the program and the skills required of certified teachers, it is safe to say that if we include singing, movement, and keyboard activities that foster music exploration and creativity, along with parental involvement when children are young, we will be providing children with ways in which to engage with music for years to come. As children get older and develop piano technique, we must remember to scaffold skills and introduce new learning sequentially so they can continue to develop music literacy and performance proficiency. The program reminds us that the music does not necessarily need to be classical in order to foster a lifelong love of music. So we might create group-piano curricula and RMM programs for children that are less classically oriented or include nonclassical and non-Western music in our existing curricula.

## North American Influences

In addition to the programs explored in what follows, Harmony Road and Music Together are programs available for children up to the age of 4 and their parents. As with the other programs outlined, unless teachers are certified, they will not have access to materials or be able to teach through the program. All of these programs feature developmentally appropriate curricula and provide students with opportunities to explore musical instruments and sing and move to music, and often require significant parental involvement. These basic philosophies should be explored if one is considering teaching young beginners and preschoolers in a group-piano setting.

### *Kindermusik International*

Inspired by German music-education programs, Dan Pratt, the American founder of Kindermusik, designed an early-childhood music and movement curriculum that launched in 1978. The curriculum is influenced by music educators we have explored (Orff, Kodàly, and Suzuki) and developmental psychologists and educators who espoused discovery learning (Montessori), scaffolding (Vygotsky), and accommodating for children's developmental and cognitive stages (Piaget). In 2005, Kindermusik began a Kindermusik@school program, in which teachers bring special curricula to students enrolled in daycare and early childhood development programs. The majority of Kindermusik's programs, however, take place with the parents present for all or part of the class time. The philosophy of the program recognizes that a parent or caregiver is a child's most important teacher, and the love of music can be nurtured in the home if parents know which activities to play and which songs to sing.

Kindermusik offers developmentally appropriate curricula from birth through age 7. Curricula are designed based on educational research and undergo extensive piloting with actual children before they are brought to the market. In recent years, curricula have been developed for children who are learning English as a second language and for children with special needs. During classes, children explore music through movement and singing and by playing age-appropriate instruments. There are musical accompaniments parents and teachers can access digitally, and stories and themes run through each individual curriculum. In the beginning, parents are present for the entire class (with infants, the parents may take turns swinging baby in a hammock while singing, and with toddlers, they sit in the singing circle with their child on their lap). As children get older and gain more independence, they work in groups with the teacher for a block of time, say 30 minutes; then the parents enter the room and join their children for a recap of the activities for the final 15 minutes of class. Class meetings get longer as the children age.

Teachers purchase packets for each curriculum that contain all materials for each course, including detailed lesson plans. Teachers are encouraged to adhere to lesson plans, which have been carefully constructed. They work well, so there is no need to deviate from prescribed activities. Once families have registered for the class, teachers purchase student kits containing codes for digital materials, simple instruments, songbooks, and other pertinent materials and distribute these to the families. Private or studio Kindermusik educators who are not involved in the Kindermusik@ school program typically teach in community schools, churches, or commercial studio spaces where there is room for movement activities, waiting rooms for families, easy access, and ample parking. More information about Kindermusik International can be found at www.kindermusik.com.

## Musikgarten

Musikgarten has music programs for babies and children through age 7 but also offers curricula in group piano, adult group piano, sacred music classes, and piano partner lessons. Training can be done in person, through workshops, and through individual webinars, making it accessible for teachers who live in remote locations or far from scheduled workshops. The stated mission of Musikgarten is to encourage children to develop a love for music and the ability to express it. Classes typically include singing, listening, movement activities, and use of various instruments. Parents receive CDs of the songs from class so they can be sung throughout the week, and guidebooks help foster the child's love of music and learning at home. The curriculum has been adapted for use in about 10 countries across the globe. The original curriculum was designed by a music educator, Dr. Lorna Lutz Heyge, and Audrey Sillick, an early childhood specialist and Montessori teacher trainer.

The philosophy is similar to Kindermusik in that they believe that music is beneficial for children, it is accessible to all children, and families should be involved in fostering the love of music. They use a carefully sequenced curriculum, with quality musical instruments, and include movement and singing from the start. However, teachers are given more flexibility than Kindermusik educators with respect to deviating from individual lesson plans. Many of the programs offered for older children are specific to the piano. But if a child wished to pursue another musical instrument, the foundation of music instruction in the early-childhood programs would be beneficial. More information can be found on the Musikgarten web site, www. musikgarten.org.

### Music for Young Children

Music for Young Children (MYC) is a program for children from ages 2 to 10 that was developed in the early 1980s by early-childhood specialists in Canada. There is currently a program for teens and adults as well. Students are taught in a group setting, and the piano is used as a vehicle for music making. MYC is taught on three continents, and there are almost 1,000 trained educators worldwide. Activities and experiences include singing, listening, rhythm ensembles, keyboard/piano activities, composition, and homework.

Although the "Sunrise" and "Sunshine" programs for preschoolers feature singing and movement activities, students are systematically prepared to use the piano as their primary instrument for musical expression in the Music for Young Children program. A feature of MYC is that it uses a "D-centered" approach to get students comfortable with the keyboard topography. By the time students complete the "Moonbeams 3" program (around the age of 9), they are ready to complete a grade 1 piano exam (in the Associated Board, Royal Conservatory of Music, or other equivalent examination system). More information about Music for Young Children is available on their web site, www.myc.com.

## Pedagogy in Action

1.  Choose one of the programs discussed in this chapter and learn more about it. Undertake detailed research about the program, including its methods, music, and overall philosophy. Where possible, read primary sources written by the program's founder(s) or scholarly sources written by music education specialists. Find journal articles that explore pedagogical implications and best practices associated with the program. Write a summary paper about what you have learned,

then identify three specific techniques, strategies, or materials from the program that you could include in one or more of your children's group-piano classes. If you are still interested in the program, look into the process for teacher certification or educational training and devise a timeline for how and when you would pursue this professional development opportunity. Be sure to consider expenses, including training and/or certification fees, annual certification renewal, and travel for training.

2. If possible, find a certified educator for one of the programs discussed in this chapter. Make arrangements to observe a class or two and conduct a brief interview with the teacher about the perceived strengths, weaknesses, and opportunities the program provides for students. Be sure to ask about the training and certification process, too. Write a synopsis of your findings.

# References

Anderson, W. T. (2012). The Dalcroze Approach to Music Education: Theory and Applications. *General Music Today*, *26*(1), 27–33. doi: 10.1177/1048371311428979

Aronoff, F. W. (1983). Dalcroze Strategies for Music Learning in the Classroom. *International Journal of Music Education*, *2*(1), 23–25.

Bigler, C., & Lloyd-Watts, V. (1998). *Studying Suzuki Piano: More Than Music: A Handbook for Parents, Teachers, and Students*. Van Nuys, CA: Summy-Birchard Inc. (2016 Kindle edition is available).

Caldwell, T. (1993). A Dalcroze Perspective on Skills for Learning. *Music Educators Journal*, *79*(7), 27–29. doi: 10.2307/3398612

Mead, V. H. (1996). More Than Mere Movement: Dalcroze Eurythmics. *Music Educators Journal*, *82*(4), 38–41. doi: 10.2307/3398915

Merwe, L. van der (2015). The First Experiences of Music Students with Dalcroze-inspired Activities: A Phenomenological Study. *Psychology of Music*, *43*(3), 390–406. doi: 10.1177/0305735613513485

Phuthego, M. (2005). Teaching and Learning African Music and Jaques-Dalcroze's Eurhythmics. *International Journal of Music Education*, *23*(3), 239–248. doi: 10.1177/0255761405058240

Suzuki, S. (2012). *Nurtured by Love: Revised Edition*. Translated from the original Japanese text by K. Selden with L. Selden. Van Nuys, CA: Alfred Music Publishing Company, Inc./Summy-Birchard.

# 9

# GROUP PIANO FOR CHILDREN IN THE INDEPENDENT STUDIO AND K–12 SCHOOLS

## Objectives

By the end of this chapter, you will have an overview of three typical settings in which children's group piano may take place, curricular considerations, materials that can be used, and strategies for evaluating books or materials that you wish to employ in children's group-piano settings.

## Overview of Group Piano for Children

As we have discussed in previous chapters, teaching children piano in groups is an ideal way for them to explore concepts together, learn from one another, motivate each other, learn to perform for others, and make music collectively in piano ensembles. Many teachers find that working with beginning children in a group setting is more conducive to spiraling the curriculum and scaffolding concepts than the typical private lesson. That is not to say that in a private lesson we cannot scaffold a concept such as rhythm, first by moving to it off the bench while the teacher plays, then clapping it together, notating it on the staff, identifying it on a score, and finally playing it in a new piece. But because students in group classes expect to engage in off-bench activities and to work together, it can be easier to integrate such scaffolded activities into the lesson plan. Although off-bench activities are integrated into the curriculum, group classes should have students playing the piano at the core of each class. Because there is a lot of material in this chapter, after you have read the initial philosophy, types, curricular considerations, and method sections, you may wish to distribute your reading and detailed exploration of the average-age methods and resources over several weeks. This can be done as you read other, shorter chapters in this text.

In this chapter, we will look at examples of activities that encourage exploration, discovery, comprehension, and demonstration of concepts. First, we will investigate materials that can be used in children's group-piano classes and learn how to evaluate them for potential effectiveness with a group of students. We will also look at locations for children's classes. Three typical venues where children might take group-piano classes include:

1. An independent studio that is equipped with multiple keyboards
2. A group-piano lab in a community music school or university
3. A group-piano lab in a K–12 public or private school

Depending on the setting for the group-piano class, there may be special curricular considerations. We will explore those as we look at methods and materials for students. Finally, while there are fewer group-piano classes offered for advancing students, some teachers do offer group-piano instruction at intermediate and more advanced levels. These classes can provide successful learning and performing opportunities for advancing pianists.

## Philosophy and Theory of Teaching Children in Groups

Frances Clark correctly noted that teaching students in groups is a natural way to teach any subject (Goss, 1992, p. 183). Indeed, children are accustomed to learning in groups, both in school and in extracurricular activities, such as dancing, martial arts, and soccer. Even general music classes, choir, band, or orchestra rehearsals are conducted with groups of students. Although teaching children piano through individual lessons is ubiquitous throughout the world, many piano pedagogues believe that group piano is an efficient, effective, motivating, and exciting way to learn piano. Provided that all students have similar levels of ability and lesson readiness, and if the teacher is equipped with basic group teaching skills, strategies, and carefully planned lessons, children learning to play piano in groups can develop a lifelong love of music and outstanding piano skills. I have come to believe that, taught well, group piano can be the best way for all music students to begin learning and to make beautiful music. I have also seen many students thrive musically with group instruction for many years.

However, group-piano teachers need to be aware that the group setting may not be the best learning environment for every student. This is why screening interviews are advisable. Some students may progress at a different pace than the others in the class and may need to be moved into a more appropriate group. Students need to understand the ground rules for the group, be willing and able to participate with classmates, and know that disruptive behavior will not be tolerated. In turn, teachers must make parents and students aware of the ground rules, manage the class, and create an environment in which each child has an opportunity to participate, share, and learn. Teachers should devote time to analyzing and improving their group-teaching techniques and prepare thoroughly for each class. The sequencing and pacing of activities is also very important when working with children in groups. We will explore these topics in Chapter 12, but if you can provide opportunities for students to experience a concept broadly, in various contexts, and then specifically in their repertoire (with just the right amount of time devoted to each activity), students will likely remain engaged, transfer learning, remain motivated, develop as musicians, and stay on task during class.

### Typical Types of Group Piano for Children and Curricular Considerations

As we saw in Chapter 1, there are many types of groups for children. However, for children who learn piano only in a group setting, they are most likely to take lessons in an independent studio, through a community school or university, or in a K–12 institution. Features of these three types of group-piano settings follow.

1.  An independent studio that is equipped with multiple keyboards

Independent teachers who teach children only in groups tend to have space in their studio for a small electronic keyboard lab (sometimes with as few as four keyboards), or they have a hybrid studio equipped with several keyboards (which may or may not be connected by a controller system) and an acoustic piano or two. I have seen teachers with both of these studio setups in their homes, in a dedicated room for teaching, and in studios that are located in commercial spaces within their communities. Either setup can be effective, but the teacher should consider the types of group activities in which students will engage, both at the keyboards and off bench, to ensure that there is ample space for movement and keyboards are situated for optimal group work.

Generally, studio teachers cover the same basic concepts that they would in traditional private piano lessons, but there is added focus on group activities, on having students perform, listen, evaluate, and assess together, and on ensemble repertoire. Some teachers of beginning group piano have students perform only ensemble repertoire at end-of-semester recitals. Others have children enter solo festivals and perform solo repertoire at the end of each semester. I would suggest that all students in a group should be learning and performing solo repertoire for each other during class. If these students will be performing solos at recitals and competitions, the teacher may need to devote more time during each class to perfecting and performing repertoire. It may be tempting to work on solo repertoire with students individually over headphones or individually at an acoustic piano while the other students are busy with another activity. Indeed, there can be some individual work. However, I have witnessed outstanding group teachers work on different solos with each student while the others listen and contribute to the evaluation and performance improvements. Students who participate in evaluative activities tend to transfer these skills to their individual practice at home, which makes them much more independent and autonomous learners than many of their private-lesson peers.

Independent teachers who instruct piano in groups should carefully consider the concepts and skills that they want students to be able to demonstrate by the end of each semester and design the curriculum and individual lesson plans accordingly. Once a teacher knows which concepts need to be covered, she should review and evaluate potential methods and materials to see which will enable her to meet her educational goals for the semester. Most teachers find that they need to supplement with additional materials, either for repertoire, theory, or other musical skills. Thus, the best group teachers I have observed tend to use materials from two methods that complement each other. Finally, games and other supplementary resources will need to be gathered for each class.

2. A group-piano lab in a community music school or university

Group classes in community schools or universities tend to take place in digital piano labs. However, I have taught group piano in a community school, where we used several acoustic and electronic pianos. Regardless, the goals and curricular considerations in these settings are usually similar to those of the independent studio teacher. The exception is that often, children's groups in a university are demonstration classes, where pedagogy students are completing internships and learning how to teach group piano. Usually, these classes are led by experienced piano pedagogues. The pedagogy students observe and assist in the teaching and gradually prepare short instructional segments and practice teaching. The interns receive weekly feedback on their teaching and make adjustments throughout the semester. This setting is an ideal way for teachers to experience and learn how to teach group piano. Occasionally, there are time constraints, and these demo classes may only take place for a few weeks rather than the entire semester. If that is the case, the goals and objectives for student learning will be adjusted to fit within the timeframe of the class. If you are a novice teacher or an experienced teacher who is considering becoming a group-piano teacher, you might inquire as to whether participating in such an internship at your local university is a possibility.

3. A group-piano lab in a K–12 public or private school

As we learned in our introduction to group piano, piano classes were first introduced in the public schools in the United States during the second decade of the 20th century. While some independent teachers and community music schools continued to develop the pedagogy of teaching piano in groups throughout the mid to latter half of the 20th century, group piano declined in the public schools during that time. However, piano class offerings in K–12 schools have experienced a resurgence and have become increasingly popular among students in recent years. Because keyboard labs are technology driven, principals can often locate funds to install them. Where money is not available, local business partners and music dealers are often willing to assist with setting up keyboard labs in public schools. I have seen such partnerships between local stakeholders who support music education for impoverished school districts flourish in my own community. Beginning piano classes can be offered starting in the elementary grades through high school. The age and developmental and intellectual abilities of the children need to be considered as teachers choose books and materials to use in such classes. There are additional curricular considerations of which teachers in K–12 schools should be aware.

Most countries have music or arts-educator organizations that outline core learning concepts and outcomes that must be met. In the United States, for example, music educators have a set of guidelines from the National Association for Music Education (NAfME). Detailed criteria for each grade level, and specifically for the piano, can be found at NAfME's web site www.nafme.org. Core musical competencies, often called standards, that students must display include creating, performing, and responding. NAfME published a list of standards for keyboard and harmonizing instruments that sets forth 11 anchors around which students must display competency. Thus, teachers need to choose materials and design curricula that enable students to generate, develop, evaluate, and refine original work at the piano. They must also be able to choose, prepare, refine, interpret, and perform works by other composers. Thus, the K–12 group-piano curriculum may emphasize improvisation and student composition more than an independent studio curriculum does. Depending on how the music curriculum is integrated with other classes at a particular school, there may be special emphasis on non-Western music or music indigenous to the region or local culture. While independent studio teachers and group-piano instructors at universities and community schools might include such activities, generally there is less emphasis on such topics outside of the K–12 environment.

Because many of the traditional group-piano methods emphasize technique and repertoire from the Western classical canon, group-piano teachers in a K–12 school setting may need to create their own materials and find supplemental resources to address creative and non-Western cultural competencies. It is anticipated that during the next few years, some of these teachers will begin to publish their useful materials. Teachers will need to seek out and evaluate materials specifically designed for composing and improvising at the piano, use educationally sound resources from the web, and evaluate new comprehensive printed or online materials designed by music educators for the K–12 piano lab as they come into the market.

## Methods and Materials for Children in Beginning Group Piano

Although competent group-piano teachers can make almost any piano method work for children learning in the group setting, there are materials that have been specifically designed and marketed for beginning group-piano instruction for children.

I will highlight several resources and offer an annotated bibliography of the books and materials for the remainder of this chapter. But the best way to discover each resource referenced is to spend time exploring the materials individually, playing the music, and trying some of the activities with students or peers. Thus, having a general template for evaluating group-piano methods is beneficial for organizing one's thoughts and perceptions. You will find a template for evaluating children's method books in Appendix D.1. As an example, I have completed sample evaluations for the Alfred Basic Piano Library (ABPL) *Group Piano Course*. (See Figure 9.1)

As you become more experienced with teaching group piano, you may choose to add categories to this evaluation template. As group piano for children becomes more

**Alfred's Basic Group Piano Course, Books 1–4**    **Publisher:** Alfred Publishing Co., Inc.

**Ancillary Materials:**
- Accompaniment CDs/MIDI
- Musical Adventures Board Game
- Game Cards for Books 1 & 2; Game Cards for Books 3 & 4
- Teachers Handbook for Books 1 & 2; 3 & 4

Are the **Concepts** presented **Systematically & Spiraled?** __✓__ Yes _____ No

Is there **Ample Reinforcement** within the text? __✓__ Yes _____ No

**Comments:** The pace is slow. There is ample reinforcement for average students. Students who do not practice regularly might need additional reinforcement of these concepts.

**Level/Book:** ____1____    *(1 evaluation completed per book/level)*
**Overview of concepts in Book 1:**

| Reading Approach | Off-staff black keys (4 units) <br> Off-staff Middle C & C position (units 5-7) |
|---|---|
| Pitch & Interval/ Reading Concepts | Off-staff reading encourages intervallic reading (on black keys) |
| | White-key names written in note heads (may discourage intervallic reading); Uses full range of the keyboard |
| Rhythmic Concepts | Quarter, half, dotted-half, and whole note patterns |
| | 4/4 meter throughout; 3/4 introduced in unit 8 |
| | Rhythm drill flashes in units 1, 2, 3, 5, 6, & 7 |
| Aural Skills | Integrated into each unit; Reinforces musical concepts |
| Sight Reading | Integrated throughout; Short SR flashes in units 2, 3, 5, & 7 |
| | Reinforces reading & rhythm concepts |
| Technique | Four units of black-key music (using fingers 2, 3, 4) encourages relaxed hand positions; Teachers can reinforce full-arm weight throughout; Specific technique pages in units 1, |
| Musicality | Several familiar tunes (i.e. Merrily We Roll Along, Alouette, & Jolly Old St. Nicholas) included; many original solos include words to help develop phrasing or reinforce concepts; accompaniments are simple and emphasize the meter, though not overly creative. |
| | Teacher CD/MIDI accompaniments are attractive & motivating. |
| | Four-part ensembles in units 3, 5, & 7 (great idea to have copies of these to use as supplements to other method books in a group class too!) |

*Figure 9.1* Completed Children's Method Evaluation for Alfred's Basic Group Piano Course, Books 1, 2, 3, and 4

| Creativity | Improvisation/Composition activities (that reinforce concepts) in units 1, 2, 3, 5, 6, & 7 |
|---|---|
| Theory | Short exercises directly related to the unit concept(s) integrated into each unit |
| Supplementary Materials | *Musical Adventures Board Game* (with Game Cards corresponding to each book) is fun but additional games and music that reinforces concepts will likely be needed. |
| | *Teacher Handbooks* contain lesson plans & student assignment suggestions and provide valuable information about scheduling groups, organizing lessons, classroom management, and more. Info about MIDI technology is dated for contemporary keyboard labs. |
| Online Resources | None at this time |

**Strengths of this Method:** Systematic approach and gradual introduction and reinforcement of basic rhythmic, pitch, and musical concepts.

**Potential Weaknesses of this Method:** Additional musical and supplemental resources will be required for most student groups. Because each book has 7 units (and semesters tend to last longer than that), teachers may be able to get through 2 books per semester or need to slow the pace but add additional solo and ensemble repertoire.

**Additional Comments & Notes:** This would be a good book to use at a week-long Piano Boot Camp or Summer Camp for beginners.

Alfred's Basic Group Piano Course          Level/Book: ___2___
Overview of concepts in Book 2:

| Reading Approach | Individual treble or bass staff (2 units) |
|---|---|
| | Grand staff Middle C & C position (units 2-7) |
| Pitch & Interval/ Reading Concepts | 2nds & 3rds reinforced (units 1-5); 4ths (unit 6); 5th (unit 7) |
| | Melodic & harmonic intervals |
| Rhythmic Concepts | Quarter, half, dotted-half, and whole note & rest patterns; Ties |
| | 4/4 meter emphasized; 16 examples in 3/4 (units 3-7) |
| | Rhythm drill flashes in units 3, 5, & 6 |
| Aural Skills | Integrated into each unit; Reinforces intervals |
| Sight Reading | SR flashes in every unit (more flashes than bk.1) |
| | Reinforces intervallic reading & rhythm concepts |
| Technique | More focus on finger independence; Legato introduced (unit 3); Specific technique pages in units 3, 5, 6, & 7; SR makes good technique exercises; LH developed as much as RH |
| Musicality | Few familiar tunes; many original solos include words to help develop phrasing or reinforce concepts; accompaniments are simple but not overly creative. |
| | Teacher CD/MIDI accompaniments are attractive & motivating. |
| | Only 2 four-part ensembles (units 5, & 7) |
| Creativity | Improvisation/Composition activities (that reinforce concepts) in units 3, 5, & 6 |
| Theory | Theory pages in each unit (directly related to the unit concept(s) |
| Supplementary Materials | *Musical Adventures Board Game* (with Game Cards corresponding to each book) is fun but additional games and music that reinforces concepts will likely be needed. |
| | *Teacher Handbooks* contain lesson plans & student assignment suggestions and provide valuable information about scheduling groups, organizing lessons, classroom management, and more. Info about MIDI technology is dated for contemporary keyboard labs. |
| Online Resources | None at this time |

*Figure 9.1* (Continued)

**Strengths of this Method:** Systematic approach and gradual introduction and reinforcement of basic rhythmic, pitch, and musical concepts.

**Potential Weaknesses of this Method:** Additional musical and supplemental resources will be required for most student groups. Because each book has 7 units (and semesters tend to last longer than that), teachers may be able to get through 2 books per semester or need to slow the pace but add additional solo and ensemble repertoire.

**Additional Comments & Notes:** This would be a good book to use at a week-long Piano Boot Camp or Summer Camp for beginners starting 2nd year or for beginning-level transfer students.

**Alfred's Basic Group Piano Course**    Level/Book: _____3_____
**Overview of concepts in Book 3:**

| Reading Approach | Grand staff Middle C & G position (units 1-7) |
|---|---|
| | Sharps & Flats (unit 2-7), More hand independence required |
| Pitch & Interval/ Reading Concepts | 2nd through 5th reinforced throughout |
| | Melodic & harmonic intervals |
| Rhythmic Concepts | Continuation of previous patterns; Half rest reinforced; Anacrusis |
| | Beamed eighth-note pairs introduced (unit 7); 2/4 meter (unit 7) |
| | Rhythm drill flashes in units 1, 2, 4, 5, & 7 |
| Aural Skills | Integrated into each unit; Reinforces scales, broken chords, sharps, flats, staccato, legato, crescendo, diminuendo, & eighths |
| Sight Reading | SR flashes in every unit |
| | Reinforces intervallic reading, rhythm, & new concepts |
| Technique | Focus on finger & hand independence |
| | Specific technique pages in units 1, 3, & 5, though may exercises develop technique throughout; LH developed as much as RH |
| Musicality | Solos still include words; Tempi (unit 6); Rit. & a tempo (unit 7) MIDI accompaniments & CDs similar to previous books |
| | Only 2 four-part ensembles (units 3 & 7) |
| Creativity | Improvisation/Composition activities (that reinforce concepts) in units 1, 2, 4, 5, & 7 |
| Theory | Theory pages in each unit (directly related to the unit concept(s) |
| Supplementary Materials | *Musical Adventures Board Game* (with Game Cards corresponding to each book) is fun but additional games and music that reinforces concepts will likely be needed. |
| | *Teacher Handbooks* contain lesson plans & student assignment suggestions and provide valuable information about scheduling groups, organizing lessons, classroom management, and more. Info about MIDI technology is dated for contemporary keyboard labs. |
| Online Resources | None at this time |

**Strengths & Weaknesses of this Method:** Similar to books 1 & 2.

**Additional Comments & Notes:** This would be a good book to use at a week-long Piano Boot Camp or Summer Camp for students entering into their second year of piano study.

**Alfred's Basic Group Piano Course**    Level/Book: _____4_____
**Overview of concepts in Book 4:**

| Reading Approach | Grand staff; new G & middle D position; 8va sign (unit 1) |
|---|---|
| | Half & whole steps (unit 4); Increased independence required |
| Pitch & Interval/ Reading Concepts | Tetrachords (unit 4): C & G octave scale (unit 5) |
| | Identification of notes all over grand staff |

*Figure 9.1* (Continued)

| Rhythmic Concepts | Continuation of patterns; single eighth rest & note (unit 7) |
|---|---|
| | Rhythm drill flashes in units 1, 4, 6, & 7 |
| Aural Skills | Several integrated into each unit; Reinforces scales, broken chords, sharps, flats, staccato, legato, crescendo, diminuendo, & eighths |
| Sight Reading | SR flashes (units 1, 3, & 6); SR required throughout |
| | Reinforces intervallic reading, rhythm, & new concepts |
| Technique | Focus on finger & hand independence; LH Alberti bass |
| | Specific technique pages in units 1, 3, & 6, though many exercises develop technique throughout; LH developed as much as RH |
| Musicality | Pedal (unit 1); More movement around the keyboard; More intricate articulation (staccato & legato within a phrase) |
| | Sonatina (unit 6); Accompaniments similar to previous books |
| | Only 2 four-part ensembles (units 2 & 7) |
| Creativity | Improvisation/Composition activities (that reinforce concepts) in units 1, 4, 6, & 7 |
| Theory | Theory pages in each unit (directly related to the unit concept(s) |
| Supplementary Materials | *Musical Adventures Board Game* (with Game Cards corresponding to each book) is fun but additional games and music that reinforces concepts will likely be needed. |
| | *Teacher Handbooks* contain lesson plans & student assignment suggestions and provide valuable information about scheduling groups, organizing lessons, classroom management, and more. Info about MIDI technology is dated for contemporary keyboard labs. |
| Online Resources | None at this time |

**Strengths & Weaknesses of this Method:** Similar to first three books.

**Additional Comments & Notes:** This would be a good book to use at a week-long Piano Boot Camp for second year students between fall & spring semesters.

*Figure 9.1* (Continued)

prevalent in our society, publishers will likely update and produce new materials, perhaps even some that are culturally relevant for specific countries around the world. I encourage you to use the evaluation template to assess the strengths and weaknesses of future materials. You will note that I have included a place to list the price of each book on the evaluation form. I find it helpful to have this included in my assessments, as the price will be a factor when assigning books each semester.

## Average-Age Beginning Methods

*Alfred's Basic Piano Group Piano Course*
Willard Palmer, Morton Manus, Amanda Vick Lethco, Gayle Kowalchyk, & E. L. Lancaster
MIDI accompaniments and CDs available.

This all-in-one method is designed for use with either electronic pianos or acoustic instruments. Each book contains seven units that include theory, ear training, rhythm drills, sight reading, composition/improvisation, technique, solos, and ensemble pieces. There are 74 to 75 student pages in each of the four books. Pages are relatively uncluttered but with attractive and relevant drawings. New concepts are introduced in highlighted boxes and reinforced henceforth. Clever icons represent drills for ear training, rhythm, sight reading, theory, technique, and so on (i.e., big-eared rabbit for ear training). Teacher handbooks are helpful for novice group-piano teachers. See Figure 9.1 for completed evaluation forms for Books 1 through 4.

*The Music Tree*
*A Time to Begin*, Parts 1, 2A, and 2B (Book and Activities)
Frances Clark, Louise Goss, & Sam Holland
MIDI accompaniments available.

These materials may be used in a group or private setting. However, they were developed and tested at the New School for Music Study, where most students enroll for both weekly group and private lessons. I have found that the materials work very well in this format, where major concepts are introduced and music is explored together in the group, and ideas are reinforced later at a private or partner lesson. One of the features of this method is that it encourages whole-keyboard exploration and large, relaxed arm movements from the start. Music can be taught by rote (sound before sight).

The pages are uncluttered, important concepts are highlighted and sequenced brilliantly, questions on the page encourage students to listen to and evaluate their sound, and ancillary materials and activities can easily be introduced to reinforce and spiral concepts. The reading begins with off-staff notation. Since intervallic reading is encouraged, through the use of landmark notes, pitches are first introduced on limited staves. In the last unit of the first book (*A Time to Begin*), students are reading on treble, bass, and grand staves with the landmark G and F lines highlighted. The activity books correlate and encourage students to explore concepts in a variety of ways. Basic rhythmic patterns for 4/4 and 3/4 are used throughout the first book; rests are not introduced until *Music Tree Part 1*. When I use this method in my group classes, I tend to supplement with another book of solos or ensemble music that incorporates a similar reading approach. This is an outstanding and pedagogically solid method book. However, teachers need to plan carefully for each class and for the entire semester, as the authors expect teachers to supply important information (not everything is on the page for the students).

### *Other Methods That May Be Used*

As noted earlier, almost any method can be used in a group-piano class as long as the teacher gives thought and preparation to the sequencing, pacing, and supplementing of in-class activities. Apart from those mentioned already, several individual methods that excellent group-piano teachers have used with success include Bastien (*Piano Basic* and *New Traditions All-in-One*), *Piano Adventures* by the Fabers, and the *Hal Leonard Piano Library*. Some teachers even use one method as the primary lesson and theory books but supplement repertoire or technique from another series. Please remember that you will need to evaluate each of these resources carefully, keeping your targeted student group in mind, as the levels differ among publications, and some reinforce concepts more completely or move more quickly than others.

## Resources for Advancing Groups

As we have noted, many teachers like to keep students studying in groups throughout the elementary and intermediate levels in order to maintain motivation, to make the most of teaching resources, and to foster student autonomy during practice. Method books can be used as students continue to progress. However, other resources are helpful as students advance. While not comprehensive, the following overview of resources should provide you with information about the types of resources that are available and where you might look to find additional teaching aids and materials for your group classes.

### *Ensemble Resources*

We begin our review with piano ensemble music, as I believe that students studying piano in groups should be making music together. The beauty of piano ensembles is that for many of the easier ensembles, students can be assigned music that is slightly easier than their technical ability. But because each student is responsible for a specific part, they are responsible to the entire group for learning it and performing it well. This is not unlike the expectations placed on wind and brass players in a band or orchestra. During rehearsals, students learn to listen to and respond to one another. Under the teacher's guidance, they learn to communicate with each other about the music and through the music. Ensemble performances can be extremely rewarding, as the overall musical performance is often more musically sophisticated than any individual could accomplish by himself or herself.

*Alfred Basic Piano Library Ensemble* Books 1, 2, and 3
Palmer, Manus, Lethco, Kowalchyk, & Lancaster, Alfred Music

*Complete Levels 2 and 3* book also available
*Alfred Basic Piano Library Christmas Ensemble* Books 1, 2, and 3
Ancillary materials: MIDI accompaniments.

These books were designed to supplement the Alfred's Basic Piano Library (ABPL) by providing four-part keyboard ensembles children would find fun and engaging. Each book contains about five ensembles (the complete Book 2 and 3 contains 10 selections) that correspond to concepts in the lesson, recital, theory, and solo books. There are simple line drawings for each piece that support the character or mood but that do not clutter the page. There are also suggestions for general MIDI sounds for each part in the ensemble. I find that once students have rehearsed with the suggested sounds, they can explore other potential keyboard sounds that would work for each part, and we can discuss range, timbre, and balance and listen for those concepts. The MIDI accompaniments are attractive and add sophistication to the ensemble. These are useful resources for beginning students (all music is notated on staff). For similar off-staff easy ensemble repertoire, the ABPL Group Piano books (see evaluation earlier in this chapter) contain good ensemble repertoire.

*Hal Leonard Student Piano Library Piano Ensembles* Books 1–5 Hal Leonard
*Hal Leonard Piano Library Christmas Piano Ensembles* Books 1–5
Ancillary materials: MIDI accompaniments.

These books correspond to the lesson, solo, and other books in the Hal Leonard Student Piano Library series. Each of these books contains between four and five different four-part ensembles. These can work on two or more acoustic pianos or keyboards. These arrangements are outstanding, engage students of all ages, and work particularly well on electronic keyboards and digital pianos. I would also recommend purchasing the MIDI accompaniments, as they add to the overall performance and help students as they collaborate on learning the music. I have seen teachers use these digital accompaniments as students perform on acoustic instruments. Each ensemble has an optional teacher's accompaniment (in the conductor's score), which is extremely useful. Especially at the beginning levels, the musical reading and concepts are simple enough for students to perform without becoming cognitively overloaded. Even the easiest ensembles are extremely musically satisfying. Having correlated Christmas ensemble books provides teachers with even more options to reinforce concepts.

*Ogilvy Music Ensembles*
Jim & Susan Ogilvy and others, www.sospace.com

More than 300 pieces of keyboard ensemble music are available at the Ogilvy Music Ensemble Gallery web site. These keyboard ensembles range from early elementary to advanced, and most ensembles or arrangements have between 4 and 12 parts.

Concerti, two pianos and keyboard ensemble, and iPad ensembles are available also. There are suggestions for general MIDI sounds to be used for each part and accompaniments are available. The music is very effective with students of all ages and abilities.

*Ensemble Music for Group Piano*, 4th Edition
James Lyke & Geoffrey Haydon, Stipes Publishing

While this book is for students who have been studying for at least one semester and is most often used in university piano labs, it can be used by independent teachers who teach children. Because this book was originally designed for use with adult students, there is no artwork cluttering the page. Eighty-one of the 120 pages are devoted to arrangements or original duets based on well-known classical melodies, and they become progressively more difficult. While the authors claim that the last third of the book contains multiple keyboard arrangements, most of these are essentially duets. There are six arrangements for three to six keyboards at the end of the book. I keep multiple copies of this book in the piano lab and have found that students of all ages enjoy working on these ensembles.

*Piano Teams®*
N. Jane Tan, www.wppinstitute.com

There are several books (each with one ensemble piece) from the elementary to advanced levels available. These ensembles are designed to be played on acoustic pianos but can be used on electronic keyboards too. Some of the arrangements are more effective than others.

*World Gems* (see detailed description under music history and world music)

One of the few resources featuring arrangements of ensemble music from different cultures. These are early-intermediate and more difficult than the Alfred Basic Piano Library or Hal Leonard level 1 to 3 ensembles.

There are numerous other duet and trio books from various publishers available. Some of these can be adapted or used in the group-piano setting. As these types of materials frequently go in and out of print, they will not be reviewed here. Teachers are reminded to consider new ensembles for use in group piano as they come to market.

### *Games*

While the majority of class time should be devoted to making music at the piano, group classes provide perfect opportunities to enhance the learning and reinforce concepts through educational (and fun) group games. Theoretical concepts are often featured in music games. In our evaluation of Alfred's Basic Group Piano books, we noted that there is an accompanying board game.

Many of the best educational games and activities were designed by teachers who needed supplemental activities in their studios. For many years, these were available through the Music Educator's Marketplace (which is located at the Keys to Imagination LLC web site). While Keys to Imagination (www.keystoimagination.com) also sells traditional games and manipulatives, this LLC was created by a piano teacher and features technology-driven activities that can enhance or supplement your curriculum. Examples of traditional manipulative games that can easily be incorporated into group classes include "Whirligig games," which are short enough to be played in class, rely on knowledge rather than speed, and reinforce specific theory concepts. On the same web site, the "Double-Click Curriculum" is an example of a technology enhancement that correlates with the *Faber Piano Adventures* and *Alfred Premier* methods. While probably not ideal for facilitating group work in a piano class, students could use the Double-Click apps and activities as at-home supplements to reinforce concepts learned in class. There are music history and world music resources too. It is recommended that you explore the Keys to Imagination web site to see videos of students using some materials and to discover new activities and curricula that might be useful in your piano classes.

The Three Cranky Women have created and published, through Kjos Music Company, almost 20 games and activities at all levels for use in group settings. They have a number of videos on their YouTube channel that show students playing various games (https://www.youtube.com/channel/UCOT_0WFBWmOqYg3XTX5SoHQ). The Music in Motion web site and catalog (www.musicmotion.com) also has many useful resources available for purchase. Among other teaching aids, they sell large-sized floor keyboards and staves that can be used with younger children, games, whiteboards, and simple instruments that can enhance experiential learning in the group-piano class. For example, a one-octave stair-step bell set can help students see and hear the ascending notes as they play from left to right, ascending both the scale and the ladder. Since some of these materials can be expensive, I find it helpful to keep a wish list of games and resources. Each semester, I try to budget for the purchase of an item that will enhance the group experience for children in my classes.

Additionally, there are several books available that describe games and activities that can be used in a group-piano class. I have found that many games (including those not designed specifically for music) can be adapted for the piano class. I have had students create Jeopardy boards and various decks of question cards related to musical concepts. Students can play these games in teams. I've seen local teachers use an "enhanced" Twister game to reinforce musical concepts. I've used homemade airy-fabric scarves to allow children to move to my playing and really feel how half notes and whole notes take up more "space" than quarters and eighths. The possibilities are endless as long as we remain creative in our thinking.

*Teacher Books on Games*

These easy-to-use books can function as useful references for teachers looking to plan a short game that reinforces a specific concept during the piano class. Necessary materials or game pieces can be created from items in the studio.

*101 Music Games for Children* by Jerry Storms
*101 More Music Games for Children*

As the titles suggest, there are 101 games per publication. These are designed for children ages 6 and older. The author provides a helpful table at the beginning showing which games are appropriate for young children, older children, teenagers, or all ages. Some of the games incorporate percussion instruments, props, or recordings, and many encourage collaboration among the students and develop listening and concentration skills. There are 10 categories of games: listening games, concentration games, expression and improvisation games, rhythm games, sound games, dance and movement games, relaxation games, multicultural and intercultural games, game projects, and card and board games.

*A Galaxy of Games for the Music Class* by Margaret Athey and Gwen Hotchkiss

Although this book was published in 1975, these games still work well. They were designed to be used in school music classes (and are classified according to grade level for age appropriateness) but work in the piano class. The games are grouped by category into 11 chapters: games for rhythmic response, reading and writing rhythm, reading and writing melody, learning music notation, ear training, developing singing, games for learning about composers and literature, musical instruments, for general review, musical word games, and games just for fun. The table of contents makes identifying a useful game easy, with information about the grade level, number of players, equipment required, and skill involved. The appendix provides detailed information about playing cards teachers can make for the games.

## Useful Books for Theory, Improvisation, Composition, and Music History

*General Resources for Teachers*

*101 Ideas for Piano Group Class*
Mary Ann Froehlich, Summy-Birchard/Alfred Music

The author of this 84-page book (Froehlich, 2004) clearly states in the introduction that she believes serious piano can only be taught in a one-on-one setting and that the ideas are not intended for piano-lab-type settings. However, the five chapters at the core of her book offer some suggestions for topics or themes of monthly or every-other-month group classes. Many of these suggestions are repertoire or music history oriented, though there are brief references to ensemble and improvisational activities for more advanced and older students. There are accessible introductions to cooperative learning, traditional children's music programs, and inclusion of children with special needs. As the author was a Suzuki piano teacher and music therapist, some teachers may wish to peruse this volume.

## *Theory*

### *Resources for Group-Piano Teachers*

Music MasterMINDS: The Ultimate Cross-Curricular Connection of Music Puzzles and Games
Cheryl Lavender, Hal Leonard

This activity book contains about 60 pages of puzzles and answer keys to engage students in group classes. The book is designed for teachers. The author (Lavender, 2006) gives teachers permission to reproduce all pages for in-class student activities. Topics include tone color, tempo and dynamics, rhythm, lyrics, pitch and melody, symbols and terms, composers and styles, and music careers.

*Piano Teacher's Resource Kit*
*Tic-Tac-Toe Music Games*
Karen Harrington, Hal Leonard

Created by a piano teacher (Harrington, 2008, 2010) who recognized that students enjoy and need engaging activity pages that reinforce musical concepts, these books contain "reproducible" games. *Tic-Tac-Toe Music Games* includes 10 game cards for each of the following theory concepts: symbols, notes, rhythm, intervals, key signatures, and tempi. The *Piano Teacher's Resource Kit* contains different types of worksheets, games, and puzzles (including numerous sudokus and crosswords). There are more than 80 different pages that encompass five grade levels. I use these pages as supplemental material when groups need specific concepts reinforced throughout the semester and have even assigned different pages to students within the group as homework, based on individual needs.

### *Books for Students*

*Theory Gymnastics*, 11 Levels (for Different Ages and Paces)
Laura Zizette, Charlene Z. Shelzi & Kathleen Lloyd, Kjos Music

These books, authored by the teachers also known as the Three Cranky Women (see game section earlier in this chapter), work exceptionally well because teachers can choose a book that is not just at the appropriate theory level but also the right age level. Book titles have attractive musical names such as *Spirito*, *Con Moto*, and *Con Fuoco*. While there are 11 unique books, with corresponding teacher guides, teachers should carefully research which book will work for each piano class. For example, at the beginning level (Level A), there is a *Brillante* book for students aged 4 to 7 but an *Animato* book for students aged 8 to 11. While each of these books covers the same concepts, materials, page layout, and activities are age appropriate. Additionally, there is an *Accelerando 1* that covers levels A and B at an accelerated pace.

While some of these pages can be undertaken as in-class activities, I have also seen group teachers use them effectively as at-home workbooks in which they assign 2 weeks of homework pages, collect the books at the beginning of class for individual grading, and return them with the next 2-week assignment at the following group lesson. There are age-appropriate activities, appealing characters, drawings, and visuals that reinforce important concepts throughout.

*Piano Bridges*, Books 1 and 2
Meg Gray, Alfred Music

Written by a group-piano teacher, each book contains 40 pages of activities that reinforce reading, writing, listening, and playing skills. There are 36 projects in Book 1. These could be used during the first year of on-staff study or as an activity book during a piano camp during the summer before the second year of study. Book 2 has 45 projects, many of which focus on intervals up to an octave, C, G, D, A, and F five-finger patterns, musical expression markings, and staccato and legato articulation. Book 2 could be used during the second year of study or during a boot camp prior to the third year of piano study.

### *Improvisation*

*Pattern Play*, Books 1–6
Forrest Kinney, Fredrick Harris Music

Forrest Kinney's series of six progressive books provides students with experiences that encourage them to expound upon their knowledge of scales, chords, and modes through creative improvisation. Students can play and experiment in pairs (duets) and trios, where they take turns playing patterns. Then they are encouraged to go on "vacations" from those models, listening and responding to one another. In the first books, students arrange familiar tunes with various triads, inversions, and seventh chords and improvise on black-and-white keys and special scales. By the last book they are experimenting in various modes, keys with up to three sharps or flats, and more complex harmonies such as 11th and 13th chords. There are many helpful ideas, pictures, and quotes for student reflection interspersed throughout. These books could be started in the third year of a children's group or possibly sooner with teenagers and adults.

*Creative Chords: Keyboard Improvisation Method,* Books 1 and 2
Bradley Sowash, Kjos Music

These books include the "interactive practice studio" at the publisher's web site, where, after entering a code found in the book, students can access some video lessons, backing tracks (accompaniments) for every piece and most exercises, record and save files of their playing, and download and print extra worksheets or information. Each book contains theory tools, practice steps, workouts, and new or familiar tunes that elaborate upon core concepts. Students are encouraged to P-L-A-Y (Prepare-Learn-Add-Your Way) during each unit. In Book 1, students learn about and elaborate upon primary chords and inversions, pentascales and octave scales in C, G, and F, and learn several accompaniment styles and rhythm ideas for 4/4 and 3/4 meter over the course of five units. Book 2 contains six units and introduces A, D, and E minor scales, minor, augmented, and diminished chords and inversions, reading slash chords and lead lines (fake book style), and improvising with various accompaniment patterns, and has students creating accompaniments for well-known classical and folk melodies. They also embellish melodies. Book 2 is more challenging than Book 1, so teachers may want to take time off to help students increase core technical and theoretical skill sets before introducing the second book into the group-piano curriculum.

### Composition

*Books for Teachers*

*Piano Teacher's Guide to Creative Composition*
Carol Klose, Hal Leonard

Authored by the late composer and pedagogue Carol Klose (2011), this book is an 80-page guide for teachers who wish to learn more about the compositional process in general. The book contains five parts that cover the broad topics of laying the groundwork for creative composition, student's library of compositional tools, mapping a composition, lesson plans, and refining a composition.

There is also an appendix containing six pages of useful resources. This book is a concise but comprehensive resource for teachers and contains numerous intermediate to advanced examples of compositional styles and activities. While there are some elementary activities, the book is aimed at broadly exploring important topics at various levels rather than covering specific topics in depth. There is a five-page "composer's toolbox" that covers basic topics such as form, rhythm and meter, pitch, melody, and harmony and expanded elements including character, transitional techniques, and special effects. While this book might work for some more advanced students, I would suggest that the resources covered in this book are more useful for the teacher who teaches composition as part of the group-piano curriculum. Also, this book would be an excellent resource for teachers wishing to explore ways to add compositional activities to the weekly lesson.

*Books for Students*

*Creative Composition Tool Box*, Books 1–6
Wynn-Anne Rossi, Alfred Music

These are excellent workbooks for student composers. The books range in difficulty from "early elementary" (beginning with creative off-staff piano notation) through "late intermediate" (where students begin to compose using secondary dominants, modulation, lead sheets, and even in canon)! The books are sequential, building gradually upon concepts that have been explored previously. Activities are simple and straightforward enough to take up minimal lesson time. Each compositional activity is preceded by a "model" composition written by Rossi so that the student can explore the concepts within the context of an elementary work. Then, through a series of succinct directions, students create their own piece. Manuscript and measures are provided, along with helpful parameters (e.g., starting pitches or motives). Each piece contains a "toolbox tip" and a "composer connection," in which a few sentences describe important composers in history.

These books are designed to be integrated into any well-sequenced piano curriculum, and concepts used in each composition reinforce concepts that are likely being explored during the regular group class. Composition pages may also be assigned for homework, as the activities are so well designed and thought out that students should achieve success and thus be motivated to complete the activities and explore composition at home. I have found that when students share their compositions with the group during class, they get ideas from each other and learn more than in a typical individual lesson. Sharing compositions or working on small-group compositions can also help students who are less comfortable exhibiting creativity and risk taking at the piano.

142

## *Music History and World Music*

More than 25 years ago, when I first started offering group-piano classes, I began with monthly music history and performance classes. We would feature a composer of the month, display pictures of the composer and maps of his or her homeland throughout the studio, engage in games related to that composer or significant compositional styles of the time, and perform his or her music for each other. Later, I began including an occasional world music class, in which we would listen to traditional music on authentic instruments, learn a folk song or two, and perform ensemble arrangements from that country.

Now, I incorporate music history and world music into my curriculum through regular (if not weekly) segments in my lesson plans. You may still wish to gradually collect books about famous composers (written for various ages of children and comprehension levels) and have a selection of representative print and recorded music, along with traditional instruments, available for these segments. But, there are several excellent materials available, and more continue to be printed as publishers recognize that piano teachers want to include music history activities and world music experiences into their curricula.

*Meet the Great Composers*—Books 1 and 2 by June Montgomery & Maurice Hinson, Alfred Music
*Meet the Great Composers Repertoire*—Books 1 and 2 (composers correspond to the main books)
Supplementary materials: CDs of musical excerpts and repertoire available.

Each book contains 17 units, with one composer featured per unit. Units begin with a "story" of the composer, representative music or pertinent information about the time period and keyboard instruments of the day, and an activity that tests the knowledge acquired in the unit. The title page of each unit contains an attractive sketch of the composer, birth and death dates, major compositions, interesting facts, and suggested listening. While the first book contains only white, male (mostly European) composers, the second book includes several American composers and females such as Gershwin, Barber, Clara Schumann, Fanny Mendelssohn, and Amy Beach. At the end of each book is a music history timeline that places these composers in context. The repertoire books correlate with the main books. They feature an intermediate one- or two-page original or arrangement of a composition widely associated with each composer.

*My Own Music History*
Karen Koch, Music Educators Marketplace; Keys to Imagination

Teacher version, teacher consumables pack, and downloadable student packs.

This is an expandable kit that centers around a timeline of history, where students place important events in American history alongside the composers about whom they are learning. At the core, students each have a binder with their timeline on the cover and information pages that they complete and create for each composer studied. The music periods important for keyboard instruments (Baroque, classical, Romantic, and contemporary) are color-coded, and students complete repertoire sheets for each time period as they learn repertoire. I think of this binder as each student's core music history reference. As they collect materials, learn about new composers, and expand upon what they already know, they hang that new history information onto the core music history "hooks" within each section of the binder. Rather than making music history abstract, these materials allow students to link new knowledge to previously learned historical facts, both musical and general. *Meet the Great Composers* can easily be incorporated into this curriculum, as can any other resources that a teacher chooses to use. There are composer stickers, color-coded highlighters, and other materials available in the teacher consumable packets.

*The World at Your Fingertips*, Books 1 and 2
Deborah Brener & Tom Gerou, Alfred Music

Divided into six units per book (one unit per country), these books explore the country, culture, music, and instruments of each country. There is an activity page at the end of each unit and an intermediate piano arrangement of a traditional folk song. While our colleagues in the world of general music education have been teaching students about music of different cultures for years, piano teachers have had few resources specifically suitable for piano students. These books fill this gap in resources.

*World Gems: International Folksongs for Piano Ensembles*
Amy O'Grady, Hal Leonard

While this is actually a piano ensemble book (two- and three-part keyboard or acoustic piano arrangements), the six ensembles represent music from Africa, Haiti, the Andes, Mexico, Japan, and China. There is a short paragraph about the origin of each selection, and each piece gives intermediate-level students an opportunity to experience rhythms and scale patterns unique to each culture.

*Journey Around the Globe—Are We There Yet?*
Michelle Sisler, Deborah Brener, & Portia Johnson, Keys to Imagination

This is an interactive curriculum about music in different cultures that is used by general music educators. There is an impressive video, audio, and interactive Smartboard component, which makes the overall classroom version and teacher kits quite expensive. However, there are also $10 piano books or piano accompaniment books available that could be useful during group classes.

## Materials Designed for Group-Piano Camps

While any of the aforementioned materials can be used by teachers who offer and create week-long piano camps for their students, there are some commercially available materials of note.

*Piano Camp*, 5 Books (Primer through 4)
June C. Montgomery, Alfred Music

As the title implies, these books are designed for week-long piano camps that would last about 2 hours per day. There are eight pages per day that include an introduction of core concepts, activity pages, sight reading, aural skills, solos, and ensemble music. Students would work through the entire book by the end of the week. Montgomery provides one page of helpful suggestions at the start of each book. These materials, she says, could be used as a prefall boot camp to remind students about concepts learned during the previous year or even during the break between fall and spring semesters. The primer level begins with off-staff reading and moves to the staff by day five, while Book 4 is deemed early–intermediate. These books correlate with the Alfred's Basic Piano Library (ABPL). Teachers will need to have additional materials and activities available and carefully prepare the lesson plans for each of the classes to ensure maximum student engagement and learning throughout the class.

## Books Specifically for K–12 Piano Classes

While current online searches do not turn up any readily accessible results for student books for K–12 group piano classes, I know several teachers who have created their own curricula, and I have reviewed new materials for potential publication that use chords to improve creativity and improvisation during class. So if you teach in this setting, be on the lookout for new resources and keep in touch with colleagues. Due to the arts standards, which emphasize demonstrating competency of musical concepts through creating and performing, even independent studio teachers would find these materials useful for improvisation and creative activities as they become available to the general public.

## Pedagogy in Action

1. Review two levels of June Montgomery's *Piano Camp* using the Group Method Evaluation Template (Appendix D.1). Be sure to play the music (including any accompaniments) as you assess how motivating the music might be for students

to play and how it might contribute to their development of musicality. Sing the words as you play to discover if they might help students with appropriate phrasing, musical line, and motivation.

2. Choose one of the books that you reviewed in #1 and design a curriculum for a 5-day children's piano camp. Write a detailed lesson plan (including time you expect to devote to each activity) for each day of your camp. If you need supplemental resources, include those in your plan.

3. Gather four (or more) of your classmates and do a peer-teaching demonstration of your first lesson plan (from question #2). Video yourself and review it within 24 hours of your peer teaching. Use one of the self-assessment forms from Appendices E.1 through E.5 to evaluate your teaching. Interview your peers to see what they felt worked well during your teaching demo and if they have any suggestions to improve a specific teaching strategy.

4. Explore either of the music-game books to identify a game that would be useful in your class. Create/find any of the materials needed and try to play it with your peers. Alternatively, purchase one of the commercially available games and play it with your peers. Once you have played the game, make a list of skills and/or music concepts that students would develop by playing this game.

## References and Teacher Resources

Athey, M., & Hotchkiss, G. (1975). *A Galaxy of Games for the Music Class*. West Nyack, NY: Parker Publishing Company.

Froehlich, M. A. (2004). *101 Ideas for Piano Group Class*. Van Nuys, CA: Summy-Birchard.

Goss, L. (Ed.). (1992). *Questions and Answers: Practical Advice for Piano Teachers by Frances Clark*. Northfield, IL: The Instrumentalist Company. Currently available through the Frances Clark Center for Keyboard Pedagogy www.keyboardpedagogy.org

Harrington, K. (2008). *Tic-Tac-Toe Music Games*. Milwaukee: Hal Leonard Corporation.

Harrington, K. (2010). *Piano Teacher's Resource Kit*. Milwaukee: Hal Leonard Corporation.

Klose, C. (2011). *Piano Teacher's Guide to Creative Composition*. Milwaukee: Hal Leonard Corporation.

Lavender, C. (2006). *Music MasterMINDS: The Ultimate Cross-Curricular Connection of Music Puzzles and Games*. Milwaukee: Hal Leonard.

Storms, J. (2001). *101 Music Games for Children*. The Hague: Uitgeverij Panta Rhei (in the USA published as a Hunter House SmartFun Book, Berkley: Publishers Group West).

# Section 4

# THE GROUP-PIANO INSTRUCTOR

# 10

# ADVANTAGES AND DISADVANTAGES OF GROUP TEACHING AND ADDITIONAL THOUGHTS ON ASSESSMENT FROM THE INSTRUCTOR'S PERSPECTIVE

## Objectives

By the end of this chapter, you should be able to list advantages and disadvantages of teaching group piano from the instructor's perspective and describe ways to provide effective instruction. You should understand how to assess students in groups.

## Advantages of Group-Piano Teaching

Throughout the first three sections of this book, we have explored many of the advantages of learning to play piano in groups. We have noted that for almost a century in the United States, some children have been exploring the fundamentals of piano technique and repertoire in group settings. We have also seen that the activities included in a comprehensive group-piano curriculum for children are not unlike what they might experience in a school music classroom. In group piano, they explore fundamental musical concepts using the keyboard as the vehicle for expression. We have also explored how excellent group-piano teachers avail of research and techniques from learning and group theories and put group dynamics to use in the piano class. It has been noted that children and adults who study in the group-piano environment often progress more quickly, cover more topics more deeply each semester, can perform as well as peers studying individually, and remain motivated to practice in preparation for weekly classes. But we have not looked closely at group piano from the perspective of the instructor.

Because teaching piano to groups of students requires the development of a specific skill set (see Chapter 11 for characteristics of effective group-piano teachers), this teaching format may not be for everyone. However, many teachers note that the challenges and the adventures experienced in the piano lab make the experience worthwhile. The ability to reach more students each week than would be possible through private lessons is one advantage of teaching piano in groups. Another often-cited benefit is increased income. Teachers should be aware, however, that teaching groups of students requires as much or more preparation time as teaching the actual class. So once preparation time is factored in, increased income may actually be a myth. What is true is that group-piano teachers likely have less student-contact time than they would teaching the same number of students individually. Without having to teach long hours during traditional vacation times, teaching group piano by offering piano camps (i.e., during the summer or holidays) can be an effective way to keep most students engaged in music making during times when they would normally take a break from the instrument and lose valuable skills attained throughout the school year.

The challenge of creating lesson plans and engaging students throughout the entire instructional period is a gratifying creative activity for many group-piano teachers. Because there are so many combinations of student personalities and learning styles, no two classes are ever the same, which creates a stimulating environment for the teacher. Witnessing groups of students (at any age) work together, learn together, and make music together is rewarding. Because most scenarios in which we teach group piano involve some technology, learning about and staying up to date with educational technology trends is also exciting for many group-piano teachers.

In short, group-piano teachers can never rest on their laurels. There is always more to learn and ways to improve our group-teaching technique. Although the musical concepts that we teach remain constant, group teachers tend to be innovative, creative, and deeply concerned about finding meaningful ways to connect with every student in their classes. Effective group-piano teachers are true lifelong learners who enjoy assessing their skills, evaluating the effect their strategies are having on their students' learning, and modifying their techniques to maximize their efforts. To that end, many teachers work to increase their teaching skills and achieve the Group Teaching Specialist designation through MTNA (Music Teachers National Association. Group Teaching Specialist Program, n.d.). This designation shows potential and current students that the group-piano teacher has successfully completed projects related to teaching philosophy, lesson planning for the group, and understanding the group and has demonstrated successful group teaching through video examples evaluated by national specialists in the field. More information about the MTNA Group Teaching Specialist Program can be found at (www.mtna.org).

## Disadvantages of Teaching Group Piano

Many of the reasons cited as benefits of teaching group piano can be seen as drawbacks by some teachers. Thus, before embarking upon group teaching, both the positive and negative aspects of working with students in groups should be considered. Although it may be possible to teach more students per week, scheduling and filling classes can be problematic, especially if one's studio is not well established. Students today are busier than ever, and the times at which you offer specific classes and levels may not be convenient for everyone who is interested in those courses. Thus, teachers need to decide what the minimum student enrollment will be in order for the class to be viable. For example, you might ask yourself if partner and trio lessons will work for the curriculum that you have planned. Or will you only run a class if there are at least four or six students enrolled? Income also factors into this decision. If you offer group classes at a significantly lower rate than your private lessons, how many students will you need to earn the same amount of income for an hour of instruction?

Two other critical factors that impact enrollment are studio space and technology, both of which can be expensive. Some teachers who have studios in their homes have enough space to teach groups of students effectively. This includes room for pianos and keyboards, room for movement activities (especially with children), portable whiteboards or other means of conveying visuals to the group, and tables for writing and games. Many teachers cannot accommodate such a teaching setup in their home. Additionally, if groups of adults need to park automobiles or children are being dropped off and picked up by parents at the same time, parking space and neighborhood traffic or zoning restrictions must be considered.

Due to limited studio size and zoning restrictions, many group-piano teachers purchase or lease studio space outside of the home, often in commercial buildings where they can renovate the teaching space to suit their needs and where there will be ample parking and easy access to the studio. Such property can be expensive, however, and this may not be a viable option for all teachers. In my local community, I have colleagues who have formed teaching consortia so that they can pool teaching resources and share studio expenses, such as leasing pianos and building space. If one wishes to teach using a piano lab, with multiple digital pianos that are connected to the teaching console via a controller, this technology is expensive to purchase, and a maintenance budget will be necessary. While digital pianos do not require regular tuning, the initial start-up costs can be more than anticipated. Teachers should have a contingency fund for repairs, which will be needed if the lab gets regular use. While I believe that a business plan and annual budget are important for all professional piano teachers, it is critical for group-piano instructors.

Group-piano teachers must remain organized from a preparation perspective, staying on top of all curricular issues, tracking and adapting multiple lesson plans, and doing preparation work outside of class, such as theory grading and selecting or creating ancillary activities. But they must also keep organized business records, which can be numerous when teaching large numbers of students. During actual classes, group teachers must be able to multitask, sequence and pace learning experiences, keep all students engaged in group work, keep students on task throughout the entire class, facilitate learning of individuals within the group, and assess individual progress, often while students are participating in group music-making activities. Some teachers thrive in this kind of environment; others wisely recognize that the group instructional setting may not be for them and leave this important work to those who are willing to develop and hone their group-teaching skills.

## Assessment

Throughout the first three sections of this book, we have discussed competencies that students should meet in various group-piano contexts. However, it can be challenging to know whether our students are actually learning in our classes. Assessment and accountability have become buzzwords of the 21st century. In general education, schools and teachers are rewarded based on how their students score on various standardized tests. By now, you are likely familiar with the proposition that teachers "teach to the test," since that is how student learning tends to be measured in our culture. However, most thoughtful educators agree that how students apply and transfer their knowledge is a more accurate assessment of student learning. But this type of assessment can be more challenging to carry out in large groups. In fact, even in higher education, I would argue that some intelligent students learn how to study and meet the expectations for each of their professors. They excel, passing all of our quantifiable means of assessment, without really digesting the new material or applying the new information in meaningful ways. We want to avoid this surface learning in group piano.

Think for a moment about our own profession of piano teaching. Many of the common means that parents and students use to evaluate our teaching do not reflect the process of learning that takes place. Positive or negative evaluations of our teaching are most frequently based on how well our students perform at contests or in recitals. In other words, our teaching is being evaluated *solely* based on how well a student performs in any given instance. While assessing performance is important in a performance-based medium such as music, it does not necessarily reflect how well someone has internalized or learned musical skills and concepts. It may represent how well a student has learned how to execute a specific skill or piece of repertoire at the piano, but it does not tell us if that student will be able to apply that particular skill in a similar situation on his own in a future musical encounter. I can think of many students who learned to perform four or five pieces well in one year but who could not sight read or learn any other music on their own. Therefore, I would question how much that student had really learned. Meanwhile, a lot of good learning that may not lead to the ultimate performance might be occurring in our studios. We should consider how we measure deep learning and how we convey its importance to our students and their families.

That is not to say that we or our students should not be judged on how well they perform. A recital performance *can* be a relevant display of how well various skills, concepts, and techniques have been synthesized. But it should not be the *sole* or only means of evaluating whether learning has taken place, especially if the student did not arrive at any of the creative or musical decisions on her own. Dutifully following a teacher's instructions or replicating a master performance of another displays a kind of procedural knowledge, but it does not necessarily demonstrate that learning has taken place. Robert Duke (2005) offers a helpful definition of learning. He states that learning "requires that the student apply knowledge or skill or both in some meaningful way" (p. 12). In other words, the new material must be worked with, manipulated, and made meaningful to the learner in working memory and subsequently stored in long-term memory where it will later be retrieved and applied in a related application, processed again, and stored even more completely.

In the case of learning to play the piano, there is the added burden of not only understanding how and when to apply the declarative knowledge but then applying this information procedurally. Ultimately, knowledge exhibited through complex motor skills, which must be developed based on auditory and kinesthetic feedback from the student and possibly from the teacher, is then rehearsed until the new musical gesture becomes automatic during performance. A student may understand key musical concepts but still be working on the associated motor skills associated with them. At this stage in the learning process, it would be a mistake to say that learning has not taken place, for the student may have a fine understanding and declarative knowledge base for the new concept. However, a traditional performance would not reveal the student's understanding of the technique or concept since the associated motor skills have yet to be refined.

Thus, what we must do as music educators is learn to evaluate students' learning "along the way" so that flawed learning is not reinforced. We must remain cognizant of each student's physical abilities throughout the learning process and acknowledge successful learning at its various stages. Learning to play the piano is not a linear process, and our evaluation of a student's learning must reflect this. Group-piano teachers must continually evaluate, assess, and provide appropriate feedback both to the group and to individuals. This type of individual assessment within the group context is a skill that is developed gradually and over time. Thoughtful self-reflection and video assessment of our teaching can help group-piano teachers improve assessment and feedback techniques.

Our teaching philosophies and evaluation practices should account for and reflect the learning that is exemplified through performance, as well as the incremental and critical learning that takes place when concepts are strategically and meaningfully scaffolded onto a student's prior knowledge base. With our adult students, we can explain that learning is not linear, due in part to the complex motor skills that must be refined throughout piano study. With our younger students, we avoid the pitfalls of discouragement during the slow pace of motor-skill development by designing new tasks and learning activities that build upon the previously learned skills and that can be achieved with some degree of success at regular intervals by the students. In other words, we design our curriculum in such a way that students can achieve short-term objectives and experience success at the piano while in the pursuit of the long-term goals they will need to rehearse and internalize for many days or weeks before they will synthesize and demonstrate complete success through performance of repertoire.

## Pedagogy in Action

1. Consider how much you will charge for private and group instruction. You may consult web sites of teachers in your region for typical rates. Create a projected-income spreadsheet that shows how much you expect to earn from each type of lesson, how many students you need to enroll to make group piano viable, and expenses associated with teaching groups.

2. Using the self-evaluation form in Appendix E.4 or E.5, watch a recent group-piano class and evaluate how well you assessed individual and group learning. Briefly describe three ways in which you will work to improve student assessment in future classes.

## References

Duke, R. A. (2005). *Intelligent Music Teaching: Essays on the Core Principles of Effective Instruction.* Austin, TX: Learning and Behavior Resources.

Music Teachers National Association. Group Teaching Specialist Program http://www.mtna.org/programs/teaching-specialists/

# 11

# CHARACTERISTICS OF EFFECTIVE GROUP-PIANO TEACHERS

## Objectives

At the conclusion of this chapter, you should be able to list the characteristics of effective group-piano teachers, identify traits you wish to develop, and know of resources for improving group-teaching techniques.

## Effective Group Teachers

Teaching piano to students in the group setting can be an excellent way to reach large numbers of students each week, introduce more material during each lesson, and involve students in collaborative learning techniques. However, simply purchasing requisite technology and scheduling students into group time slots does not guarantee an optimal experience for the students or teacher. In previous chapters, we have considered theories of learning, group techniques, group dynamics, philosophies for various age groups, psychosocial, cognitive and developmental characteristics, and desired outcomes with respect to grouping students and choosing materials. But how does this knowledge translate into effective group teaching?

In this chapter, we will explore these ideas through the lens of identifiable characteristics of effective group-piano teachers. In Chapter 12, we will approach this topic from the flip side and explore typical mistakes that novice group teachers make and how we can avoid them. We will begin this exploration by categorizing traits of effective teachers and learners in their classes and pinpoint specific attributes we can develop in our own teaching. Broad categories into which we can cluster effective teaching characteristics include curriculum, lesson planning and realization, group engagement, measurement of individual outcomes, and student motivation. We will explore these using examples from actual classes and examine specific strategies teachers use effectively with various groups.

### *Curriculum*

A well-designed music curriculum organizes and sequences musical experiences so students will develop understanding and performance skills (Colwell, 2011). Effective group teachers create and provide a curriculum of comprehensive musicianship from beginning through advanced levels. Further, they have clear, well-articulated, long-term goals for the anticipated progress of the group for the entire year (ordinarily two semesters). Then they divide each of these goals into manageable weekly objectives and have benchmarks against which they can measure the results. They choose a method and ancillary materials that will allow them to accomplish their objectives and spiral the curriculum so students have opportunities to construct their own meaning or understanding and to elaborate and expand upon previously learned musical concepts. Good musical technique and pedagogically appropriate repertoire are at the heart of this curriculum.

Comprehensive musicianship implies that students are doing more than just learning specific pieces each week. Rather, through their individual work at home and their group activities during class, they are developing technique, sight reading, aural abilities, harmonization, improvisation, and other essential musicianship skills. Then they transfer these skills to new musical learning and situations. Thus, teachers must clearly articulate end goals for the students and work backward to figure out how to create a curriculum and learning activities that will develop the necessary skill sets. As we saw in Chapter 9, teachers in public K–12 schools have national standards and guidelines for what children should be able to do at each grade level. In college music classes, group-piano teachers have a set of loosely agreed-upon competencies that all music majors must meet at the piano (see Chapter 5 for specifics). However, since independent studio teachers and group teachers of non-music major adults do not have an overarching set of national standards to which they must adhere, there is more autonomy and flexibility. However, as we see with beginning students learning to improvise, sometimes too few guidelines can lead to incoherent or underdeveloped curricula. The default some teachers use is to pick a method book and design the curriculum around it. This is not an unreasonable place for novice group-piano teachers to begin. However, if we choose our method book first and develop the curriculum second, we run the risk of passively accepting the musical and curricular goals of the book's author(s). Since few method books are as comprehensive as we might like for the group-piano class, I encourage all novice group-piano teachers to write down their broad curricular goals first then choose the method books that will provide the most tools and exercises to help the students achieve those goals.

Since this can seem like a daunting task, I recommend taking the broad categories of musical skills and concepts (such as sight reading, aural skills, technique, harmonization/improvisation, theory, and specific musical goals that would be displayed through performance) and setting reasonable goals for each of these for the end of the semester. For example, one technical skill I might want a beginning group of middle-aged adults to be able to do by the end of the semester includes primary chord progressions. Let's assume that by the end of the 14-week semester, I want them to be able to perform melodies with block or broken primary-chord accompaniments in the keys of C, G, D, and F. This competency includes both declarative and procedural knowledge. In this case, declarative knowledge includes basic theoretical understanding of primary chords and recognizing which chords are appropriate for a given melody. The procedural knowledge includes being able to perform the primary chords in any of these keys, being able to read and play the melody, and finally, the ability to perform the specific example with the correct left-hand chords and accompaniment pattern. In order to help students develop the requisite skills, I would look at how the written theory, technique, sight reading, harmonization, improvisation, and repertoire chosen for each class and weekly practice assignments support the development of that goal throughout the semester. I begin by outlining the correct sequence of activities that will help students learn and increase understanding and technical abilities, from the first class through the last class of the semester. Then, after consulting the method book chosen for the course, I usually find (or create) supplemental activities to support the motor skill acquisition and development. We will discuss how to create meaningful lesson plans that include these activities in the next section.

While piano performance should be at the center of the curriculum, teachers need to accommodate the age or developmental stage of each group by choosing appropriate materials, activities, and teaching strategies. Thus, while the musical outcomes might be similar for a beginning group of 20-year-olds and another group of 6-year-olds, the curricular design would be different for each group. Using the harmonization exercise as an example, most 6-year-olds cannot develop the manual dexterity to form a full three-note-chord within one hand by the end of the semester, so unlike the adults, I might only ask for a single-note tonic or dominant (or a harmonic fifth and sixth if the students are a little older) to harmonize the melody. See Figure 11.1 for examples of how different age groups might be expected to harmonize the same melody by the end of a semester.

Developing such a detailed and structured curriculum takes an inordinate amount of time and work. Teachers who are new to the group-piano format should not underestimate the preparation time required. Even master group-piano teachers who have taught successfully for decades report spending a lot of time planning curricula and preparing for individual lessons.

### *Lesson Planning and Realization*

Incorporating various activities and exercises takes thoughtful planning. While our piano method books tend to be sequenced superbly, do not assume that you can just turn the page and the students will be able to achieve competent performance without intermediary learning activities. Students should not move haphazardly from one activity to the next. Rather, each activity should set the student up for success by being scaffolded onto already known concepts and skills. Additionally, exceptional

# Camptown Races

Traditional

*Figure 11.1* Examples of Appropriate Harmonization Exercises by Age-Group and Motor-Skill Development

group-piano teachers tend to consider the individuals and the dynamic of each group when planning weekly lessons. Personally, although I now have a general set of lesson plans for each age group of beginning students I teach (developed through extensive self-observation, feedback, and "tweaking"), I still modify the specific activities and consider how I will partner or group students for exercises within each lesson so that they achieve success.

The sequence of activities in the lesson should flow logically from one activity or musical example to the next without the students feeling as though one segment of the class has ended and now they are moving on to something different. For example, let's imagine that I want to introduce a new rhythm to my group of 7-year-olds. Note that they know each of the individual note values that they will encounter; they will just experience them in a new rhythmic pattern. At the start of class, I may gather a group of second-semester, beginning 7-year-olds around the white board to march and learn a new chant by rote. After we have learned the chant, we try to clap the rhythm of the chant while marching to the beat. Once I see that they have performed it successfully, I invite each student to notate a measure of the rhythm of the chant on the board. (Note: My chant has been chosen because it will lead to the next activity, but it must be long enough to give all students an opportunity to notate the rhythm.) As students write, everyone is encouraged to check the work for accuracy, and we might review the chant periodically to ensure that we are recalling it accurately. Once we have the rhythm notated, we clap and chant again, this time marching in place and following the notation (I point to the notes on the board as we chant and clap). Then I might circle a specific two-measure motive on the board and ask them to clap this isolated rhythm. I suggest that they memorize the rhythmic pattern because they will need to identify it in a new piece in a moment. Then I give them 30 seconds to quickly walk to their pianos, put on their headphones, and find the rhythmic example. Once they have found it, they may circle it. I give them another 30 seconds to try to locate the pitches on their keyboards and to play it on their own. Then I pair them up, and they compare performances for both rhythmic and pitch accuracy. Finally, together over headphones (with me playing the model and each student listening to himself or herself on headphones), we sight read the entire phrase.

I would never ask students to quickly find the pitches if they hadn't previously demonstrated that they could locate their hand positions and starting notes. Everything I did prior to moving to the piano was to help them experience the rhythm. First, they marched to the big beat then chanted the rhythm while marching. This was followed by clapping and chanting to the beat, then trying to identify and write the symbols that we use to notate the rhythm. They experienced the rhythm through their bodily movements first, they clapped it (sound before sight), then they notated it, before identifying and performing it to specific pitches in a new piece. The entire string of activities was sequenced for student success and allowed the students to make meaning of the rhythm through kinesthetic, aural, and visual modes. The entire learning experience only lasted about 6 minutes. I didn't waste time with lengthy explanations; rather, I modeled and they copied, and because the activity was sequenced well, they remained on task and succeeded at each step in the process. The lesson plan for the class from which this segment was excerpted is shown in Figure 11.2. Video segments of appropriate sequencing with a beginning children's class are available online (www.pameladpike.com).

Pacing is usually appropriate for each group when effective teachers begin the class by introducing the most important concept for the day. Then they lead students through discovery activities in which they master small components of the concept and immediately apply them to the next musical puzzle, building upon prior knowledge. Good teachers know that students tend to focus (and remember) best at the

**Concept:** quarter notes and half notes
**6-Minute Teaching Segment with 7-year-olds:**
Experience rhythmic patterns through: chanting; movement; clapping; notation; recognition/identification; playing
**Book:** Music Tree: Time to Begin by Clark, Goss, & Holland

| Book & Page/Activity | Plan | Assessment/Objectives Met |
|---|---|---|
| p. 12 – *New Kite* chant | Entire Group:<br>• demonstrate chant by rote<br>• have group move and chant in circle<br>• have group march & clap with chant | • all will chant correctly<br>• all will clap correctly<br><br>• students feel pulse while chanting & clapping |
| Notation of chant | Entire Group:<br>• invite students to write one measure each (2-3 notes/person) one whiteboard<br>• others evaluate & correct work | • students notate correctly<br><br>• students catch mistakes |
| • Clap notated rhythm<br>• Identify patterns of quarter and half note groupings | Entire Group:<br>• Everyone claps & chants<br>• Circle 2 rhythmic groupings<br>• Challenge: go to pianos & find those patterns on p. 6 & circle each | • all clap correctly<br><br>• students quickly move to pianos & correctly identify patterns |
| p. 6 – *In a Canoe* | Individuals/Pairs:<br>• Find hand position & play on own<br>• In Pairs: play for each other & compare (correct mistakes); move lower on keyboard<br>• Entire Group: Play over headphones (I demo correct model with them as they play) | • students find correct hand positions<br>• students perform for each other and evaluate correctly<br><br>• students follow my example & relaxed technique (large-arm movements)<br>• students play correctly |

*Figure 11.2* Sample Lesson Segment Reinforcing Rhythmic Patterns and Pulse through Various Activities

beginning of class. After initial priming activities or brief review of concepts that were practiced throughout the week, effective teachers dive into the most challenging material first. But they break it down so students achieve success along the way. When you observe classes with effective teachers, students remain engaged and on task, in part because they are experiencing success, but also because the pacing is appropriate. Many teachers teach in 20-minute segments with a 10-minute focused activity, a complementary 3-minute downtime or movement activity, and then a 7-minute focused segment again. Young children cannot focus for as long as older children (or most adults). A good rule of thumb is that children can usually focus for the same number of minutes as their age. Be sure to consider this when working with 5-year-old beginners!

One final note about pacing pertains to transfer of learning and skills. Successful group teachers ensure that students have mastered a small concept before introducing the next step. As students meet with success, they are encouraged to apply the concept in various contexts. This keeps them engaged as the level of difficulty gradually increases but maintains their focus as they meet with success and the activities integrate seamlessly from one to the next. Teachers may have up to 11 activities from which they can choose to reinforce new ideas including technique, harmonization, transposition, improvisation/composition, sight reading, aural skills, score preparation, solo repertoire, ensemble repertoire, theory, and games (Pike, 2013). While teachers do not use all of the activities at each class, they do cycle through many of these regularly throughout the semester. Because group classes tend to be longer than private lessons, they can explore more material each week.

Good teachers know what the students must master during the instructional period in order to successfully complete the assignment and ensure that they have experienced success before they leave the class. Rather than trying to cover too many concepts or pieces at a surface level, they have students work deeply with these skills. Generally, students who have worked together and who have discovered concepts for themselves (with guidance) are empowered and successfully practice throughout the week on their own.

Due to the need for student success to be experienced, effective group-piano instructors create detailed lesson plans, and they ensure that every activity addresses the concepts and skills that are the focus of that class. While they are willing and able to deviate from the plan as needed, they know what students must accomplish and set them up to attain the weekly objectives. Stated simply, clear goals and objectives for the curriculum translate into specific objectives for each class. I list my main objectives for the class at the top of each lesson plan. I know that regardless of how the class unfolds, students need to demonstrate understanding of these objectives if they are to be successful practicing on their own at home. Then if I modify my plan, I know that the students will still be able to practice effectively throughout the week.

## *Group Engagement*

Good group-piano teachers engage students in group work for the majority of the lesson time. Even if they are working on solo repertoire, they include the other students (or small groups of students over headphones) in the evaluation and problem-solving process rather than simply spending time with individuals while the other pupils also work individually. If individuals spend time working alone during class, usually they are involved in some sort of quick preparation that will subsequently be used for a small-group activity in which group success depends on preparation of each student.

Group engagement throughout the class serves several purposes. First, it permits students to learn with and from one another. They make meaning of new material together, thereby constructing meaning collectively. This is a much more effective teaching strategy than simply telling students what to do and tends to lead to greater understanding over time. Second, if each student has a role to play in the activity, they are more likely to remain on task and focused throughout the class. Third, students become better listeners, evaluators, performers, and collaborators. Many of the components of these skills are required for problem solving, learning, and self-regulation when practicing at home. Finally, when each person is responsible for the group outcome, it keeps individuals motivated to focus, practice, and learn. Many students find working together to be inherently more enjoyable than working alone, which also improves motivation and learning. They usually spend 6 days practicing alone at home, so they look forward to the opportunity to engage in group work during the piano class. When performing ensemble music, the final product is more musically satisfying than anything the students would be able to achieve individually. Being able to explore music and concepts together with others in the group setting provides balance between solo homework and in-class group work. Performing with others also takes some of the spotlight off of individuals; many students appreciate this when playing for audiences.

## *Measurement of Individual Outcomes*

Although the students do much work together, effective group teachers are keenly aware of the individual progress and learning outcomes of each student in the class. Although the lesson generally moves at the pace of the average student in the class, group activities are tailored to involve faster and slower learners, making the most of their abilities and giving them opportunities to excel. Effective group teachers do not include games or activities just for the sake of entertaining the students. Rather, each endeavor undertaken during class is purposefully chosen to facilitate and improve student understanding, skill, and knowledge. Activities may be enjoyable and engaging, but the educational purpose and learning outcome for each student in the group has been considered before the task was chosen for inclusion in the lesson. As we noted in Chapter 3, in order for group work to be effective, students must be held accountable for both individual and group work (Cohen & Lotan, 2014). In K–12 and classes for college credit, there is formal assessment. The majority of these assessments are of individual work, but group work can be included in the final grade. For example, while my students engage in group work in every class, the majority of their grade is derived from individual performance assessments. However, I assign about 15% of the group-piano course grade to collaborative assignments in which success depends upon the students working together, even if they are still graded individually.

In private studios or recreational classes, where formal assessment is less likely to occur, outstanding group-piano teachers are keenly aware of how each individual is performing, and individual outcomes are assessed informally during class in order to know when students can move from one activity to the next. Some group-piano teachers choose to have students perform solos in recitals and festivals, and their individual performance preparation is incorporated into the group work during class time. At the beginning stages, I like to have students perform ensemble music only at recitals, but they are still encouraged to perform repertoire for one another and engage in reflective evaluation during class. See Appendix A.1, A.2, or A.3 for sample assessment pages that children at various ages can use when first learning to listen to and evaluate peer performances. In classes in which outstanding group-piano teachers are guiding students, I have noticed an interesting (and perhaps unexpected) effect of group work. Although the majority of the in-class activities are undertaken by the entire or small subgroup, the students display individual understanding and learning. That is, when students engage in musical activities together and help one another, they assimilate the information in meaningful ways and believe in their individual ability to learn music. High levels of self-efficacy among individuals within the group are particularly striking during the beginning stages of group-piano study, whereas students in traditional private lessons learn to rely on their teacher to teach them directly and tend not to develop independent problem-solving or self-regulation skills until they become more advanced.

### Student Motivation

We mentioned motivation under the "group engagement" heading. From a basic human psychology standpoint, when we must prepare our portion of the work thoroughly in order for the group to succeed, we tend to practice better. My experience has not been that individuals depend on others for their learning to occur but that they rise to the occasion so they can succeed alongside of their peers. Initially, teachers may need to facilitate group work and encourage all students to engage with the group through structured activities, but students quickly learn about the in-class expectations and responsibility to the group. The adage "success breeds success" has been quoted in numerous educational and popular-level articles about motivation and learning. As this catchy saying suggests, good group-piano teachers know that if we set up our students to experience success with one task and they attribute their success to specific steps they took during the learning process, they will believe they can be successful at a related activity (Sousa, 2006). When students attain the objectives set in class, because they have applied their knowledge and skill, they become empowered to continue problem solving and thus develop their skills even more.

Carol Dweck (2008) has referred to attribution of success due to effort as a growth mindset rather than a fixed mindset. Many people in the general population assume musicians possess some sort of supernatural talent rather than having honed skills through years of disciplined practice. Attributing success to an inborn ability contributes to a fixed mindset, which can discourage and demotivate students when they must persevere through challenging learning tasks, such as developing piano skills. Astute group-piano teachers help students develop a growth mindset that leads to success and motivation. During class, they praise students for their efforts throughout the process of learning and encourage them to enjoy musical challenges. The stakes of each task are relatively low. In other words, if students fail at the task initially, all is not lost, and they will be encouraged to try to solve the problem again in new ways with their peers (Duckworth, 2016). For example, a solo performance in a recital or at the end of class time should not be the first time a student has an opportunity to succeed or fail with that musical task. Such a goal is likely too big and the stakes too high. However, some of the most inspiring group-piano teachers I have observed have fostered an environment in which the group thrives on the musical tasks that require effort to solve. I've watched groups enjoy the process of experimenting with ways to solve the musical challenges and seem undaunted by the task. These teachers help students attribute their success to the effort that they put into the task. Thus, all students experience and recognize that mastering the piano takes purposeful practice, not a magical ability called talent.

## Conclusions

In this chapter, we have explored attributes of successful group-piano teachers. While something as complicated as teaching human beings cannot be easily broken down into discrete components, there are some common features of effective group-piano instructors. First, they take time to develop a comprehensive music curriculum. Then they create lesson plans that will permit students to explore making music at the piano through appropriate pacing, sequencing, and reinforcement of concepts. Then effective teachers engage students in valuable group work and musical activities but also remain cognizant of individual learning outcomes within the context of the larger group. Finally, through group work and reinforcement of appropriate attributions, excellent group-piano teachers foster an environment in which students are motivated to support each other and to work intelligently to achieve success, both within the group and individually.

With the exception of group work, I would argue that all of the skills exhibited by exceptional group-piano teachers are the same as those employed by outstanding individual instructors. The difference is that in a group setting, one cannot slide by with subpar curriculum design, lesson planning, preparation and realization, group engagement, assessment of individual outcomes, or strategies that increase students' intrinsic motivation and self-efficacy. Without planning for all of these elements, students in the group setting may not develop musical skills and performance abilities.

## Pedagogy in Action

1. Explore some of the references and resources from this chapter. Choose one topic (i.e., developing intrinsic motivation, assessing performance outcomes, developing a growth mindset, encouraging grit and perseverance) and read several sources related to it. Then list 10 concrete steps or actions you could make in your group-piano classes to increase student learning and outcomes related to your topic.

2. Choose a musical skill or component noted in this chapter (i.e., a specific technical skill, sight reading, harmonization, or improvisation) and create a timeline for how you would have students develop and reinforce this skill over a 14-week period.

3. Take your musical skill from #2 (or choose a different musical skill) and create a 10-minute sequence of activities that would help students develop this skill during a group-piano class. Decide upon the age and level of your students and the desired learning outcomes before deciding upon activities. List age, level, and outcome on your page, then describe the sequence of activities.

4. Observe a group-piano teacher in your community. Using an appropriate group-teaching evaluation form (Appendix E.1, E.2, or E.3), make a list of the top five best teaching strategies or practices you observed and briefly discuss how you could implement each of these in your own group teaching. Following the observation and evaluation, discuss your observations with a peer or pedagogy teacher if you have the opportunity.

## References and Teacher Resources

### Books and Articles

Cohen, E. G., & Lotan, R. A. (2014). *Designing Groupwork: Strategies for the Heterogeneous Classroom*, 3rd edition. New York: Teacher's College Press.

Colwell, R. (2011). "Direct Instruction, Critical Thinking, and Transfer." In R. Colwell, & P. R. Webster (Eds.). *MENC Handbook of Research on Music Learning*, Volume 1: *Strategies* (pp. 84–139). New York: Oxford University Press.

Duckworth, A. L. (2016). *Grit: The Power of Passion and Perseverance*. New York: Scribner.

Dweck, C. S. (2008). *Mindset: The New Psychology of Success*. New York: Ballantine Books.

Pike, P. D. (2013). Profiles in Successful Group Piano for Children: A Collective Case Study of Children's Group-Piano Lessons. *Music Education Research*, *15*(1), 92–106.

Sousa, D. A. (2006). *How the Brain Learns*, 3rd edition. Thousand Oaks, CA: Corwin Press.

## *TED Talks Online*

Grit (persistence) by Angela Duckworth (2016): https://www.ted.com/talks/angela_lee_duckworth_the_key_to_success_grit?language=en

The Growth Mindset by Carol Dweck (2008): http://www.ted.com/talks/carol_dweck_the_power_of_believing_that_you_can_improve

## *Video Segments of Concept Sequencing with a Beginning Children's Class*

www.pameladpike.com

# 12

# COMMON PITFALLS OF BEGINNING GROUP-PIANO INSTRUCTORS AND HOW TO AVOID THESE MISTAKES

## Objectives

By the end of this chapter, you should be able to list common pitfalls encountered by group-piano teachers and have strategies to prevent these common mistakes.

## Introduction

Many teachers did not have the opportunity to participate in high-quality group-piano classes during their formal education. Others did not consider teaching piano in groups until they were removed from educational settings. As a result, these teachers often make common mistakes when they first start teaching group piano. Unfortunately, these mistakes can lead to ineffective teaching and learning, which can result in student attrition, teacher burnout, or complete abandonment of group teaching altogether. Since there is a considerable up-front investment in teaching space and technology required for a group-piano studio, it would be beneficial for novice teachers to be aware of and prevent some of the more common group-teaching pitfalls. In this chapter, we will explore common difficulties experienced by beginning group-piano teachers and suggest ways to avoid falling into these traps.

## Policy and Procedural Issues

Several of the problems that surface in classes taught by novice group-piano teachers result from ineffective or unenforced policy and procedures within the studio.

### *Lesson Scheduling and Length of Term*

Scheduling the wrong amount of time for classes or the incorrect number of classes within a semester can result in an inability to achieve stated goals and trouble attaining appropriate student outcomes. Generally, group classes will be longer than the typical private lesson. However, consider the age of the students with whom you will be working. If you schedule an hour-long piano class for a group of beginning

6-year-olds, you are likely to discover that regardless of how many activities you plan, you will not be able to keep them engaged for the entire time. For average-aged beginning children and novice teachers, a 40- to 45-minute class is a good starting point. As children get older and become more technically advanced, group teachers typically offer 60- to 90-minute classes.

Beginning adult classes tend to last from 50 to 60 minutes, in part because the attention span of adults is longer than that of children. However, you will still need to remain cognizant of keeping each adult student's attention throughout the instructional period. Refer to Chapters 2, 4, and 11 for tips on pacing and keeping students engaged during class. As adult groups advance or spend more time working on ensemble repertoire, it is not uncommon for instructional periods to last for 2 hours (with short breaks and changes in activity). There is more information about scheduling group classes in Chapter 14.

Another benefit of group teaching, often referenced in texts, is that students progress more quickly than they might in private lessons. However, this does not necessarily mean that you can plan on offering shorter semesters. If you do choose to have abbreviated semesters or short, week-long piano camps, expect to adapt your learning goals and outcomes accordingly. Teachers sometimes offer an abbreviated semester to introduce beginners to the piano and to provide them with an opportunity to discover if they would like to continue with lessons. Experienced group-piano teachers set appropriate learning objectives and tailor the curriculum for such classes. I have observed numerous novice teachers offering such experiences in which the curriculum and materials did not match the stated goals. Even if students cannot articulate why such classes don't work, they recognize that the learning experience does not live up to its potential, and often these students do not continue with lessons.

The final issue with scheduling has to do with finding enough students to make the class feasible. When teachers first begin or switch to the group format, they may have trouble finding enough students at the same level who are available at any given time to participate. As a result, it can be tempting to place multiple levels in one group or to not do student placements to ensure that everyone is at the same level. I have taught at community schools in which a director or coordinator scheduled the groups, and I had to make the best of it when students clearly were not operating at the same level (developmental or musical/technical). This situation is not ideal, and even experienced group-piano teachers have trouble creating effective learning situations for all of the students in this environment.

Novice group-piano teachers should avoid such situations. It is hard enough when we first begin teaching group piano to design effective lesson plans, monitor pacing and student learning, and keep all students on task—even when all students are equally matched. The task becomes almost impossible if students are not grouped appropriately. I believe that it is better to have small groups of well-matched students when you first start teaching group piano (and teach more classes each week) than to have fewer teaching hours (i.e., fewer classes) of mismatched students. You may earn less income initially, but the positive teaching experiences will allow you to become a better group-piano teacher, and in the long run, you will have the potential to earn more income, be a better teacher, and have more satisfied, competent, and returning students.

### *Unclear or Unstated Expectations for Students and Families*

Because you will be expecting students to work independently during the week and together during class in order to accomplish objectives, you will need to clearly communicate your expectations for students and families prior to the first class. You may find that you need to reiterate and reinforce these expectations periodically throughout the semester. Many times when I have observed group-piano classes in which novice teachers struggle to maintain student attention and focus, the trouble stems from not setting ground rules from the outset (Pike, 2014). If you expect students to arrive on time, not miss classes, and prepare practice assignments so they will be able to complete in-class and group activities, they must be made aware of their responsibilities before the class starts.

In children's classes, parents must assume some of the responsibility for ensuring that their children attend class regularly and arrive prepared to participate. You must enforce these expectations. If children are frequently absent, they can delay the progress of the group or not assimilate within the larger group. Speaking with parents outside of class to find ways to prevent absences and tardiness is imperative. Find ways to make your families partners in the learning process. Additionally, there must be ground rules for participation during class. If students exhibit disruptive behavior, teachers need to patiently but vigorously stop the inappropriate behavior. Often, when students exhibit poor behavior during class, it is because they are not engaged, do not understand the task, the activity is too hard or too easy, or the time allotted for the activity is too long. Teachers will need to thoughtfully reengage a disruptive student as soon as possible. After exploring and modifying the learning environment, if the child is not able to follow the rules, he or she may need to switch from a group-piano class to a private lesson in which the full attention of the teacher can be given to that student for the entire time.

If you teach a college class, ground rules should be outlined in the class syllabus. If you expect students (and you should) to prepare practice assignments prior to coming to class, then testing them on exercises from the assignment and having them engage in group work should begin at the second class. Our students learn a lot about what we expect of them based on what we do during class. If students do not practice and you regularly give them time to practice in class, they soon learn that they do not have to prepare outside of class time. If you ask a question and immediately provide an answer, they learn that they do not have to think about or give an answer.

Be thoughtful about what you expect of your students, and be consistent in reinforcing those expectations for the duration of the semester.

## Curricular Issues

### *Inappropriate Methods and Materials*

Even once the scheduling issues have been figured out, I believe that the biggest source of teacher and student dissatisfaction with group-piano arises from choosing and using inappropriate methods and materials. I would recommend revisiting Section II of this book to locate the chapters that deal with method and materials that work with specific age groups and situations. Then take time to carefully consider and evaluate the materials and supplements that you will use with each of your groups. When children are not captivated by the materials or able to accomplish performances of the music, they lose focus, motivation, and self-control, both in and out of class. When adults do not find the materials or music engaging, they are more likely to discontinue lessons or look for another teacher.

### *Lack of Specific Long-Term Goals and Objectives*

We explored the need for defining clear short-term objectives and long-term goals for group-piano classes in Chapter 11. Novice group-piano teachers who have trouble designing curriculum or individual lesson plans or maintaining student attention during class often lack clear goals and objectives. Each and every activity during class and assigned for at-home practice must contribute in a clear and measurable way to the weekly objectives and, ultimately, to the long-term goals that the teacher has set. If teachers remember that objectives for each class should be well defined, possible within the time-frame allotted, and measurable, planning curriculum, lessons, and activities becomes more focused and sustainable. If students are not meeting these objectives, teachers should pivot to another teaching strategy and reflect upon how the next lesson can be improved.

### *Inadequate Reinforcement*

As we have noted throughout this book, providing ample opportunities for reinforcement is essential for effective student learning. Rarely do methods provide ample examples or enough different ways for students to experience musical concepts. This is not a critique of method books. Rather, teachers will know much more about the types of activities, music, and materials that should help their specific students learn effectively. However, novice group-piano teachers sometimes forget to include varied activities or additional music that would provide students with opportunities to experience concepts in numerous ways. As a result, some of the weaker students or those who learn differently from the majority of the group members sometimes do not achieve mastery of a concept. Even those students who do exhibit adequate procedural knowledge may still benefit from additional and varied experiences. Recall that knowing is not the same as understanding. Any time we provide students with opportunities to apply knowledge in many contexts, elaborate upon their skills, and demonstrate their understanding in novel ways, we are offering them a chance to make the musical concepts personally meaningful and applicable to future situations.

## Teaching Difficulties, Issues, and Assessment Concerns

In a large study that looked at preservice and experienced teachers' beliefs about the importance of musical, personal, and teaching skills (Teachout, 1997), experienced teachers ranked two musical skills (maximizing time on task and maintaining student behavior) and two personal skills (being enthusiastic and being patient) much higher than novice teachers did. It was noted that music education programs do a good job of preparing young teachers for initial success when they begin teaching. Piano pedagogy classes familiarize students with methods and materials they will use when teaching privately. Good programs provide supervised teaching experiences in which students receive feedback. However, many schools are not equipped to offer students the opportunity to practice teaching piano in groups. Additionally, many undergraduate piano majors do not realize that group teaching is a viable option; thus, they do not avail of opportunities to learn about or develop effective teaching techniques for group piano during their formal education.

Good teaching is good teaching, regardless of the environment. However, many teachers who have not developed strong teaching skills in private lessons struggle to maintain student attention, focus, and motivation during group instruction. Expert teachers set up specific tasks for students, provide precise and concise explanations, ask questions that require thoughtful responses, listen to student performances and responses, and provide immediate and specific feedback to students. In music education, this is known as a complete pattern or sequence of direct instruction. It has been shown that expert teachers complete more of these teaching sequences than teaching interns or novice teachers, and they place more emphasis on expressive performance during rehearsals (Goolsby, 1997). In private piano lessons, more effective teachers model and provide more feedback to students, and the pace of the lesson moves faster, often with students performing shorter segments of music but receiving precise and immediate feedback (Siebenaler, 1997). In group-piano settings, keeping students engaged in specific tasks and encouraging them to become involved in evaluation will maintain attentiveness.

The remaining pitfalls are related to teaching techniques and assessment. One of the biggest issues for novice group-piano teachers is that they teach the group much as they would a private lesson. They tend to lecture, be unclear or inconcise, or diverge from the immediate task, and not engage students in enough discovery learning. We will look at several common issues briefly.

### Telling, Not Teaching

Frances Clark used to say, "telling is not teaching." Unfortunately, new group-piano teachers fall into the trap of lecturing or of telling students everything they need to know rather than leading them to discover concepts and ideas on their own. This happens sometimes when the teacher teaches as she would in a private lesson, where she gets individual feedback from the student. Teachers often continue to teach in the same way, but the individual feedback is difficult to discern in the group-piano setting, so they are not flexible in adapting to students' needs.

### Pacing, Flexibility, and Wasted Time

Unfortunately, when teachers are lecturing, students' attention will wander, and they become disengaged. If tasks are too hard, too easy, or not specific enough, they will move off task. If the pacing is too slow, students will divert to off-task and potentially disruptive behaviors. Teachers should plan how they will switch from one activity to the next so that there are no opportunities for students to lag behind or waste time. If students understand what is expected of them and know they have a limited amount of time to accomplish the goal, they will stay focused until it is complete.

If teachers watch videos of their classes, they should note the number of total minutes when they talked and the number of total minutes in which students were playing or engaged in musical activities. Teachers may even notice students engaged in off-task behavior on the video that may have gone unnoticed during the actual class. Too much talking and off-task behavior creates a less-than-optimal learning environment. When observing your teaching video, look for activities that were too hard or too easy, for nonspecific instruction and feedback, or for other cues that lead to poor use of class time and work to prevent these problems at future classes. (See Appendix E.4 and E.5 for self-evaluation forms.)

### Too Few Group Activities and Little Serious Learning or Musicianship

A group-piano setting provides a unique opportunity for students to work and learn together. Therefore, it should not look like a private piano lesson. Students should not spend excessive amounts of time working individually over headphones. They should be exploring concepts in diverse ways and engaging in group music making. Teachers need to have contingencies for keeping everyone involved in the activity. For example, if a student masters a concept well before her classmate, the teacher should give her a specific but related task to keep her working on the problem. It might involve helping a peer. Depending on your goals and learning outcomes, students of like abilities can be partnered for an activity, or students of varying abilities can work together on a task, provided they each understand their specific roles. Likewise, if a student lags behind, the teacher should find ways to simplify the task so that he can continue to work with the group.

Ensemble music, with parts of varying technical levels, is particularly effective at engaging all students in listening to each other, responding to one another, and evaluating the overall expressiveness while participating at their own skill and comfort levels. For each of the activities during class, teachers should plan contingencies to accommodate different learning styles, preferred learning modes, and individual variability.

Novice teachers sometimes do not avail of technology and materials to full effect. Often, technology in the piano lab can facilitate group work, evaluation, and feedback. Students can work in small groups over headphones. They can record their performance, listen to and evaluate it, and then suggest ways to help one another improve. Using different MIDI sounds can promote accurate articulation. Nontechnological materials such as rhythm instruments, flashcards, games, and ensembles can be created to elaborate upon skills and generate new ideas. Group piano should engage students in activities that could not occur during typical private piano lessons.

Some new teachers want students to have fun during class and resort to providing too few serious learning or musicianship opportunities. After several classes, the result is usually opposite the teacher's intention. Students who are not engaged in serious learning and who are not stretched to become better musicians often become demotivated, do not practice or seek to improve piano skills, and even exhibit poor behavior during class. Learning can be fun and engaging, even if it requires some effort. The group-piano setting is a wonderful place for students to discover and develop musical and general learning techniques that can be applied to other areas of life.

### Classroom Management

Classroom management can be one of the most difficult tasks facing a young, inexperienced group-piano teacher. Teaching a group-piano class requires personal traits such as leadership skills, maturity, confidence, and organization. Teaching skills include setting expectations and maintaining appropriate student behavior, maximizing time on task, motivating students, maintaining positivity, and involving students in the learning process, preferably through discovery. Musical skills instructors must demonstrate proper piano technique, musicality, singing, movement, and aural skills. Feedback about musicality and technique should be immediate and precise so students can improve. Being less absorbed in one's lesson plan and more focused on the students' actions and musical expression contributes to class management. Every student deserves a safe, secure learning environment. The teacher is responsible for getting all students to follow her lead, engage in all activities, and become the best musicians possible.

## *Individual and Group Assessment*

Many of the issues outlined here are rooted in the fact that teachers are not assessing individual competency accurately. Beware of simply having students do activities and assessing their enjoyment rather than skill level. Your expectations also have a great impact on students. If they receive general praise or compliments for substandard work, students quickly learn that they do not have to give their best effort, and they gradually lose motivation to improve. Much off-task behavior occurs when students are not challenged enough or if the challenge is perceived as being too great. Therefore, teachers need to know what each individual is capable of (at any given time, with any given discrete musical skill) and set up the learning tasks appropriately. When working on ensemble music or even individual solos, accurate assessment of musical performance and precise feedback is imperative. If you provide good feedback, your students will learn from your example and become better listeners and better learning partners for their peers.

## Final Thoughts and Ideas

While there are any number of mistakes that we can make when we begin teaching group piano, I have tried to highlight some of the more common pitfalls and actions that can be taken to avoid them. By carefully planning and strategizing before teaching your first class, you will avoid some of these problems. Yet regardless of how much you prepare, as with any new learning or endeavor, there will be setbacks along the way. The first step is to identify your particular challenges. Remember that you will not be able to fix all problems in your teaching immediately. Rather, identify the top three issues and set clear objectives for how you will fix each. Work on one problem at a time, but be persistent and deliberate as you work to change your teaching behaviors. I recommend videoing your teaching and taking notes as you watch the video soon after the class (see Appendix E.4 and E.5 for evaluation forms). Then you will be able to identify and work toward fixing perceived teaching concerns.

Some novice teachers find watching their videos to be discouraging at first, as they notice student and teacher behaviors that had gone undetected while teaching. However, many of us frame such video evidence as empowering and recognize how valuable videographic evidence can be—it can lead us to clarify problems and help us to improve our teaching technique. Before you video your teaching, however, you should obtain written consent from the students and their parents (if the students are minors). Even if you are only using the video for your own professional development, obtaining student/parental consent and child assent is a professionally responsible action. A sample consent form can be found at the MTNA web site: http://www. mtna.org/media/24961/videoauthorization.pdf.

If you are fortunate to live close to a college or university where group demonstration classes take place, you might consider enrolling for continuing education or certification credit. When you have the opportunity, observe master group-piano teachers in person or on video. Use the group-teaching evaluation form to assess the teaching and learning, and be sure to list your takeaways: what do you wish to improve, what will you work on, and how will you go about making these improvements? Be specific in your self-feedback and in your observation of others and work gradually and persistently on your stated goals. With time, practice, and reflection, your group-piano teaching will improve.

## Pedagogy in Action

1. Imagine that you are about to start teaching a class of beginning 7-year-old students. You have completed interviews with each student, and you believe that they will be capable of working together and learning piano in the group setting. Compose a one-page handout you will give students to take home following the interview that outlines expectations for members of the group (and their parents). Think of this handout as preparation for the norming stage (see Chapter 3); it should establish the guidelines for participation in the group-piano class. You might call this policy page "rules of engagement" or create a clever title that will capture your students' attention and encourage them to embrace proper group participation.

2. Create a similar one-page set of guidelines for a beginning group of 30-year-old students who have registered for your piano class. This class is not for credit.

3. Share your "rules of engagement" with a classmate and discuss similarities and differences in your policies. Be sure to assess whether your statements were age appropriate, were clear enough, and didn't come across as too negative. Be sure to adapt your policy page if you discovered some good ideas from your colleagues!

4. Observe a group-piano teacher in your community. Use an appropriate group-teaching evaluation form from Appendix E.1, E.2, or E.3. Without being overly negative, note one strategy that you observed that might not have had the intended effect during the instructional period. Briefly discuss what you think the teacher was trying to accomplish and why it might not have worked and give one possible option you think might have worked in this instance (and explain why). Following the observation and evaluation, discuss your observations with a peer or pedagogy teacher to flesh out your observations and ideas.

# References

Goolsby, T. W. (1997). Verbal Instructions in Instrumental Rehearsals: A Comparison of Three Career Levels and Preservice Teachers. *Journal of Research in Music Education, 45*(1), 21–40. doi: 10.2307/3345463

Pike, P. D. (2014). The Differences between Novice and Expert Group-Piano Teaching Strategies: A Case Study and Comparison of Beginning Group-Piano Classes. *International Journal of Music Education, 32*(2), 213–227. doi: 10.1177/0255761413508065

Siebenaler, D. J. (1997). Analysis of Student-Teacher Interactions in the Piano Lessons of Adults and Children. *Journal of Research in Music Education, 45*(1), 6–20. doi: 10.2307/3345462

Teachout, D. J. (1997). Preservice and Experienced Teachers' Opinions of Skills and Behaviors Important to Successful Music Teaching. *Journal of Research in Music Education, 45*(1), 41–50.

# 13

# ESTABLISHING TRUST
# WITHIN THE GROUP

## Objectives

By the end of this chapter, you should have an understanding of how to create an environment in which you can facilitate effective group work and have ideas for collaborative activities.

## Introduction

At a keynote plenary session at the 2015 National Conference on Keyboard Pedagogy, Jane Chu, the 11th chairman of the National Endowment for the Arts, reminisced about her college group-piano classes. She said, "I quickly saw that the piano classes . . . were able to bring people together socially while they simultaneously learned from each other" (Wachter, 2016, p. 32). Within the context of general music classrooms, practitioners and researchers have noted that exploring creativity and group music making is critical for helping students develop their social and musical skills, but the teacher provides a crucial learning link for the students (Burnard, 2013). Regardless of the age of the students in your piano group, if they do not believe the environment is a safe space in which they can experiment with others and succeed or fail together, effective group work will not be possible. Group work, in which students learn together and from each other, enables students to process new concepts and information more meaningfully than they typically would individually or in a teacher-centered environment.

## Teacher's Role

Learning to set up and facilitate effective group work takes preparation and practice. Initially, you may not be completely successful at assigning and facilitating group work. Following each class, reflect on what worked and what did not and persevere in your use of group activities. I have observed many novice group-piano teachers give up on group work prematurely when their initial attempts to engage the students were met with resistance or were not as effective as they might have been. I encourage instructors to record their classes and review the video before planning the next lesson. If the camera captures a wide-angle view of the room, teachers often see student behaviors or problems that went unnoticed during class. Then these issues can be addressed and prevented at the next session.

Students do not necessarily come to class equipped with the skills necessary to communicate with each other and to collaborate effectively. But they can develop these skills. The first step, I believe, occurs during the initial student interview. Among the requisite skills you are assessing during the placement is the ability of the student to follow directions and work with another person at the piano. During the interview, providing opportunities for the student to improvise or make music with you, respond correctly to rhythmic clapbacks, and execute simple playing tasks will help you to discover if he or she will be well-suited for the group. Not all students work well in a group-piano setting. Although many can learn to function within the group, the interview should serve as a chance to discover if the student will be able to function musically with others. It is better to provide an opportunity for individual instruction to students who will not be able to focus on the assigned task or who appear to need a great deal of individual attention in order to function at the piano.

The placement interview is also a time to educate the student (and his or her parents if the student is a child) about the expectations of at-home and in-class work and about what happens during classes. Most of the group activities my students engage in during class require that they have mastered the materials and skills from the weekly practice assignment. If the students do not practice, they will not be able to participate fully in the group work and may actually hold back their peers. My students take this responsibility to the group seriously and complete their weekly practice assignments, in part because this is a basic expectation for participation in the class but also because they enjoy working with their peers. Initially, many students do not know what to expect during piano classes, so the teacher's explanations can alleviate concerns or fears and create a sense of excitement about the group-piano environment.

At the very first class, teachers should be mindful of including group work in which the students can be successful. But it should be implemented from the outset so that students understand that working with others will be an expectation. With children, I like to incorporate group activities that include everyone so that I can foster cooperation and gently redirect any inappropriate behavior from the outset. At the very first class, I use music games and group "skillbuilder" activities (Cohen & Lotan, 2014) that encourage the students to communicate with each other and become comfortable expressing themselves through music. In my adult classes, I introduce partner work (over headphones) during the initial class meeting. Even though most adults have engaged in group work in other settings, their experiences and opinions of it may be varied. So I listen in to groups and give prompts over the headphones, or I walk around and provide feedback while standing next to groups. I find it essential to monitor the groups vigilantly during these first sessions, keeping individuals on task, keeping everyone engaged in the group activity, modeling appropriate verbal responses, and ensuring that the group space feels safe for each student. If students feel threatened by their peers or the teacher, they will be less likely to engage in and learn during group activities.

One of the most important benefits for piano students engaged in group work is that they share the cognitive load (thus, can process information more effectively), they learn to listen critically and assess playing, and they learn to create solutions to the problems they have identified. These are all skills essential for effective practice during the week. Offering constructive criticism is a skill that must be learned. If criticism is given thoughtlessly, it can cause some students to feel uncomfortable working with the group. Consider ways you provide feedback that is both encouraging yet honest. Then model this behavior to your students during class and help them learn to give similar feedback to their peers. In some of my classes, I engage the group in coming up with a list of acceptable phrases that we will use when pointing out errors so that we are kind and respectful of each other. I am gratified when I hear students communicating using "I feel" or "I think" statements to defuse conflict or to discuss errors that they have detected in others' playing. If a student hears a mistake, effective feedback might be, "I think that you played a dominant instead of a tonic chord in measure 4" or "I thought I heard you play an F# in measure 2, is that correct?" Such carefully worded phrases will elicit more effective communication and teamwork than bluntly saying, "You played the wrong chord in measure 4" or "Don't play F# in measure 2."

When assigning group work, it is essential that students know what the objective of the exercise is, how long they will have to work on it, how it will be assessed (or how they will know that they have completed the task successfully), and what each individual's role is within the group for creating the final product. Initially, you may need to assign specific roles to individuals, though it may be more helpful to guide a discussion among the students in which they have to figure out how to break down the project into manageable tasks and who might be best suited to each role within the group. I try to remember that from the first group activity, I am laying the foundation for future work, so I want to avoid making students dependent upon me. Anything I can do to enable student independence and facilitate effective communication and collaboration among group members expedites effective group development. Also, if the students know they have a limited amount of time to complete the group work, they can prioritize objectives and procedures to facilitate their work. This tends to create effective learning outcomes and successful group projects.

When students experience success working together, they become more resilient and eager to try increasingly complex group work. Some subgroupings of students work more effectively than others, in general, but the type of task may also have an impact upon which students will work well together. While I offered some suggested groupings based on different processing and learning styles in Chapter 4, I would recommend observing which student groups work well together within any given class and experiment with different groupings for different types of activities (i.e., sight reading, improvising, harmonizing, etc.). As students mature and become accustomed to working together, you will likely find that most student combinations for collaborative work will be effective.

## Sample Student Activities

Although the types of activities and group work you design are only limited by your imagination, there are two criteria that typically exist with effective group learning activities:

1.  The learning requires conceptual thinking.
2.  The group has the resources and skills necessary to complete the task, though they may not be able to do so individually.

(Cohen & Lotan, 2014, p. 9)

Additionally, practitioners and scholars (Kagan & Kagan, 1994) point out that group work is generally most effective when the individuals:

*   are participating equally and simultaneously
*   are individually accountable to the group
*   are dependent upon one another for successful completion of the task

### *Rehearsing Ensemble Repertoire*

One example of such group work in the piano lab would be having students prepare a short ensemble piece to perform for the class. This project meets the basic criterion for an effective group project because it is conceptual in that the students will have to listen to and assess their performance and work on finer points of musical expression together, and no individual would be able to perform all parts individually. We are assuming that the students have experienced a successful modeling of ensemble music previously, probably with the teacher soliciting student feedback and helping them tease out the problems and identify how to fix specific problems. As the students work together on the ensemble, because each part is equally important, they are accountable to the group and positively dependent upon each other for a successful performance.

In a group of eight students, I would begin by assigning each group a short four-part ensemble (such as one of the ensembles that we referenced in Chapter 9). Depending on the makeup of each group and the difficulty of each part, I might assign individual parts or let the students choose their own parts once they begin working together. I would group each quartet together over headphones and then monitor their progress. Initially, they would need to work on simply getting the parts together, with everyone playing the correct notes and rhythms. I would encourage all members to participate in identifying problem spots and potential group rehearsal strategies. Then I would encourage the students to work on musical aspects of the repertoire, such as articulation, phrasing, dynamics, and other interpretive details. Students would need to work together to solve any number of musical issues that might arise.

One musical problem could be a ritardando indicated on the score. Students would need to decide who should serve as the leader and determine this based on the musical inferences in the score. So if three of the four parts are holding half notes at the cadence where the ritardando is indicated, but one person is playing a melody in eighths or quarters, the students should figure out that the group member playing the melody will need to be in charge of leading the group slowing. Other group members could provide feedback to the leader on the appropriateness of the pace of the deceleration and on the effectiveness of the musical cues. In effect, they would all be experiencing and learning this skill because they would each be actively engaged in the learning process. After solving this musical problem, the group might experiment with alternate instrumentation for each part and work together to achieve optimal balance and musical expression. Finally, the group will perform its ensemble out loud for the rest of the class, and the students who are listening can provide feedback on technical and musical aspects of the performance.

### *Improvising Accompaniments*

Another example of an effective group activity might be having students work on improvising two-hand accompaniments in pairs. Each group might proceed using different steps, depending on their abilities, learning preferences, and needs. For example, one group might decide to play the melody together first, then talk through possible chord choices. After settling on a chord progression, they could play the chords together before finally splitting up and taking turns playing the melody and accompaniment. Another group might decide to record the melody on one of the keyboards and then experiment with potential chord options. A third group might begin with one student playing the melody while the other improvises an accompaniment. Then the person playing the melody could point out passages that worked well or not and offer potential solutions for the problem spots. Finally, they could switch roles. Groups that quickly complete the exercise might decide to alter instrumentation, articulation, or even the accompaniment pattern in order to expound upon the exercise. Others might decide to challenge themselves by transposing the exercise to distant keys. Regardless, the pairs are working together, learning from one another by completing the feedback loop, deepening understanding and meaning, and creating a product that would not have been possible individually.

For additional activities, see Fisher's (2010) instructional strategies, which he has divided by category into beginning, intermediate, and advanced activities. The point of suggesting ways teachers can foster effective collaboration and mentioning sample group activities for the piano class is to remind us that in order for effective group work and learning to take place, each person in the group must feel like he or she has something of value to provide to the project, the learning, and the finished product. If a student does not feel safe in sharing opinions, concerns, and successes with his or her peers, effective group work will not take place. If groups are operating optimally, students are more engaged in the project or task, they take command of their learning, they learn skills and concepts more completely, their individual musicianship improves, and they will be motivated to take responsibility for their practice outside of class and to contribute to the group during class. Effective group work allows students to benefit not only from an educational standpoint but provides opportunities for students to make music with others—which many pianists who take individual lessons rarely experience.

## Pedagogy in Action

1. When you facilitate group work, you will need to monitor multiple groups simultaneously and be ready to offer suggestions and prompts quickly and efficiently. If you have some prompts prepared for various situations, you will be able to focus more on the students in your class. Prepare a list of five prompts or suggestions for students that will facilitate in-class group work for each of the following situations:
   - Harmonization exercise
   - Improvisation exercise
   - Sight-reading exercise
   - Simple accompaniment exercise
   - Short four-part keyboard ensemble
2. Imagine that you are starting a beginning piano class with 7-year-old students. There are eight students registered for the class. Six of the students attend the same school and know each other well, while the other two students attend different schools during the day. Create and describe three group activities you will use during the first class meeting to help all students get to know each other (especially the two students from different schools). Be specific about the actual game or activity, what the students will do, and how you expect it to foster student interaction.
3. Write down five phrases you will encourage children in your group-piano classes to use when they communicate with one another about perceived errors or

misunderstandings. Will these phrases work with adults, too, or should the language be adapted? If you need to adapt these sentences for adult students, write these down too.

4. Write a brief script for how you would quickly defuse the following situations.

  • In a first-semester music-major college class, you have paired students to work on improvisation over headphones. Even though the students can hear one another, they do not look at each other or speak but instead practice on their own individually.

  • In an adult leisure class, you group three students to work on an ensemble piece. One student seems to be taking charge, making all of the suggestions and correcting the others. Meanwhile, the other two students seem to be taken aback by the self-appointed leader's brashness and appear to be uncomfortable with the situation.

  • In a group of 8-year-old beginners, you put them into subgroups of four to work on rhythm ensembles at their keyboards (over headphones). One student has turned his keyboard up to a loud volume, has chosen an obnoxious percussion sound that is drowning out the other students, and is refusing to listen to and play in time with the others.

## References

Burnard, P. (2013). "Teaching Music Creatively." In P. Burnard, & R. Murphy (Eds.). *Teaching Music Creatively* (pp. 1–11). London: Routledge.

Elizabeth G. Cohen & Rachel A. Lotan, (2014). *Designing groupwork: Strategies for the heterogeneous classroom*, 3rd Edition, New York: Teachers College Press.

Fisher, C. (2010). "Instructional Strategies." In *Teaching Piano in Groups* (pp. 113–173). New York: Oxford University Press.

Kagan, S., & Kagan, M. (1994). "The Structural Approach: Six Keys to Cooperative Learning." In S. Sharan (Ed.). *Handbook of Cooperative Learning Methods* (pp. 115–133). Westport, NT: Greenwood Press.

Wachter, M. (Ed.). (2016). "A Conversation with Jane Chu." In *Proceedings of the National Conference on Keyboard Pedagogy* (pp. 31–38). Princeton: NJ: The Frances Clark Center for Keyboard Pedagogy.

# 14

# LOGISTICS OF TEACHING GROUP PIANO

## Objectives

By the end of this chapter, you should have concrete ideas about scheduling and marketing group-piano classes and understand how to maintain a studio environment that is conducive to learning. You will know which ancillary materials can be useful and where to find them.

## Scheduling

### Surveys

Scheduling group lessons can be one of the trickiest activities for the novice group-piano teacher. Some teachers ask parents to complete surveys, highlighting times when their children are available. This can be done during the interview using a paper survey or online via a free Doodle-type poll (i.e., www.doodle.com). If you have a returning group of students who want to remain together, a survey may be an effective way to identify mutually agreeable times, as these families are often motivated to be flexible with their availability in order to keep the children together. However, you may find that you are still unable to accommodate everyone or that you need to spend some time negotiating with a family or two in order to find a suitable time.

### Optimal Time of Day

I prefer to think about days and times that I would like to offer a particular class and set those in my schedule first. I then work private students around the group times. See Figure 14.1 for a sample weekly group schedule. Some teachers like to avoid Mondays for group classes, since many national and civic holidays fall on Mondays. If you are only teaching a class once a week, it should be possible to avoid such teaching disruptions. If you are fortunate enough to offer a class twice each week, try to schedule it so that there are about the same number of practice days between classes. For example, you might schedule the group for the same time on Tuesdays and Fridays.

You will find that there may be optimal times of day for various age groups to engage in intensive learning activities. Thus, I take time of day and age of the group into consideration when setting times. For example, I prefer to offer my beginning classes for children shortly after school, before the evening meal, so that I am not teaching young people when they are tired or hungry. Classes with only home-schooled students may be scheduled during morning or afternoon hours if parents view group-piano as a critical component of their child's overall education. I schedule many of my adult classes after evening dinner, when they are more likely to be free of family obligations. Third-age classes for retirees can be offered earlier in the day, when many of them prefer to engage in activities and so they won't have to drive after dark.

In the example in Figure 14.1, you can see that the majority of my weekly teaching is done in a group setting. I have two groups of first-year and second-year students, grouped according to age. By year three, I only offer one group-piano class. There may be some attrition by year three, but other students are better served by moving into private lessons at this time. In my studio, private students are still expected to participate in regular performance classes, but I hold those during the weekend. I work all of my private lessons around the group schedule.

In this scenario, I only allow a 10-minute break between two of the classes. This keeps students moving but gives them a few minutes to greet each other as they enter and leave the studio. I have ample parking and space for the class change. But it can be mentally taxing to teach two groups back to back. I suggest that novice teachers allow a little downtime for rest and review of the lesson plan between classes. I should also note that if I have a group of students that will continue together from one semester or one year to the next, I keep them in the same time slot. So I may have to adjust the times of my year one and year two classes on my master schedule from one year to the next. I have found that parents will work other activities around effective and enjoyable piano classes. However, I recommend setting the dates and times early and publicizing those well before the registration deadline. I send home paper reminders about scheduling to returning students. I include class schedules in my online newsletter, and these are posted prominently on my studio web site.

|  | Monday | Tuesday | Wednesday | Thursday | Saturday |
|---|---|---|---|---|---|
| 10-11 a.m. | Third-Age |  |  | Third-Age | Year 3 10-year-olds |
| 3:30-4:30 p.m. | Year 1 (group 1) 6-year-olds | Year 2 (group 1) 7-year-olds | Year 1 (group 2) 8-year-olds |  | Late-Interm Perf Class |
| 4:40-5:40 p.m. | Year 3 8-year-olds | Year 2 (group 2) 9-year-olds |  |  | Advanced Perf Class |
| 7:00-8:00 |  | Year 2 Adult Class |  | Year 1 Adult Beginners |  |

*Figure 14.1* Sample Weekly Group Schedule

If you offer occasional group classes in conjunction with private lessons or regular group theory classes, you may find that a weekend class is easier to schedule. If publicized in advance, parents can put these classes on the family calendar and work other activities around the group-piano class. Scheduling all lessons and classes early is particularly important if you do not offer private lessons during the week of the group meeting. A benefit for the teacher of this type of scheduling is that he or she will have time during the week, when lessons typically occur, to prepare for the group classes. Many teachers also use this time to practice and pursue professional development activities.

Some teachers set up their weekend groups with some flexibility for families. For example, if the Saturday sessions are performance classes and the studio is large enough, there may be several classes from which parents can choose (say an intermediate-level class at 10 a.m. or another at 2 p.m.). I like to have about the same number of students at each class, so I recommend having families sign up for specific classes if you choose this approach. Then you can avoid having 3 students at the 10 a.m. class and 10 at the 2 p.m. session! Some teachers who are willing to work on Sundays find that Sunday-afternoon groups are easier for families to accommodate. Regardless of the type of class offered (performance, theory, group lesson) you will want to have the correct number of materials prepared and have games and activities that will work with the number of students in the class. Thus, having firm numbers ahead of time is essential for preparation and learning success during class.

Finally, teachers need to remember that group teaching is hard work. While it can be tempting to schedule classes for every day of the week, few teachers can sustain this level of preparation and intense teaching in the long term without suffering from professional burnout. Even if teaching group piano is among your favorite activities (as it is for me), remember to schedule downtime and rest for yourself. In the long term, you will be able to maintain higher teaching standards, intensity, and motivation if you work rest into your weekly schedule.

## *Marketing*

When first starting your group-piano studio, marketing will be crucial. You will want to explore numerous ways of advertising and letting potential students know that you are offering classes. Furthermore, the marketing needs to occur as early as possible so you know whether a class can happen (and you will have time to make accommodations for students who have registered if the class does not have adequate enrollment). While one type of marketing may be more effective than others in your particular community, you will want to get the word out using several different venues. The timing of advertising may vary slightly depending on the venue.

Advertising in neighborhood newsletters or newspapers during the summer months can be effective, whereas these sorts of print ads may be less cost-effective during the school year. You will want to be sure that your upcoming class schedule is prominently featured on your studio web site. Post flyers in music stores and other places in your community where future students congregate. Consider reaching out to school music teachers too, as parents sometimes ask for referrals. And be sure to let your local music teachers' association colleagues know that you are offering group-piano classes. Some organizations have teacher-finder tools on their web sites, and many established teachers are delighted to refer parents to young colleagues who are just starting out and building studios. Some teachers set up information booths at local farmers' markets or arts fairs, or offer short, free introductory classes to give students a sample of what group piano is like.

Depending on where and how you advertise, you will need different materials (which all convey the essential information in different ways). For example, you may need trifold brochures for an arts fair, a camera-ready ad for a community newspaper, and business cards and a set of materials for each student at a demonstration class. There will be a cost associated with purchasing booth space or ad space in newsletters. Keep track of your expenditures and reassess your marketing strategies at least twice per year to ensure that you are making the most of your marketing budget. It can be difficult to know how effective your efforts are, so always ask students and parents who email or call with inquiries about classes how they found out about you. Knowing which methods are effective in your community can help you make future marketing decisions. Regardless, you will want to factor costs associated with advertising into your annual studio budget. Once your group-piano studio has been well established, your marketing may shift from actively pursuing new students to keeping the studio on the radar of members of your community.

## Space in the Studio—Considerations

When deciding on how many students to accept into each class, teachers should consider their ability to engage, supervise, and assess students at any given age. Teaching your best should take precedence over making money. Students and families who are pleased with their group-piano instruction will spread positive comments about your studio throughout the community. It is better to have smaller but well-taught classes at the beginning than larger classes of students who do not learn much and who are not satisfied with their experience. Your reputation as an effective teacher is on the line. At the beginning, working with groups of three or four students can be a good way to develop group-teaching skills.

Once you have discerned your comfort level with teaching groups of students, the actual studio layout, equipment, and supplies you own will need to be taken into account when considering optimal enrollment.[1] In this regard, physical space in the studio and the layout of the space should be of primary concern. Consider movement activities and games in which the students will engage. While a single acoustic piano can be used to teach small groups of young students, they will need room to work safely with manipulatives and games. Too much space or clutter can also be a problem. I once taught general music in a large classroom shared with the art teacher. The many art supplies, brightly colored artwork, and tables provided too much stimulation for some students. So the careful placement of room dividers, musical instruments, and games became critical for student engagement.

Even now, in my ideal studio, I use Mylar dots with students' names to assign seating in our activity circle. Some teachers use carpet squares to help children know where their "spot" is. We use this floor space for many of our movement explorations, rhythm activities, and games. When students enter the room, I have only materials that I will use during each class available, and these are not always out and on display when students arrive. I find that if they follow my cues, young children are very intrigued and stay focused as I create a Velcro staff on the floor, for example. Thus, this does not necessarily need to be set out before class begins.

I have big baskets in my studio in which I keep the materials that we will need for each class. I also have smaller baskets and containers for student supplies such as pencils, crayons, and writing materials so they can quickly and easily return everything to the proper place. The actual physical environment should be free of clutter and be a safe space for everyone. I also ensure that students have a task for every minute of the lesson. For example, you will need to consider how you will keep children focused on a task as they move from a floor activity to the piano. The more directly and quickly they can move from floor to piano, the more on task they are likely to remain. Thus, having a really large space is not always ideal. Ask yourself what Goldilocks would want in a studio; given the size and age of your group, how can you set up the space so that it is "just right" for optimal student learning?

## Ancillary Materials

### Books and Multiple Copies of Music

Most teachers do not ask students to purchase a lot of extra materials beyond the method books and ensemble book each semester. But there are many times when supplemental materials will be needed when working with the group. It can be helpful to have multiple copies of frequently used supplemental music or books available for each student during class. For example, I like to have enough copies of sight-reading and ensemble music for each student so we can work on these activities during class time. These are not items that I expect them to practice at home, so they do not need to purchase these. Rather, I have several copies of each book that I can recycle from one semester to the next with many student groups. I have some resources specifically for adults, as I don't like them to have to play from children's materials (with pictures and childish writing). I have also created numerous exercises, harmonization, and sight-reading examples of my own over the years. I have these examples stored on my computer as Finale files but always have enough printed copies available for student use. If single sheets, such as these, will get a lot of use, I have them laminated or mounted on stiff cardboard so they do not flop around on the music stand, and they last for several years. Having filing cabinets or shelves where these materials can be easily accessed but stored out of sight is important. I also have my sight-reading and harmonization creations filed on my teaching computer and project those to monitors at each student keyboard when needed.

### Games and Manipulatives

When working with groups of beginning children, I have numerous games, flash-cards, and items that can be reused with various groups or employed over several weeks with specific groups. At first, I created many of these items myself (Athey & Hotchkiss, 1975; Harrington, 2008; Storms, 2001). For example, large foam poster boards can be used to create stock game boards for Jeopardy or tic-tac-toe, and index cards can be used to create questions sets for various concepts or age groups. This is cost-effective, and it ensures that every activity meets the specific needs of my students, my teaching preferences, and my individual curriculum. Again, laminate anything (such as game pieces or cards) that will be handled by many students to increase the longevity of these manipulatives.

Having various rhythm instruments and a set of resonator bells can be an asset when working with young children. Individual 9 × 12 magnetic/dry-erase white-boards (which have the grand staff on one side and space for rhythm work on the other) can be used during group classes, too. Some teachers have just one of these boards, and students take turns using it to solve problems, while other teachers like each student in the class to have their own board. Commercial versions of these boards range anywhere from $6 to $25. As the quality of these products may vary, consider the frequency with which you will use these objects, as you may need them to stand up to a lot of use. I have found that purchasing high-quality equip-ment and materials pays off in the long run when I do not have to replace them. See Music in Motion or Keys to Imagination web sites to purchase high-quality materials.

Large-scale floor keyboards and staves with plastic musical alphabet letters and dots for notes are also a must in classes for young children. There are several differ-ent brands available for purchase, some that are made from cloth and others made from vinyl. Both of these materials enable regular cleaning, which is recommended so that your studio does not become an incubator for germs. Having a large dry-erase board with staff lines is also important when teaching groups. Some teachers begin by making their own chalk boards with special paint created for that purpose until they can afford to purchase a commercial-grade board. Other teachers use software that allows them to show staves and keyboards, but a projector or large screen/monitor will be necessary for display. When first starting out, I suggest that teachers keep a "wish list" of potential teaching aids and prioritize those wishes based on necessity. Then each semester, part of the student registration or studio fee can be put toward building the library of teaching tools, games, books, and manipulatives that will be enjoyed by all students.

## Pedagogy in Action

1. Imagine that you are going to offer three group-piano classes in your studio next semester. Think about which classes (age, level, etc.) you will offer and when you will schedule each. Create a chart that shows when these classes will be offered. Next, create a multipronged marketing strategy. List at least three different ways you will get information about your classes out to the surrounding community. Be sure to list the budget for each of these, the materials that will be necessary, and a timeline for effective marketing with each strategy. Create a set of marketing materials for at least one of these venues (i.e., camera-ready ad, brochure, web site content, etc.).

2. Share your schedules and marketing materials and strategies with your peers and discuss what is effective and what might be less effective. Make any necessary changes to your materials based on your group reflections.

3. Create a wish list of materials you would like to have in your ideal studio. Check local music stores and online music educator sites for prices and include these in your wish list. Then think about your teaching needs (or anticipated needs) and prioritize your list for future purchases.

4. Identify a specific group class or age group that you are teaching and create a game you can use for several weeks with that specific class. (Reminder: there are more ideas about games in Chapter 9, or refer to the reference list at the end of this chapter.)

## Note

1 See Chapter 15 for discussion about music technology and equipment for the group-piano studio.

## References

### Books about Games

Athey, M., & Hotchkiss, G. (1975). *A Galaxy of Games for the Music Class*. West Nyack, NY: Parker Publishing Company.

Harrington, K. (2008). *Tic-Tac-Toe Music Games*. Milwaukee: Hal Leonard Corporation.

Storms, J. (2001). *101 Music Games for Children*. The Hague: Uitgeverij Panta Rhei (in the USA published as a Hunter House SmartFun Book, Berkley: Publishers Group West).

## *Web Sites and Music Stores for Teaching Materials*

Music Educators Marketplace teaching aids and games at www.keystoimagination.com

Music in Motion: www.musicmotion.com

# 15

# TECHNOLOGY FOR THE GROUP-PIANO INSTRUCTOR

## Objectives

By the end of this chapter, you will know about basic technology and software that can be useful in the group-piano setting. You will have thought about how to budget for technological purchases and maintenance and know how to keep abreast of changes in educational music technology.

## Introduction

When group-piano teaching began in public schools in the 1930s and '40s, the classrooms equipped with MIDI technology and digital pianos that have become ubiquitous with group-piano labs in the 21st century were not available. I remember in graduate school in the 1990s watching video of Frances Clark and Louis Goss teaching group piano at the New School for Music Study, where students rehearsed new techniques at desks using plastic silent keyboards and then gathered around an acoustic grand piano to take turns trying out the finger patterns and music. Even a few years ago, I observed one of the best group-piano teachers that I have ever seen teaching a group of beginning 6-year-olds using mostly a single grand piano.

Although outstanding group-piano teachers can design innovative, creative, and stimulating educational experiences in almost any setting, and some individual studio teachers avail of technology, we are likely to find more technology used in the group-piano studio than in many private studios. However, before deciding on which technological components you will purchase, lease, and integrate into your group classes, remember to consider the educational benefits or drawbacks. Technology can be a powerful learning tool in group-piano instruction and learning. But it should not be used for its own sake. Rather, it should only be employed if the teacher can clearly articulate the benefits for the students of integrating technology into the curriculum. A digital keyboard lab permits students to collaborate with one another if used properly. Other technology may promote interaction, but for some students, it may be superfluous or even distract from the learning. In this chapter, we will look at technology that many group-piano instructors use and discuss ways teachers can keep abreast of a medium that changes quickly.

# Basic Technology

## *Digital and Electronic Pianos*

I consider the modern acoustic piano, with hundreds of intricate moving parts, to be a technological wonder. However, it may not be the first instrument that comes to mind when we think about group-piano teaching. Consider the piano lab, where students can work on digital pianos, individually or in small groups, using headphones. In such a piano lab, there are some basic components to the setup. These include digital pianos for students and the teacher, MIDI technology, and recording devices. There will be student keyboards—anywhere from 2 to 6 keyboards in an independent studio and somewhere around 16 in a university or community school piano lab. The student keyboards should be touch sensitive so that proper technique, dynamics, and musical nuance can be pursued and assessed during classes. There is a teaching console, which consists of a digital piano for the teacher, and a controller. Most digital pianos today have onboard MIDI sequencers, players, and rhythm machines. In older labs, or with less sophisticated keyboards, the teaching station may have separate MIDI player and drum machine components. Including a controller in the setup allows students to work together in small groups or pairs over headphones without disturbing other groups. The MIDI player allows the teacher to play MIDI accompaniments or rhythm tracks at varying speeds as the students play. If everyone is working over headphones, the teacher can also configure the sound so that each student can hear himself and the teacher. This provides students with critical feedback as they compare their playing to the teacher's model without having to play aloud with the entire group. One additional benefit of using digital pianos is that students can experiment with different instrumental sounds, textures, and timbres. Even though students enjoy playing with these, I find that specific instrumental sounds can help students hear articulation more accurately and improve. For example, a woodwind instrument, whose tone does not decay as quickly as that of a piano, can help students to hear slurs, legato, and staccato and adjust technique accordingly. Choosing appropriate instrumental settings also makes the experience of playing high-quality keyboard ensemble music more musically satisfying and fulfilling for both performers and audience members.

Current digital pianos permit students to record their playing and listen to it, which can help with self-evaluation. Students can create and record their own compositions through simple one-button recordings or by setting down more sophisticated layers of MIDI tracks. Recall that MIDI stands for musical instrument digital interface, and it allows various instruments and computers to communicate with each other across platforms. When stored, standard MIDI files take up relatively little space, making them convenient for file sharing among musicians, educators, and publishers. Most group-piano texts and many individual methods come with MIDI accompaniment files (often available through an online app) that students can play along with at the tempo of their choosing.

Group-piano teachers find that MIDI accompaniments can be useful for motivating students, for filling out simple-sounding elementary pieces, and for developing a sense of pulse and rhythmic continuity in students' playing. Thus, many teachers who do not teach in digital keyboard labs have at least one instrument in the studio capable of MIDI playback. Another option for teachers who have electronic keyboards without onboard sequencers is to import and playback MIDI files using the Home Concert Xtreme computer program (available for less than $100 from www.timewarptech.com). MIDI files are displayed on a score on the computer screen, but more importantly for group teaching, the tempo of the audio can be adjusted to match student needs.

### Computers and Audio and Visual Aids

Audio and video recorders and playback devices can also be assets when teaching group piano. Not long ago, this meant investing in expensive equipment. Today, even students have recording devices in their pockets. If teachers use mobile phones, computers, or tablets for recording purposes, they may wish to have a good-quality Bluetooth speaker in the room so students hear high-quality audio. Some teachers like to have a computer/tablet station (or two) that students can use to work on theory, aural skills, sight reading, and other skills using online apps or specialized software. In a group setting, it is important for students to work collaboratively. This should be taken into consideration before teachers purchase computer stations. Often there are relatively inexpensive apps or other types of nonvirtual games that can be just as engaging, educational, and more conducive to group interaction.

In college-level classes, I have found that having a computer and a Smartboard or an ELMO document camera connected to a data projector at the teaching station is beneficial. This allows me to project important visual information, preview and mark scores, and conduct any number of teaching activities from the front of the room. I keep extra manuscript paper on hand to project notation, making the whiteboard obsolete. Similar visual technology is useful in K–12 piano labs. Smartboards and data projectors are commonplace in many schools, and some school districts have special funds for teaching technology.

For the majority of teachers who run independent studios or work in community schools or in music stores, Smartboards, ELMOs, and data projectors are not economically feasible. Because having large-scale visuals of the keyboard and grand staff is so valuable when teaching, savvy teachers have created reasonably priced software that can be used in place of Visualizers and data projectors. As previously noted, Timewarp Technology (www.timewarptech.com) has several software programs that are Mac or PC compatible and work well in the group-piano lab. Classroom Maestro

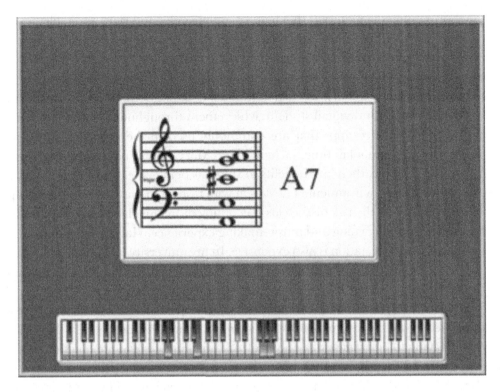

*Figure 15.1* Screenshot of Classroom Maestro Intelligent Music Display Software

retails for under US$70. It runs on a computer, connected to a MIDI keyboard using a USB-MIDI cable, and shows the keyboard and notes on the staff as they are being played. See Figure 15.1 for a screen shot of Classroom Maestro. The display, which is a virtual whiteboard, can be used to show single notes, scales, chords, progressions, even hand positions on the keyboard. In college classes, teachers project the display from a data projector. Many independent studio teachers connect their computer to a large-screen television display to project the images. This is much more cost-effective than purchasing a data projector, and it works quite well.

Finally, for both adult and children's classes, I believe that having an acoustic piano in the lab is essential. Even though digital piano technology has improved dramatically and there are many benefits to using it for the majority of class, students need the opportunity to perform for each other on an acoustic instrument.

## Additional Technology to Enhance the Learning Experience

While not required, many college-level group-piano teachers have individual computers and monitors at each student piano, essentially creating individual student learning stations. Some instructors use online or e-books or practice apps in their classes, where students work on materials over the Internet via each computer. One such set of multimedia materials that features online video tutorials, audio files, exercises, flash cards, printed drills, and assignments to develop keyboard skills is eNovative Piano (www.enovativepiano.com). Other teachers who work in labs where each student has a computer and keyboard at her station post lessons and assignments for students in individual folders on each computer desktop. Some even use programs or apps that monitor individual student achievement throughout the class or during extra lab time. Practice apps that are commonly used in the group-piano setting (especially for individual lab time) include Piano Marvel and Piano Maestro.

As you can imagine, there are benefits to students being able to work and learn in such a personalized environment. The caveat with respect to these types of lab setups is simply that there is the risk of the class becoming individual lab time rather than a collaborative group-learning and music-making experience. Having individual computers at each student station is also expensive. In my university lab, I have individual video monitors daisy-chained from my teaching-station computer to each student keyboard. I use the monitors to provide supplementary materials for students to work on together during class, such as sight-reading examples or flashes, harmonization examples, score-reading exercises, and other musical materials as needed. This saves me from having to purchase extra copies of materials and provides me with freedom to adapt my teaching to the needs of specific classes.

Many K–12 and independent studio group-piano teachers will want to incorporate creative and compositional activities into the curriculum. Individual student computer/electronic keyboard stations with sequencing, MIDI, and music-notation programs can be a real asset in such group-piano environments. For suggestions on technology and activities that can be used in K–12 piano labs, Barbara Freedman's (2013) book contains numerous suggestions and solutions. Independent teachers often find resources and suggestions from other teachers within their communities or states. Some teachers find that they can use multiple digital pianos for the majority of the instructional time and only need one computer with notation software that can be shared by all students during the final stages of each compositional activity.

## Keeping Up with Technological Change

We live during an exciting time when technology has become integrated into our lives so fully that it ceases to be novel. This is particularly true for our younger students. For teachers who make the investment of education, time, and money to set up a digital piano lab in their studios, it can be easy to get comfortable with the technology we use daily and not keep up with emerging trends. I am not suggesting that we need to become early adopters, adding another technological element every time something new is released. However, even top-of-the-line technology will age and need upgrading. And we need to be aware of trends and advances in our field.

This way, when we must upgrade or require a new program to enhance the learning experience, we will know what we need and how much it will cost.

The piano magazine *Keyboard Companion* and journal *American Music Teacher* both feature short, regular technology columns written by leaders in the field of piano pedagogy and technology. As technology becomes increasingly important in day-to-day life and educational settings, these periodicals often feature full-length articles on practical applications of music technology for piano teachers. Since both of these are recommended reading for all piano teachers, these columns can serve to keep us aware of important innovations and educational uses of music technology.

The more scholarly *Journal of Music, Technology & Education* features research articles by educators from around the world who are integrating technology in both classroom and private-lesson settings, and the *MTNA e-Journal*, while not specifically geared toward technology, often publishes articles related to technology and group-piano teaching. Many independent teachers find blogs and online teacher groups to be useful sources of information on technology that can be used in group-piano. While new sites come online from time to time, at the time of this writing, there are many popular and useful groups that are curated by educators and technology enthusiasts. The September/October 2016 volume of *Keyboard Companion*, for example, included a brief article that evaluated 25 teacher Facebook groups (Haxo, Huston, Reinhardt, & Thickstun, 2016).

Finally, pedagogy-related conferences such as the Music Teachers National Association national and state conferences, the National Conference on Keyboard Pedagogy, and the Group Piano—Piano Pedagogy (GP3) Forum regularly feature sessions (if not entire day-long workshops or preconference sessions) on technology that can be used in teaching group piano. While attending these conferences takes an investment of time and money, the expenses are often tax deductible, and the professional development experience will enhance your teaching, the effective use of technology in your classes, and your students' learning outcomes. I recommend making a commitment to attend one or several of these conferences regularly.

## Pedagogy in Action

1.  Research equipment you would need for a six-student electronic piano lab. Visit your local music store or piano retailer and explore technology web sites. Compare prices for several types of digital pianos you could use (remember to think about the type of teaching console you would like and cables and controller systems that will be needed to connect the keyboards together.) Consider if you will use software such as Classroom Maestro or online books and tutorials in your studio. Create a master list of the technology you envision needing, along with a price list. Write a detailed plan for how you will purchase or lease and upgrade essential equipment.

2. Make arrangements to visit a piano lab at a local college, music store, or independent studio and meet with the teacher. Observe a class, if possible, to see how the teacher uses the technology throughout the class. Then interview the teacher about which technology he or she uses regularly and regards as critical for effective group teaching. Write a summary exploring what you have discovered and explain how this field trip has affected your technology wish list for your own group teaching.

3. Find three articles or columns about teaching technology in any of the journals referenced in this chapter. Summarize each article and note which journal or magazine you think will help you keep abreast of technological change.

4. Spend time investigating the National Conference on Keyboard Pedagogy and the MTNA National Conference technology offerings. Using conference web sites, conference proceedings, and affiliated journals from the past few years, explore technology offerings and sessions at national music conference programs. Decide which conference would be most beneficial for your professional development in terms of using technology effectively, look into expenses associated with that conference (registration fee, airfare/transportation, hotel, meals, etc.), and create a travel budget. Remember, some preconference workshops, in which day-long technology sessions are offered, require an additional registration fee. Describe how you could budget to make conference attendance possible.

## References and Teacher Resources

### *Books and Articles*

Be aware that these become quickly outdated with technological advances, but they can provide good educational overviews of how to incorporate technology in the group-piano or computer lab.

Freedman, B. (2013). *Teaching Music through Composition: A Curriculum Using Technology*. New York: Oxford University Press.

Haxo, C., Huston, A., Reinhardt, J. L., & Thickstun, K. (2016). Problem Solved! Seeking Solutions Online: Facebook Groups for Teachers. *Keyboard Companion, 8*(5), 46–49.

### *Journals*

*American Music Teacher* (peer-reviewed journal published 6 times/year by MTNA).

*Clavier Companion* (piano magazine published 6 times/year by Frances Clark Center for Keyboard Pedagogy).

*Journal of Music, Technology & Education* (peer-reviewed journal published 3 times/year by Intellect Books).

*MTNA e-Journal* (peer-reviewed journal published 6 times/year by MTNA).

## *Software and Online Teaching Tools*

The following is only a sample of programs and apps on the market. These are used extensively by teachers at the time of this writing and have received good reviews from educators.

Classroom Maestro & Home Concert Xtreme www.timewarptech.com
eNovative Piano online multimedia resource www.enovativepiano.com
Piano Maestro (assessment/practice software) www.joytunes.com
Piano Marvel (assessment software) www.pianomarvel.com

## *Professional-Development Teacher Conferences*

Music Teachers National Association (holds national conference annually, sponsors the GP3 Forum in even-numbered years, and an annual collegiate symposium): www.mtna.org
National Conference on Keyboard Pedagogy (meets every other year, in odd-numbered years) and is sponsored by the Frances Clark Center for Keyboard Pedagogy: www.keyboardpedagogy.org

# Appendix A.1

## STUDENT PERFORMANCE EVALUATION SHEET

### Young Beginners

**Performer Name:** _____     **Date:** _____

**Your Name:** _____

1. Circle the **tempo** of the piece.

Fast                                              Slow

2. Circle the **dynamic** at the **beginning**.

Loud                                              Soft

3. Did the piece start **high** or **low**?

High                                              Low

4. Circle the **dynamic** at the **end**.

Loud                                    Soft

5. Was the piece **staccato** or **legato**?

Staccato                                Legato

6. How was the **bow**?

     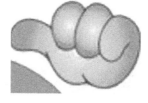     

# Appendix A.2

## STUDENT PERFORMANCE EVALUATION SHEET

### Average-Age Beginners

**Performer Name:** _____     **Date:** _____

**Your Name:** _____

### Read the Questions and Circle What You Heard!

1. What was the **tempo** of the piece?
   Slow          Moderate          Fast

2. What was the **dynamic** at the **beginning**?
   p          mp          mf          f

3. Did the piece start **high** or **low**?

4. What was the **dynamic** at the **end**?
   p          mp          mf          f

5. Was the piece **staccato** or **legato**?

6. How was the **bow** at the end of the piece?
   Keep Working!          Fantastic!

# Appendix A.3

# STUDENT PERFORMANCE
# EVALUATION SHEET
## Late-Elementary and Intermediate Students

**Performer Name:** _____  **Date:** _____

**Composer Name & Title of Composition:** _____

**Your Name:** _____

1. Describe the character or mood conveyed by the performer. If it changed during the piece, list each change.

2. Was there a melody throughout? If so, which hand was it in? Did the performer project the melody?

3. If there was no melody, what was the main feature of the piece? (Arpeggios? Chord progression? Other?) Describe this feature and how the performer brought it out.

4. Were there any sudden dynamic changes? Where did they occur?

5. Did the performer use pedals?

6. Describe the best thing about this performance.

7. If you have a tip for the performer, list it here (remember to use positive statements).

# Appendix B
# RESOURCES FOR PIANO CAMPS

## Books and Methods for Children's Beginning and Elementary Levels—Ideal for Camps

- *Alfred's Basic Group Piano Course*, Books 1–4 (Alfred Music)[1]
- *Piano Camp*, Books Primer–4 by June C. Montgomery (Alfred Music)

## Ensemble Music for Electronic Keyboards

- *Alfred Basic Piano Library Ensemble*, Books 1, 2, and 3; complete Book 2 and 3 also available (Alfred Music)
- *Alfred Basic Piano Library Christmas Ensemble*, Books 1, 2, and 3 (Alfred Music)
- *Hal Leonard Student Piano Library Piano Ensembles*, Books 1–5 (Hal Leonard)
- *Hal Leonard Piano Library Christmas Piano Ensembles*, Books 1–5 (Hal Leonard)
- *Ogilvy Music Ensembles* by Jim & Susan Ogilvy and others (www.sospace.com)

## Games, Creativity, Improvisation, and Activity Pages for Groups

- *Creative Chords: Keyboard Improvisation Method*, Books 1 and 2 by Bradley Sowash (Kjos)
- *Creative Composition Tool Box*, Books 1–6 by Wynn-Anne Rossi (Alfred Music)
- Evaluation Pages for Peer Performances (Appendix A)
- Keys to Imagination web site for Music Educator's Marketplace and other materials (www.keystoimagination.com)
- *Meet the Great Composers*, Books 1 and 2 by June Montgomery & Maurice Hinson (Alfred Music)
- Music in Motion web site for various teaching products (www.musicmotion.com) Especially useful resources:
  - Keys to Music Activity Kit (floor keyboard, beanbags, musical alphabet)
  - King Keyboard and Music's My Bag (floor keyboard and grand staff with accessories)
  - Re-Markable Staff Boards
  - Color Dots Spot Markers

- • Step Bells and Rhythm Instruments
- • Games for Groups (Velcro KidsPlay name-a-note and symbol games, magnetic boards and games, cubes/dice, etc.)
- • Music history DVDs
- • Studio posters, flashcards, and so forth
- • Scarves for movement
- *Music MasterMINDS: The Ultimate Cross-Curricular Connection of Music Puzzles and Games* by Cheryl Lavender (Hal Leonard)
- *My Own Music History* by Karen Koch (Music Educator's Market Place/Keys to Imagination)
- *Pattern Play*, Books 1–6 by Forrest Kinney (Fredrick Harris Music Company, Ltd.)
- *Piano Bridges*, Books 1 and 2 by Meg Gray (Alfred Music)
- *Piano Teacher's Resource Kit* by Karen Harrington (Hal Leonard)
- *The World at Your Fingertips*, Books 1 and 2 by Deborah Brener & Tom Gerou (Alfred Music)
- Three Cranky Women games, over 20 games of various types, concepts, and levels (Kjos Music)
- *Tic-Tac-Toe Music Games* by Karen Harrington (Hal Leonard)
- *World Gems: International Folksongs for Piano Ensembles* by Amy O'Grady (Hal Leonard)

## Books on Games

- *101 Music Games for Children* by Jerry Storms (Publishers Group West)
- *101 More Music Games for Children* by Jerry Storms (Publishers Group West)
- *A Galaxy of Games for the Music Class* by Margaret Athey & Gwen Hotchkiss (Parker Publishing Company)

## Note

1  There are annotated references for many of these resources in Chapter 9.

# Appendix C.1

# GROUP-PIANO LEARNING STYLE PREFERENCE SURVEY

**Name:** _____      **Date:** _____

1. I prefer to work with classmates when working on new material in class.
   ___ Yes      ___ No

2. When working with others on new material in piano class (sight reading, harmonization, transposition, improvisation), I prefer to think through the theory behind the material before or as I am working on the material.
   ___ Yes      ___ No

3. When working with others on new material in piano class (sight reading, harmonization, transposition, improvisation), I prefer to play on the keyboard as I am working on the material.
   ___ Yes      ___ No

4. When working with others on new material in piano class (sight reading, harmonization, transposition, improvisation), I prefer to play on the keyboard *and* use my ear as I am working on the material.
   ___ Yes      ___ No

5. I prefer to work on my own when working on new material in class.
   ___ Yes      ___ No

6. When working on new material on my own in piano class (sight reading, harmonization, transposition, improvisation), I prefer to think through the theory behind the material before or as I am working on the material.
   ___ Yes      ___ No

7. When working on new material on my own in piano class (sight reading, harmonization, transposition, improvisation), I prefer to play on the keyboard as I am working on the material.
   ___ Yes      ___ No

8. When working on new material on my own in piano class (sight reading, harmonization, transposition, improvisation), I prefer to play on the keyboard *and* use my ear as I am working on the material.
___ Yes  ___ No

9. When working on new material in piano class, I may not always be able to explain what I am doing, but I know when something sounds correct. I enjoy brainstorming at the piano with peers.
___ Yes  ___ No

10. When working on new material in piano class, I prefer to brainstorm with peers, trying lots of different options, but I like to think about the best solution from our options.
___ Yes  ___ No

11. I prefer to know the goals for the in-class exercise, figure out the needed steps and required technique, and then work through it on my own.
___ Yes  ___ No

12. I prefer to know the goals for the in-class exercise, then work with a partner or group and experiment with ways to complete it.
___ Yes  ___ No

13. I am comfortable completing improvising activities in the textbook.
___ Yes  ___ No

14. I am not comfortable completing improvising activities in the textbook.
___ Yes  ___ No

15. Place an "x" next to one statement below that best describes you in piano class:

(a) ___ I enjoy using imagination at the piano, I am comfortable trying different solutions to problems while practicing, I enjoy brainstorming with others during class, and I can often see several ways to solve harmonization/improvisation problems.

(b) ___ I enjoy using imagination at the piano, I do not need to understand why certain strategies work as long as they sound correct, I enjoy brainstorming with others during class, and I prefer to play through examples rather than thinking about them away from the keyboard.

(c) ___ I enjoy trying (playing and hearing) different solutions to a problem while practicing, I prefer practicing alone to working with others during class, and

I can often see several different ways to solve harmonization/improvisation problems.

(d) ___ I enjoy thinking through different solutions to a problem before practicing, I prefer practicing alone to working with others during class, and I can often see several ways to solve harmonization/improvisation problems.

# Appendix C.2

# GROUP-PIANO LEARNING STYLE PREFERENCE—ANSWER KEY[1]
## For College-Aged and Adult Students[2]

**Questions 1–4:** (likely comfortable with active experimentation at the piano)
*You could have those who answer **yes** to #1 skip to question 5. Those who answer #2–4 will be Accommodators and Divergers.*

#1: Accommodators and Divergers will answer **yes** to enjoying group work.
#2: Divergers (more likely); Assimilators may answer yes
#3: Accommodators (more likely); Convergers may answer yes
#4: Accommodators

**Questions 5–8:** (likely comfortable with reflective observation before playing the piano)
*You could have those who answer **yes** to #5 skip to question 9. Those who answer #6–8 will be Convergers and Assimilators.*

#5: Convergers and Assimilators will answer **yes** to preferring thinking/observing and not necessarily relying on group work.
#6: Assimilators (more likely); Divergers could answer yes
#7: Convergers (more likely); Accommodators could answer yes
#8: Convergers

**Questions 9–14:** If the answer is yes, they are likely the type listed next to each question.

| | |
|---|---|
| Question 9: | Accommodator |
| Question 10: | Diverger |
| Question 11: | Assimilator |
| Question 12: | Converger |
| Question 13: | Accommodators |
| Question 14: | Divergers |
| Questions 3 and 7: | Convergers and Accommodators (enjoy active experimentation at the piano) |
| Questions 2 and 6: | Divergers and Assimilators (enjoy objective reflection before playing) |

**Question 15:** Self-Assessment of Learning Style

(a)  Diverger
(b)  Accommodator
(c)  Converger
(d)  Assimilator

*(You may observe different reactions in class; however, this is a good place to start at the beginning of the semester.)*

## Notes

1  See Chapter 4 for ideas about how to pair these learners for specific group-piano activities.
2  Keith Golay (2003) offers quick tools for teachers to assess the learning and temperament styles of children.

# Appendix C.3

# PERFORMANCE ASSESSMENT RUBRIC
## Elementary and Intermediate Repertoire

**Student Name:** _____ **Date:** _____

**Composer & Piece:** _____

*(Make notes for the student in the appropriate box.)*

| | Excellent | Improving | Needs Work |
|---|---|---|---|
| Technique | | | |
| Pitches, Rhythms, & Continuity | | | |
| Dynamics, Articulation, Expressive Markings | | | |
| Musicality & Artistry | | | |
| Other | | | |

# Appendix D.1

## GROUP PIANO METHOD EVALUATION TEMPLATE FOR CHILDREN'S BOOKS

**Name of Method**

**Publisher**

**Book Levels**                                   **Price**

**Ancillary Materials**                **Price**

**For each book/level, complete the following:**

Are the **Concepts** presented **Systematically** and **Spiraled**? _____ Yes _____ No

**Comments**

Is there **Ample Reinforcement** within the text? _____ Yes _____ No

**Comments**

**Level/Book:** _____      *(You may wish to complete 1 evaluation per book/level.)*

**Overview of concepts at each level:**

| | |
|---|---|
| **Reading Approach** | |
| **Pitch & Interval/Reading Concepts** | |
| **Rhythmic Concepts** | |
| **Aural Skills** | |
| **Sight Reading** | |
| **Technique** | |
| **Musicality** | |

| Creativity | |
|---|---|
| Theory | |
| Supplementary Materials | |
| Online Resources | |

**Strengths of this Method:**

**Potential Weaknesses of this Method:**

**Additional Comments and Notes:**

# Appendix D.2

# GROUP PIANO METHOD EVALUATION TEMPLATE FOR ADULT BOOKS

**Title of Book:**

**Authors:**

**Date of Publication/Edition and Publisher:**

**Intended Audience for the Book** (i.e., music majors, college non-majors, leisure students, RMM, etc.):

**Number of Pages and Units of Material** (this can help you discover if there is enough material for one or more semesters):

**Supplementary Material** (include online tutorials and additional books):

**Recordings** (list whether CD only or MIDI or both; note musical features of the recordings):

**Teaching Aids** (i.e., instructor's manual—note: you might find these online at the publisher's web site):

**Topics Addressed** (include SR, harmonization, transposition, improvisation, score reading, accompaniments, repertoire, and approximate level):

**Strengths of the Book:**

**Weaknesses of the Book:**

**Other:**

# Appendix E.1

# GROUP-PIANO OBSERVATION FORM
## Children's Classes

**Children's Class**

**Level/age of students in group-piano class:** _____     **Length of Class:** _____

**Number of students in class:** _____     **Teacher:** _____

**Books used:** _____

List activities covered and number of minutes spent on each segment (i.e., SR, harmonization, etc.)

| *Activity:* | *Time:* | *Interesting teaching techniques:* |
|---|---|---|
| | | |

How did the teacher keep all students attentive throughout the class?

If students got off task at any time, how did the teacher direct them back toward the group activity?

How did the teacher address different personality styles of the learners in the class?

Additional materials (books, materials, sound accompaniments, collaborative learning, games, etc.)

Could you discern clear learning objectives? If not, how could these have been clearer?

Please use this page for any additional notes, thoughts, significant teaching strategies you observed, or techniques you'd like to remember for future reference.

Name of observer: _____     Date: _____

# Appendix E.2

# GROUP-PIANO OBSERVATION FORM
## Adult Classes

**Check one:** __ **College Music Majors** __ **College Non-Majors** __ **Leisure/ RMM**

**Level of group-piano class:** _____  **Instructor:** _____

**Number of students in class:** ____  **Text used:** _____

List activities covered and number of minutes spent on each segment (i.e., SR, harmonization, etc.)

_____

*Activity:*                          *Time:*                          *Interesting teaching techniques:*




_____

Note any special strategies the instructor used to address various types of learners in the class.




Additional materials (books, overhead materials, sound accompaniments, collaborative learning, etc.)




Could you discern clear learning objectives? If not, how could these have been clearer?




Please use this page for any additional notes, thoughts, significant teaching strategies you observed, or techniques you'd like to remember for future reference.

# Appendix E.3

# GROUP-PIANO OBSERVATION FORM
## Interpersonal Communication of Effective Teachers

**Check one:** __ **College Music Majors** __ **College Non-Majors** __ **Leisure/
RMM**

__ **Children's Class** __ **Age** __ **Level**

**Number of students in class:** _____ **Instructor:** _____

*The purpose of this observation of an effective group-piano teacher is to note how the teacher communicates with the students, how he/she relates to all students in the group, how he/she engages students throughout the class, and how students work together and communicate with each other.*

1. How did the teacher greet the students upon entering the class? Did there seem to be a routine at the beginning of class that prepared the students for piano?

2. How did the teacher include quieter learners throughout the class?

3. How did the teacher keep more vocal students from dominating class discussions and activities?

4. How did the students respond to one another when working collaboratively on projects, activities, and musical performance? Did the teacher do anything to facilitate these interactions?

5. Did the teacher seem to design the class to appeal to different learning styles and different modes of learning and to reinforce concepts through varying activities? If so, be specific about what appeared to work well.

6. List the ways students worked collaboratively (in large or small groups) during the class. What skill, concept, or technique did they reinforce or develop as a result of the group work?

7. Check the types of teaching and learning that you observed and note below how engaged students were for each.

___ Lecture-Type Explanations       ___ Discovery Questions

___ Guided Discovery Activities       ___ Student Assessment of Playing

___ Student Demonstration of Concepts       ___ Visual Contact (Between Teacher and Students)

___ Interaction with Peers through Music       ___ Student–Teacher Interaction through Music

8. Note any other observations worthy of mention, especially skills you would like to develop as a group-piano teacher.

Name of observer: _____    Date: _____

# Appendix E.4

# GROUP-PIANO TEACHING VIDEO SELF-ASSESSMENT FORM 1

**Name:**_____ **Date:** _____

_____ **Adults** _____ **Children** _____ **Level of Group** _____ **Approximate Ages**

## Specific Teaching Assignment

1.  As you observe, keep a list of all lesson activities and note beginning and ending times. You will want to list these in several columns. Be sure to be specific (i.e., teacher explains sharps—timing; student finds and plays sharps—timing; name of piece that uses sharp concept—timing). This chart should give you play-by-play notes of what happened at the lesson.

2.  Looking at your chart, describe the strengths and weaknesses of your pacing.

3.  Compare the overall amount of time that you spent talking and the overall time that the students spent playing. Discuss positive and negative implications or other concerns you have after comparing these times.

4.  Discuss strengths and weaknesses of your concept and skill sequencing throughout the lesson.

5.  Describe creative activities you included during the lesson and how they appeared to benefit the students or group.

6.  Describe how effectively you integrated discovery learning into the lesson.

# Appendix E.5

# GROUP-PIANO TEACHING VIDEO SELF-ASSESSMENT FORM 2

**Name:**_____ **Date:** _____

_____ **Adults** _____ **Children** ___ **Level of Group** ___ **Approximate Ages**

## Specific Teaching Assignment

Since space is limited, answer the following questions on a separate page.

1. As you observe, keep a list of all lesson activities and note beginning and ending times. This chart should give you play-by-play notes of what happened at the lesson. Compare this chart with your lesson plan. In a paragraph, describe why you made alterations from your intended plan and how effective or ineffective these were and why.

2. Notice the students throughout the video. Were there specific times or activities in which they were inattentive or off task? Speculate on why and describe how you will prevent the off-task behavior at the next class.

3. Were there any specific times when students demonstrated misunderstanding (through their questions, responses, or inability to complete tasks)? If yes, list these and describe how you could have been clearer in your preparation or teaching.

4. During which activities did the students appear to be actively engaged? Speculate as to why (activity, time in the lesson, preparation, etc.) and describe how you could facilitate this kind of engagement at other points during the class.

5. Did the students display improvement or mastery as a result of the in-class activities? Reflect on why or why not.

6. Did each in-class activity contribute to the students' development of a skill or concept? If not, what would you leave out or alter to increase the educational value for the students?

7. List specific group or collaborative activities in which the students participated.

8. List three aspects of your teaching you wish to improve. Give three concrete strategies you will employ for each.

# REFERENCES

Anderson, W. T. (2012). The Dalcroze Approach to Music Education: Theory and Applications. *General Music Today*, *26*(1), 27–33. doi: 10.1177/1048371311428979

Aronoff, F. W. (1983). Dalcroze Strategies for Music Learning in the Classroom. *International Journal of Music Education*, *2*(1), 23–25.

Athey, M., & Hotchkiss, G. (1975). *A Galaxy of Games for the Music Class*. West Nyack, NY: Parker Publishing Company.

Baker, V. A. (2017). Teachers' Perceptions on Current Piano Use in the Elementary General Music Classroom. *Update: Applications of Research in Music Education*, *35*(2), 23–29. doi: 10.1177/8755123315598558

Baker-Jordan, M. (2004). *Practical Piano Pedagogy: The Definitive Text for Piano Teachers and Pedagogy Students*. Miami: Warner Brothers, Inc.

Bigge, M. L. (1982). *Learning Theories for Teachers*, 4th edition. New York: Harper & Row, Publishers, Inc.

Bigge, M. L., & Shermis, S. S. (2003). *Learning Theories for Teachers*, 6th edition. Boston: Allyn & Bacon.

Bigler, C., & Lloyd-Watts, V. (1998). *Studying Suzuki Piano: More Than Music: A Handbook for Parents, Teachers, and Students*. Van Nuys, CA: Summy-Birchard Inc. (2016 Kindle edition is available).

Blanchard, B. (2007). *Making Music and Enriching Lives: A Guide for All Music Teachers*. Bloomington: Indiana University Press.

Bloom, B. S. (Ed.). (1985). *Developing Talent in Young People*. New York: Ballantine Books.

Bruner, J. (1966). *Toward a Theory of Instruction*. Cambridge, MA: Belknap/Harvard University Press.

Bruner, J. (1977). *The Process of Education*, 2nd edition. Cambridge, MA: Belknap/Harvard University Press.

Bugos, J., Kochar, S., & Maxfield, N. (2016). Intense Piano Training on Self-Efficacy and Psychological Stress in Aging. *Psychology of Music*, *44*(4), 611–624. doi: 10.1177/0305735615577250

Burnard, P. (2013). "Teaching Music Creatively." In P. Burnard, & R. Murphy (Eds.). *Teaching Music Creatively* (pp. 1–11). London: Routledge.

Caldwell, T. (1993). A Dalcroze Perspective on Skills for Learning. *Music Educators Journal*, *79*(7), 27–29. doi: 10.2307/3398612

Cartwright, D., & Zander, A. (Eds.). (1960). *Group Dynamics: Research and Theory*, 2nd edition. Evanston, IL: Row, Peterson.

Christensen, L. (2000). A Survey of the Importance of Functional Piano Skills as Reported by Band, Choral, Orchestra and General Music Teachers. (doctoral dissertation, University of Oklahoma, 2000). *Dissertation Abstracts International*, 61(6), 2229.

Chung, B., & Dillon, B. (2008). Piano Teaching—Traditional or Recreational? What's the Difference? *American Music Teacher*, 58(2), 46–47.

Coats, S. (2006). *Thinking as You Play*. Bloomington: Indiana University Press.

Cohen, E. G., & Lotan, R. A. (2014). *Designing Groupwork: Strategies for the Heterogeneous Classroom*, 3rd edition. New York: Teacher's College Press.

Colwell, R. (2011). Direct Instruction, Critical Thinking, and Transfer. In R. Colwell, & P. R. Webster (Eds.). *MENC Handbook of Research on Music Learning*, Volume 1: *Strategies* (pp. 84–139). New York: Oxford University Press.

Creech, A., Hallam, S., Varvarigou, M., & McQueen, H. (2014). *Active Ageing with Music: Supporting Wellbeing in the Third and Fourth Ages*. London: Institute of Education Press.

Duckworth, A. L. (2016). *Grit: The Power of Passion and Perseverance*. New York: Scribner.

Duke, R. A. (2005). *Intelligent Music Teaching: Essays on the Core Principles of Effective Instruction*. Austin, TX: Learning and Behavior Resources.

Dweck, C. S. (2008). *Mindset: The New Psychology of Success*. New York: Ballantine Books.

Enz, N. J. (2013). Teaching Music to the Non-Major: A Review of the Literature. *Update: Applications of Research in Music Education*, 32(1), 34–42. doi: 10.1177/8755123313502344

Erikson, E. (1963). *Childhood and Society*, 2nd edition. New York: Norton.

Fay, A. (1965). *Music Study in Germany from the Home Correspondence of Amy Fay*. New York: Dover Reprint.

Freedman, B. (2013). *Teaching Music through Composition: A Curriculum Using Technology*. New York: Oxford University Press.

Fisher, C. (2010). *Teaching Piano in Groups*. New York: Oxford University Press.

Friend, M. P., & Cook, L. (2003). *Interactions: Collaboration Skills for School Professionals*, 4th edition. Boston: Allyn and Bacon.

Froehlich, M. A. (2004). *101 Ideas for Piano Group Class*. Van Nuys, CA: Summy-Birchard.

Gagné, R. M. (1985). *The Conditions of Learning*, 4th edition. Ft. Worth, TX: Holt, Rinehart and Winston, Inc.

Gembris, H. (2008). "Musical Activities in the Third Age: An Empirical Study with Amateur Musicians." In A. Daubney, E. Longhi, A. Lamont, & D. J. Hargreaves (Eds.). *Musical Development and Learning Conference Proceedings, 2nd European Conference on Developmental Psychology of Music* (pp. 103–108). Hull: GK Publishing.

Gembris, H. (2012). "Music-Making as a Lifelong Development and Resource for Health." In R. MacDonald, G. Kreutz, & L. Mitchell (Eds.). *Music, Health, & Wellbeing* (pp. 367–382). Oxford: Oxford University Press.

Golay, K. (2003). "Staying in Tune with Learning Styles: Matching Your Teaching to Learners." In M. Baker-Jordan (Ed.). *Practical Piano Pedagogy* (pp. 149–166). Miami, FL: Warner Bros. Publications.

Goolsby, T. W. (1997). Verbal Instructions in Instrumental Rehearsals: A Comparison of Three Career Levels and Preservice Teachers. *Journal of Research in Music Education*, 45(1), 21–40. doi: 10.2307/3345463

Goss, L. (Ed.). (1992). *Questions and Answers: Practical Advice for Piano Teachers by Frances Clark.* Northfield, IL: The Instrumentalist Company. Currently available through the Frances Clark Center for Keyboard Pedagogy www.keyboardpedagogy.org

Harrington, K. (2010). *Piano Teacher's Resource Kit.* Milwaukee: Hal Leonard Corporation.

Harrington, K. (2008). *Tic-Tac-Toe Music Games.* Milwaukee: Hal Leonard Corporation.

Haxo, C., Huston, A., Reinhardt, J. L., & Thickstun, K. (2016). Problem Solved! Seeking Solutions Online: Facebook Groups for Teachers. *Keyboard Companion, 8*(5), 46–49.

Houle, C. O. (1984). *Patterns of Learning: New Perspectives on Life-Span Education.* San Francisco: Jossey-Bass.

Jacobson, J. M. (2015). *Professional Piano Teaching*, 2nd edition. Edited by E. L. Lancaster. Van Nuys, CA: Alfred Music Publishing, Inc.

Jung, C. G. (1972). *Four Archetypes: Mother, Rebirth, Spirit, Trickster.* Translated by R.F.C. Hull. London: Routledge.

Kagan, S., & Kagan, M. (1994). "The Structural Approach: Six Keys to Cooperative Learning." In S. Sharan (Ed.). *Handbook of Cooperative Learning Methods* (pp. 115–133). Westport, NT: Greenwood Press.

Keirsey, D. (1998). *Please Understand Me II: Temperament, Character, Intelligence.* Del Mar: CA: Prometheus Nemesis Book Company.

Klose, C. (2011). *Piano Teacher's Guide to Creative Composition.* Milwaukee: Hal Leonard Corporation.

Knowles, M. S., Houlton III, E. F., & Swanson, R. A. (2015). *The Adult Learner: The Definitive Classic in Adult Education and Human Resource Development.* New York: Routledge.

Koga, M., & Tims, F. (2001). The Music-Making and Wellness Project. *American Music Teacher, 51*(2), 18–22.

Kolb, D. A. (2015). *Experiential Learning: Experience as the Source of Learning and Development,* 2nd edition. Upper Saddle River, NJ: Pearson Education, Inc.

Kottler, J. A. (2001). *Learning Group Leadership: An Experiential Approach.* Boston: Allyn and Bacon.

Lavender, C. (2006). *Music MasterMINDS: The Ultimate Cross-Curricular Connection of Music Puzzles and Games.* Milwaukee: Hal Leonard.

Levinson, D. (1978). *The Seasons of a Man's Life.* New York: Knopf.

Magrath, J., & Pike, P. (2002). Polyphony. *American Music Teacher, 52*(2), 83–86.

Maslow, A. (1969/2014). *Toward a Psychology of Being.* Reprint of the first edition. Floyd, VA: Sublime Books.

Mead, V. H. (1996). More Than Mere Movement: Dalcroze Eurythmics. *Music Educators Journal, 82*(4), 38–41. doi: 10.2307/3398915

Merwe, L. van der (2015). The First Experiences of Music Students with Dalcroze-inspired Activities: A Phenomenological Study. *Psychology of Music, 43*(3), 390–406. doi: 10.1177/0305735613513485

Montgomery, J. (1998). *Piano Camp, Books Primer-4.* Van Nuys, CA: Alfred Publishing Co., Inc.

Music Teachers National Association. Group Teaching Specialist Program http://www.mtna.org/programs/teaching-specialists/

Music Teachers National Association. Video consent/authorization form http://www.mtna.org/media/24961/videoauthorization.pdf

National Association of Schools of Music. (2016). *Standards for Baccalaureate and Graduate Degree-Granting Institutions: NASM Handbook.* Reston, VA: National Association of Schools of Music. https://nasm.arts-accredit.org/accreditation/standards-guidelines/handbook/

Perkins, R., & Williamon, A. (2014). Learning to Make Music in Older Adulthood: A Mixed-Methods Exploration of Impacts on Wellbeing. *Psychology of Music, 42*(4), 550–567. doi: 10.1177/0305735613483668

Phuthego, M. (2005). Teaching and Learning African Music and Jaques-Dalcroze's Eurhythmics. *International Journal of Music Education, 23*(3), 239–248. doi: 10.1177/0255761405058240

Pike, P. D. (1999). The Adult Leisure Student. *Keyboard Companion, 13*(2), 34–35.

Pike, P. D. (2001). *Leisure Piano Lessons: A Case Study in Lifelong Learning.* Unpublished doctoral dissertation. Norman, OK: University of Oklahoma.

Pike, P. D. (2006). Addressing Individual Learning Styles in the Group-Piano Class. *Proceedings from the 27th World Conference of the International Society for Music Education* (pp. 932–947). ISBN: 0-9752063-6-2.

Pike, P. D. (2011). Using Technology to Engage Third-Age (Retired) Leisure Learners: A Case Study of a Third-Age MIDI Piano Ensemble. *International Journal of Music Education, 29*(2), 116–123.

Pike, P. D. (2013). Profiles in Successful Group Piano for Children: A Collective Case Study of Children's Group-Piano Lessons. *Music Education Research, 15*(1), 92–106.

Pike, P. D. (2014a). An Exploration of the Effect of Cognitive and Collaborative Strategies on Keyboard Skills of Music Education Students. *Journal of Music Teacher Education, 23*(2), 79–91. doi: 10.1177/1057083713487214

Pike, P. D. (2014b). The Difference between Novice and Expert Group-Piano Teaching Strategies: A Case Study and Comparison of Beginning Group Piano Classes. *International Journal of Music Education, 32*(2), 213–227. doi: 10.1177/0255761413508065

Pike, P. D. (2015). "Dismantling Barriers to Quality Music Instruction for Older Adults in Rural America: A Collective Case Study of Six Adults Taking Online Synchronous Music Lessons." *Paper presented at the Suncoast Music Education Symposium,* Tampa, FL. This paper has been adapted and will be included as a chapter in a forthcoming book entitled *The Handbook of Music Education,* edited by Bugos and Dege.

Pitts, S. (2012). *Chances and Choices: Exploring the Impact of Music Education.* Oxford: Oxford University Press.

*Proceedings from MTNA Pedagogy Saturday III.* (1999). Cincinnati: Music Teachers National Association.

Sheehy, G. (1995). *New Passages: Mapping Your Life Across Time.* New York: Ballantine Books.

Siebenaler, D. J. (1997). Analysis of Student-Teacher Interactions in the Piano Lessons of Adults and Children. *Journal of Research in Music Education, 45*(1), 6–20. doi: 10.2307/3345462

Smith, M. K. (2005). "Bruce W. Tuckman—Forming, Storming, Norming and Performing in Groups, *The Encyclopaedia of Informal Education.*" http://infed.org/mobi/bruce-w-tuckman-forming-storming-norming-and-performing-in-groups/. Retrieved: 10 October 2010.

Snowman, J., McCown, R., & Biehler, R. (2012). *Psychology Applied to Teaching,* 13th edition. Belmont, CA: Wadsworth, Cengage Learning.

Sousa, D. A. (2011). *How the Brain Learns*, 4th edition. Thousand Oaks, CA: Corwin.

Stevens, D. D. & Levi, A. J. (2005). *Introduction to Rubrics: An Assessment Tool to Save Grading Time, Convey Effective Feedback and Promote Student Learning.* Sterling, VA: Stylus Publishing, LLC.

Storms, J. (2001). *101 Music Games for Children.* The Hague: Uitgeverij Panta Rhei (in the USA published as a Hunter House SmartFun Book, Berkley: Publishers Group West).

Suzuki, S. (2012). *Nurtured by Love:* Revised Edition. Translated from the original Japanese text by K. Selden with L. Selden. Van Nuys, CA: Alfred Music Publishing Company, Inc./ Summy-Birchard.

Teachout, D. J. (1997). Preservice and Experienced Teachers' Opinions of Skills and Behaviors Important to Successful Music Teaching. *Journal of Research in Music Education, 45*(1), 41–50.

Tough, A. (1982). *Intentional Changes: A Fresh Approach to Helping People Change.* Chicago: Follett.

Tuckman, Bruce W. (1965). Developmental Sequence in Small Groups. *Psychological Bulletin, 63*(6), 384–399.

University of Vermont and PACER Center. (2008). "Stages of Group Development." Online module www.uvm.edu/~pcl/Module4. Accessed 1 March 2016.

Wachter, M. (Ed.). (2016). "A Conversation with Jane Chu." In *Proceedings of the National Conference on Keyboard Pedagogy* (pp. 31–38). Princeton: NJ: The Frances Clark Center for Keyboard Pedagogy.

Yalom, I. D. (1995). *The Theory and Practice of Group Psychotherapy*, 4th edition. New York: Basic Books.

Young, M. M. (2013). University-Level Group Piano Instruction and Professional Musicians. *Music Education Research, 15*(1), 59–73. doi: http://dx.doi.org/10.1080/14613808.2012.737773

## Journals, Periodicals, and Magazines

*American Music Teacher* (peer-reviewed journal published 6 times/year by MTNA).

*Clavier Companion* (piano magazine published 6 times/year by Frances Clark Center for Keyboard Pedagogy).

*Journal of Music, Technology & Education* (peer-reviewed journal published 3 times/year by Intellect Books).

*MTNA e-Journal* (peer-reviewed journal published 6 times/year by MTNA).

## Software and Online Teaching Tools

Classroom Maestro & Home Concert Xtreme www.timewarptech.com

*eNovative Piano* online multimedia resource www.enovativepiano.com

*Piano Maestro* (assessment/practice software) www.joytunes.com

*Piano Marvel* (assessment software) www.pianomarvel.com

## Professional Organizations for Group-Piano Teachers

Music Teachers National Association www.mtna.org

National Conference on Keyboard Pedagogy (Frances Clark Center for Keyboard Pedagogy) www.keyboardpedagogy.org

# Online Video References

## *TED Talks Online*

Grit (persistence) by Angela Duckworth https://www.ted.com/talks/angela_lee_duckworth_the_key_to_success_grit?language=en

The Growth Mindset by Carol Dweck: http://www.ted.com/talks/carol_dweck_the_power_of_believing_that_you_can_improve

## *Video Segments of Group-Piano Teaching*

www.pameladpike.com

# INDEX

Made in the USA
Columbia, SC
24 August 2024

41068544R00141